RAISING THE DUST

Beth Sutton-Ramspeck

RAISING THE DUST

The Literary Housekeeping of

Mary Ward, Sarah Grand, and

Charlotte Perkins Gilman

OHIO UNIVERSITY PRESS ∾ ATHENS

Ohio University Press, Athens, Ohio 45701
© 2004 by Beth Sutton-Ramspeck

Printed in the United States of America

Ohio University Press books are printed on acid-free paper ∞ ™

12 11 10 09 08 07 06 05 04   5 4 3 2 1

Library of Congress Cataloging-in-Publication Data

Sutton-Ramspeck, Beth, 1954–
  Raising the dust : the literary housekeeping of Mary Ward, Sarah Grand, and
Charlotte Perkins Gilman / Beth Sutton-Ramspeck.
    p. cm.
  Includes bibliographical references and index.
  ISBN 0-8214-1586-7 (alk. paper) — ISBN 0-8214-1587-5 (pbk. : alk. paper)
  1. Domestic fiction, English—History and criticism. 2. English fiction—Women
authors—History and criticism. 3. Gilman, Charlotte Perkins, 1860–1935—Criticism and interpretation. 4. Ward, Humphry, Mrs., 1851–1920—Criticism and
interpretation. 5. Domestic fiction, American—History and criticism. 6. Grand,
Sarah—Criticism and interpretation. 7. Housekeeping in literature. 8. Housewives in literature. 9. Mothers in literature. 10. Women in literature. 11. Home
in literature. I. Title.
  PR830.D65S88 2004
    823'.8093552—dc22
                                                            2004004872

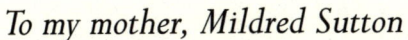

To my mother, Mildred Sutton

Mirrors may be either a distorting or a flattering medium, but women do not care to see life any longer in a glass darkly. Let there be light. We suffer in the first shock of it. We shriek in horror at what we discover when it is turned on that which was hidden away in dark corners; but the first principle of good housekeeping is to have no dark corners, and as we recover ourselves we go to work with a will to sweep them out. It is for us to set the human household in order, to see to it that all is clean and sweet and comfortable for the men who are fit to help us to make a home in it. We are bound to raise the dust while we are at work, but only those who are in it will suffer any inconvenience from it.

—*Sarah Grand, "The New Aspect of the Woman Question"*

CONTENTS

ACKNOWLEDGMENTS

My research for this book could not have been completed without library assistance. For permission to quote Ward's correspondence with her editor at Smith, Elder, Co. in the Mrs. Humphry Ward Papers, I gratefully acknowledge the Department of Special Collections, Honnold/Mudd Library, Claremont, California. I also wish to thank Kathy Stedke and Tina Schneider at The Ohio State University—Lima campus library, and I am especially indebted to the marvelous tracking skills of Lori Schleeter in the OSU-Lima interlibrary loan office.

An earlier version of a portion of the first chapter appeared as "The Personal Is Poetical: Feminist Criticism and Mary Ward's Readings of the Brontës" in *Victorian Studies*. I am grateful to the editors and to the Indiana University Press for permission to use it here. I am also grateful to Susan Gubar and Patrick Brantlinger for their advice about that earlier essay.

My research for this book was generously supported by The Ohio State University at Lima. I am grateful to the Faculty Research Committee and Dean Violet Meek for granting me research leaves, without which I might not have been able to finish the book in a timely manner. OSU also provided the support of student workers who helped me compile notes: E. C. Miller, Teresa Mullett, Tina Paullin, Emily Schlenker, Christina Snover, and Jessica Straw.

My students in seminars on literary housekeeping provided stimulus, inspiration, and insight. I gratefully acknowledge Kathleen Anspaugh, Jessica Bradshaw, Arin Burton, Lisa Clark, Michelle Claypool, Joe Dugan, Crystal Dunson, Eissa Grunden, Pam Heffner, Casey Keating, Buck Lambert, Linda Miller, Barbara Rizor-Poland, Emily Schlenker, Jen Sensabaugh, Airica Stemen, Amanda Tate-Sullivan, Elizabeth Taylor, Gina Taylor, and Corey Ward.

Members of the online VICTORIA discussion list have generously responded to many literary housekeeping queries over the years. I am grateful to moderator Patrick Leary and list subscribers Antje Anderson, Hilary Attfield,

Acknowledgments

Eva Badowska, Chris Baggs, Les Bailey, Ed Beasley, Rachel Bright, T. J. Collins, Eileen M. Curran, Terri Doughty, Megan Early, K. Eldron, Michel Faber, Rosary Fazende, Judith Flanders, Sunie Fletcher, Holly Forsythe, Kerryn Goldsworthy, Ann-Barbara Graff, Kelley Graham, Lesley Hall, David Hennessee, Andrea Hibbard, Susan Hoyle, Audrey Jaffe, Ryan Johnson, Ellen Jordan, Priti Joshi, Meegan Kennedy, Ivo Klaver, Graham Law, Ying Lee, Margot K. Louis, Jim Loucks, Susan K Martin, Timothy Mason, Michèle Mendelssohn, Doris Meriwether, Liz Miller, Peter O'Neill, M. Jeanne Peterson, Jennifer Phegley, Harriet Rafter, Dara Rossman Regaignon, Jamie Ridenhour, Meri-Jane Rochelson, Tracey S. Rosenberg, Martin Rush, Karen Sayer, SueAnn Schatz, Patrick Scott, Linda Shires, Suzanne Rosenthal Shumway, Rebecca Stern, Barbara Tilley, Jane Weiss, Stephen Wildman, Perry Willett, Chris Willis, Anthony Wohl, and Molly Youngkin.

I would also like to thank members of the Women Writers through the Ages online group: Diane Bateman, Diana Birchalls, Abigail Burnham Bloom, Fran Karlich, Judy Geater, Joanne Pope, Angela Richardson, Val Shepherd, Jill Spriggs, Patricia Stewart, Joan Wall, and especially moderators Ellen Moody and Penny L. Richards. Their 2002 discussion of Ward's *Marcella* helped sharpen my ideas about the novel.

I received valuable information, advice, and support from other scholars working on Ward, Grand, and Gilman: Sydna A. Byrne, Cynthia Davis, Ann Heilmann, Denise Knight, Teresa Mangum, Michelle Mouton, Patricia Murphy, Angelique Richardson, Gary Scharnhorst, Esther Schwartz-McKinzie, Val Shepherd, Jeff Smith, Jennifer Tuttle, Lia Vella, and Kim Wells. Dave Cheadle provided vital assistance in my efforts to obtain advertising soap cards designed by Charlotte Perkins Gilman and in explicating advertising card iconography.

Many OSU colleagues generously read parts or all of the manuscript at various stages, suggested revisions, and offered reading lists. Many thanks to Anne Bower, Jared Gardner, Marlene Longenecker, Jim Phelan, David Riede, Clare Simmons, Les Tannenbaum, and Susan Williams. I also received helpful practical advice from David Adams, Deb Burks, and John Hellmann.

I owe a particular debt of gratitude to Sally Mitchell and Talia Schaffer for their insightful responses to my manuscript.

I am grateful to everyone at Ohio University Press for seeing the book through production with efficiency, patience, and care: Thank you to Director

David Sanders, Managing Editor Nancy Basmajian, copyeditor Bevin McLaughlin, proofreader Corinne Colbert, Production Manager Beth Pratt, Marketing Manager Richard Gilbert, and, I am sure, others working behind the scenes.

Finally, special thanks to my family. Lee and Doug Sutton-Ramspeck shared the literal housekeeping while I was writing about literary housekeeping. Doug Sutton-Ramspeck has always been my most insightful and helpful advisor, reader, and critic, from the earliest brainstorming stage forward. And loving thanks to my mother, Mildred Sutton, who by introducing me to nineteenth-century women writers, by telling funny stories of 1930s Home Economics classes, and by exemplifying the art of feminist motherhood, planted the seeds of this book.

INTRODUCTION

THE DOMESTIC AND THE PUBLIC SPHERES—variously defined—
have traditionally been viewed as competing and mutually contradictory realms,
both in fact and in fictional portrayals. My study uncovers an alternative paradigm: literature engaging the public realm through the housekeeping devices
and perspectives of the domestic realm. I call this alternative paradigm "literary housekeeping."

In the mid-nineteenth century, housekeeping was viewed as a purely private activity and the home as a secluded, safe retreat from the public sphere;
by the end of the century, however, this perception had undergone a dramatic
transformation. Falling birthrates, the growth of the women's movement, the
rise of mass marketing, and the discovery of bacteria had made the home seem
far less secure. In 1876 Robert Koch demonstrated for the first time the connection of a specific bacillus to a specific disease—*Bacillus anthracis* to anthrax—
and within two decades, housekeeping had changed irrevocably. Anthrax, though
no longer lived than most bacteria, has an unusual reproductive process: it
produces spores that survive in soil for considerable periods and can withstand
boiling or freezing. Late-Victorian health experts, basing their model of disease
transmission on the behavior of anthrax, warned women that germs lurked
everywhere, especially in dirt; that germs were virtually indestructible; and
that only the most meticulous cleanliness could protect households.

Microbes, invisible and powerful, represented a terrifying threat. Disease was no longer linked only to "sewer gas," obvious filth, and sick people, but could be spread by healthy carriers, through casual contact such as kissing, shaking hands, or simply breathing. Until the development of antibiotics in the mid-twentieth century, the only way to protect one's self and one's family from these insidious attackers was prevention: vaccination, quarantine, and other forms of avoidance. As more bacteria (including cholera, tuberculosis, tetanus, gonorrhea, typhoid, and scarlet fever) were identified in rapid succession in the last two decades of the nineteenth century, daily life changed radically. Flies and mosquitoes became not just annoyances but menaces, and widespread installation of window screens began. Beards and trailing skirts excited suspicion as carriers of contagion, and fashion changed accordingly. Particularly in America, foods previously sold in the open air, from meat to bread to candy, were enclosed in "sanitary packaging," and refrigeration of meat, milk, and prepared foods represented no longer a luxury (though it long remained expensive) but a health necessity.

The panic over germs coincided with several other cultural changes: the late-Victorian eugenics movement; the popularity of the "house beautiful"; the rise of advertising, with its emphasis on brand names; and the emergence of the home economics movement. The exodus of traditionally "domestic" industries from the home continued apace, as more ready-made products became available, while more homes acquired central plumbing, gas, and electricity, as well as household technologies like washing machines, vacuum cleaners, refrigerators, and more efficient stoves. As standards for housework rose, housewives took on tasks traditionally shouldered by husbands, children, and servants. In England between 1881 and 1911, the proportion of female domestic servants fell from 218 per 1,000 families to 170 per 1,000 (Horn, 25); in the United States, the proportion dropped from 119 servants per 1,000 families in 1870 to 100 servants per 1,000 in 1900, to 57 per 1,000 in 1920 (Strasser, 163; Cowan, "Coal Stoves," 214–15).[1] All these changes created "more work for mother," in Ruth Schwartz Cowan's phrase, as middle-class women increasingly "did their own work" in the home. Yet the same period also saw increases in women's education, workforce participation, and political activism.

My study proposes that this confluence of circumstances at the turn of the century significantly affected the interrelationships between the domestic

sphere and the public sphere. In turn, portrayals of domesticity in the era's fiction and nonfiction challenged widely accepted separations between the spheres. My book explores one heretofore-overlooked literary challenge to the public-private dichotomy, the approach I call "literary housekeeping." To the three writers I discuss—Mary Augusta Arnold Ward (1851–1920), Sarah Grand (Frances Elizabeth Bellenden Clarke McFall, 1854–1943), and Charlotte Perkins Stetson Gilman (1860–1935)—housekeeping activities represent more than the small, private duties women carry out for their families. These writers reenvision housekeeping as representing responsibilities with enormous public impact: making the food supply safe, "cleaning up" society, improving the human race through "public motherhood." Moreover, Gilman, Grand, and Ward articulate an alternative domestic aesthetic of "literature as housekeeping" that sweeps away boundaries between the artistic and the practical, the personal and political, the public and private.

Literature as housekeeping is not "domestic fiction," though it owes debts to the British and American traditions of the domestic novel. Literary housekeeping differs from domestic fiction primarily in its attitudes toward interrelationships between public and private spheres. The earlier domestic novel rhetorically empowers a spiritual matriarchy that operates within the private home, as an alternative to the public world. Nancy Armstrong, in her study of late-eighteenth- and early-nineteenth-century domestic fiction, has shown that because the domestic novel, with its focus on marriage and kinship, "represent[s] sexual relations as something entirely removed from politics," it "could represent an alternative form of political power without appearing to contest the distribution of power" (28, 29). The ostensibly apolitical domestic fiction therefore exerted a covert political authority, for its emphasis on individual subjectivity, as opposed to inherited privilege, helped bring the middle class into power. Nevertheless, this earlier genre exerted power by displacing public politics into a private sphere represented as "separate." To be sure, to emphasize domestic spaces and personal emotion is not necessarily to retreat from the realities of political or economic oppression. Most famously, *Uncle Tom's Cabin* dramatizes Harriet Beecher Stowe's view that "historical change takes place only through religious conversion" (Tompkins, 133). This is why the novel ends with Stowe's admonishing her readers that the "one thing that every individual can do" to solve the problem of slavery is to "see to it that *they feel right*" (624; emphasis Stowe's). Like Stowe (for whose work Gilman, Grand, and Ward all professed admiration) and like other writers of domestic fiction, the literary housekeepers frequently wrote from a woman's point of view, primarily for women readers, with the aim "to reorganize culture from a woman's point of view" (Tompkins, 124). But domestic fiction is premised on the "conviction that parlor commonplaces were superior to the prevailing public morality" (Hedrick, 85); in contrast, the writings I identify with literary housekeeping advocate extending maternal power beyond the individual fireside and *into* the marketplace and halls of government.

The Public/Private Dichotomy and Domesticity

To fully understand literary housekeeping's challenge to the idea of separate spheres, it is necessary to examine the long-accepted dichotomy between the public and the private, especially as it has generally been applied to women's history and literature. The dichotomy is an ancient one, first articulated in detail by Plato and Aristotle, and thus providing a theoretical foundation for Western law, political science, and economics, as well as philosophy and religion, sociology, anthropology, history, communications theory, and literary history. Despite—or because of—its long history, the public/private distinction generates confusion: "[D]ifferent sets of people who employ these concepts mean very different things by them—and sometimes, without quite realizing it, mean several things at once" (Weintraub, 1–2). To begin with, the contrasting concepts may in different circumstances imply fundamentally distinct sets of "imagery": the distinction between what is concealed (secret) and what is visible or accessible, on the one hand; or, in other cases, between what is particular or pertains only to the individual and what is collective (Weintraub, 4–5). Thus a behavior, for example economic behavior, can be private in the sense of "individual" with or without being secret.

On a more broadly theoretical level, the terms "public" and "private" have been used differently within different disciplinary or conceptual models. Political philosopher Jeff Weintraub identifies four different types of private/public distinctions: (1) The "liberal-economistic model" distinguishes between the "private sector" market economy and state—"public sector"—intervention; this model dominates many current "public policy" debates. (2) In the "republican-virtue (and classical) approach," the term "public" refers to the *polis*—the site of discussion among individuals, collective decision making, and citizenship, while the "private" includes the individual, the domestic, or the marketplace (7). In this conceptual model, typified by Alexis de Tocqueville's descriptions of "political society," Hannah Arendt's discussion of the "public realm," or Jürgen Habermas's conception of the "public sphere," the "public" is nevertheless distinct from the state (3). The social-scientific or anthropological model defines the "private" spatially, as secret or intimate space, as opposed to the public realm of sociability, such as the city street, public square, or marketplace. Theorists working, in different ways, within this conceptual framework include Philippe Ariès, Michel Foucault, and Erving Goffman (4). Finally, the feminist model, the approach most explicitly concerned with housekeeping behaviors, sees the private/public distinction as between the family (private sphere) and the larger political or economic realm. Adding to the confusion among these theoretical languages is the fact that the terms "public" and "private" are used not only descriptively, but also normatively. In some contexts, in which "private" suggests the normative value of freedom from interference, the meaning of "public" will vary depending on the source of the interference. Moreover, the words "public" and "private" might either—or both—be applied to describe any particular activity or situation, depending on the model being used. So, for example, a woman at work in her kitchen might be described as engaged in a "private" (domestic) activity or as illustrating a woman's lack of "private" (individual) space; her situation might be described as "public" if she and a group of women are debating a political issue on which they intend to act, or, if the woman is a paid servant, as "public" in the economic sense—or as "private" in the economic sense. As this analysis should suggest, the terms "public" and "private," precisely because they are so widely used, are remarkably slippery terms.

The public/private distinction, along with its sister concept, "separate spheres," has influenced feminist theory from the beginning: "The dichotomy between the private and the public is central to almost two centuries of feminist writing and political struggle; it is, ultimately, what the feminist movement is all about" (Pateman, 118). Mary Wollstonecraft, for example, challenged assumptions of classic Enlightenment Liberalism that women, as denizens of the private domestic sphere, are unqualified to share decision making in the public, political sphere. Later, arguments against the Contagious Diseases Acts invoked another public/private distinction to deplore invasions of women's personal privacy by public officials; and more recently the abortion debate has invoked the right to privacy, while the problem of domestic violence has inspired demands for public protection of women in what some perpetrators have claimed as a "private matter." Thus, even within the feminist interpretive framework, the terms "public" and "private" acquire distinctive, sometimes contradictory, theoretical and normative meanings, depending on the context(s) of discussion.

In turn, contemporary feminist scholarship, especially the study of American women's history and culture, has been shaped by the public/private distinction. The proliferation of studies of women's culture beginning in the late 1960s echoed Alexis de Tocqueville's frequently quoted observation in *Democracy in America* that "[i]n no country has such constant care been taken as in America to trace two clearly distinct lines of actions for the two sexes." Feminist historians debated whether "the cult of true womanhood," in Barbara Welter's phrase, was fundamentally repressive or whether it represented the empowering "Female World of Love and Ritual," of Carroll Smith-Rosenberg's title. But either way, the assumption of separate spheres long went unquestioned. In recent years, however, feminists throughout the disciplines have identified serious flaws in the public/private dichotomy.[2] These flaws include not only the fuzziness of the terminology, but the actual inaccuracy of the dichotomy as a description of social, historical, or political reality. As recent scholarship has paid more attention to issues of race and class, the inadequacy of the concept of "true womanhood" to describe factory laborers, servants, women of color, and so on, has become apparent. Historians like Karen Hansen, who has analyzed actual interactions of men and women in antebellum New England, have cast doubt that the everyday lives of men and women were as separated or distinctive as we had come to believe. Even the ideology that held that the middle-class home was a private "haven" from the public, commercial sphere is belied by the realities of running a household, for the middle-class woman managed not only the funds that her husband earned but also her own employees: "Running the middle-class household, which by definition became 'middle class' in its possession of at least one servant, was an exercise in class management" (Langland, 8). Furthermore, as my study demonstrates, among the many women and men who believed that separate spheres existed at the turn of the century were many who were committed to sweeping away the walls between the spheres.

Prominent among these groups were the founders of the home economics movement in the United States. The American Home Economics Association (AHEA) was established in 1899 to ensure that the era's better-educated housewives had access to the latest scientific information about bacteria, nutrition, and child development. Evolving from the emphasis on education in the domestic science writings of Catherine Beecher and Harriet Beecher Stowe, the AHEA rejected the influence of those who wanted only to solve the "servant problem," focusing instead on designing advanced academic courses for upper- and middle-class women attending both land grant universities and elite institutions like the University of Chicago.[3] Despite what home economics education would become as the twentieth century progressed, the movement's pioneers set out with ambitious feminist goals. Founder Ellen Richards, a feisty Vassar-educated chemist, who twice broke the gender barrier at MIT—as its first woman graduate student and then its first woman faculty member—envisioned home economics as a means to professional careers for women. Designing high school and college courses around rigid laboratory methods and the latest scientific information, early home economists set about to bring science into individual kitchens, promoting such innovations as recipes specifying exact measurements—and standardized measuring utensils to correspond. But, more fundamentally, their goal was to move women scientists into careers in academia, nutrition, and sanitation. Women in this movement believed in essential differences between the sexes, but also believed that women's domestic skills represent not a separate private sphere but distinctive responsibilities in the public sphere, variously understood in both economic and political terms. Employing concepts from the social sciences and turn-of-the-twentieth-century progressive reform movements, the home economists aimed to empower women's contributions to the tasks of "municipal housekeeping." In the words of Gilman's friend Helen Campbell, one of the pioneering home economists, "Household Economics is the connecting link between the physical economics of the individual and the social economics of the state" (*Household Economics,* 2). Literary housekeeping, in turn, applies to literary texts this idea of finding "connecting links" between the domestic and the social.

Who Are the Literary Housekeepers?

In order to clarify the ways that "literary housekeeping" engages and departs from other traditions, it is necessary to begin with some background. First, a word on terminology. As I use the term, "housekeeping" includes tasks traditionally carried on by women within the home: child care, cooking, cleaning, and sewing, along with home design or interior design. I have chosen to call the phenomenon studied in this book "literary housekeeping" primarily because "housekeeping" is the word preferred by Ward, Grand, and Gilman. Whereas "homemaker" suggests a mother, a woman devoted exclusively to her own small world, "housekeeper" connotes a laborer, for "housekeeping" seems less about creating an atmosphere—though it may also include that—than about cooking and especially cleaning. After all, in a wealthy nineteenth-century home, a "housekeeper" was a paid employee who supervised other servants. Moreover, in the late nineteenth and early twentieth centuries—the era with which my own study is concerned—the "servant crisis" that emerged as domestic help became harder to obtain led to a merging of the roles of "housewife" and "homeworker" (Oakley, 6). The ambiguous term "housekeeper" reflects that uneasy synthesis. Furthermore, the professional quality that "housekeeper" may connote reinforces the concern with taking domestic values into the public sphere that is at the heart of "literary housekeeping." Thus, Gilman's 1910 short story "Her Housekeeper" embodies her ideal of commercialized housekeeping in a boardinghouse that makes an actress's life so comfortable that she promises her suitor she will marry him only if he can promise to give her a house like her current residence and to run it as smoothly, with no more cares for her than she currently has. At the end of the story, she and we learn that the boardinghouse owner and manager, the story's eponymous ideal, is the suitor himself. "Housekeeper" is thus redefined as limited to neither the private sphere nor the female sex. By the same token, "municipal housekeeping," a favorite slogan of early-twentieth-century civic reformers, relocated "feminine" domestic activities into the dirtiest streets and sewers, thus mixing feminine caretaking with the most ostensibly masculine tasks of urban England and America.

Since Mary Ward, Sarah Grand, and Charlotte Perkins Gilman are relatively unknown, some biographical background may clarify the origins and contexts of some of their ideas.[4] The three writers were very close contemporaries, with little more than nine years separating their births, and each enjoyed tremendous international literary success in her upper thirties, followed by decline to near obscurity. Ward, the eldest of the three, was born in 1851, the granddaughter of Thomas Arnold of Rugby and niece of Matthew Arnold. When Mary Augusta Arnold was five, her father converted to Catholicism and lost his academic position: until he rejoined the Church of England when Mary was sixteen and he obtained work at Oxford, he had difficulty finding employment whose salary could adequately support eight children. For years, the family endured "straitened means and constant struggles, . . . in dismal furnished houses" (Ward, "Memoir of W. T. Arnold," v). Because Tom Arnold could not afford to send his daughters to schools as good as those to which he sent his sons, Mary considered her time at the boarding schools she attended between age seven and sixteen "practically wasted" (*A Writer's Recollections,* 1:129), and she essentially educated herself in Oxford's Bodleian library. Her dissatisfaction over her missed opportunities inspired her lifelong devotion to promoting education.

Although only around half of women writers born in the nineteenth century married—in comparison to about 85 percent of women generally—and only 65 percent of married women writers were mothers (Showalter, *Literature,* 65), Ward, like Grand and Gilman, married relatively young and had children. In 1871, Mary Arnold, twenty, wed Thomas Humphry Ward, an Oxford tutor, later a writer for the *Times.* The Wards' three children were born two, three, and seven years into their marriage. Unlike Grand and Gilman, Ward managed successfully to combine marriage, motherhood, and literary productivity, publishing her first book, the children's book *Milly and Olly,* when her third and youngest child was only two; *Robert Elsmere,* an international bestseller about a clergyman's crisis of faith, was published in 1888, when Ward was thirty-six, her eldest child thirteen, and her youngest eight. She wrote and published at an ever-increasing rate until her death in 1920, producing twenty-five novels, the children's story, a translation, three books of war propaganda, an autobiography, and a diverse range of shorter nonfiction pieces.

Having spent much of her girlhood away from home, Ward obtained less domestic training than might have been expected of the eldest daughter in a large, impoverished family, but she somehow acquired the necessary skills by the time she married. In her autobiography, she describes young faculty wives like herself as "very fair housekeepers and competent mothers, . . . very anxious to be up-to-date and in the fashion, whether in esthetics, in housekeeping, or in education" (*A Writer's Recollections,* 1:160). Although the Wards employed a nurse and later a governess, a cook, and other servants, Mrs. Ward could "do her own work" in emergencies, such as Christmas 1891, when the cook suffered an injury and two other servants and her daughter had influenza: Mary Ward both nursed the sick and prepared the Christmas dinner (Sutherland, 185–86). In her writings, housekeeping functions in two ways, as a means to reveal character—efficient housekeeping skills augment other positive traits in Ward's admirable female characters—and in connection with larger political ideas. In arguing against parliamentary suffrage for women, Ward contended that women are "debarred from political knowledge" by the demands of motherhood ("On the Eve of the Bill," 11a); yet she also invoked women's housekeeping responsibilities to advocate their greater participation on school boards and county and borough councils, in support of children and the poor, aged, sick, and insane. At various times Ward called such work the "enlarged housekeeping of the nation" (qtd. in "Anti-Suffrage Demonstration," 9f). Such work "had to deal with all that grew most naturally and closely out of the house-hold life of women as well as men" (qtd. in "Needs of Local Government," 12d) and, she contended, would draw on the "enormous amount of shrewd home-wisdom still unutilized by the women of this country" ("A Way Out," 8e).

Sarah Grand was born Frances Elizabeth Bellenden Clarke in 1854. Her father, a naval coastguard, died when she was seven; his widow and five children afterward lived in Yorkshire. Little else is known about her childhood, but because the little we know matches so closely with the story of Grand's fictional Beth Caldwell in *The Beth Book,* biographers speculate about other parallels. The fictional Beth, at least, must wear shabby hand-me-downs and hunt rabbits to help feed her family. As with Ward and Gilman, Grand's apparently pinched childhood circumstances contributed to a frequently expressed sympathy for servants and other members of the working class; likewise, one of the main themes of Grand's books—as of Ward's and Gilman's—is the importance of girls' education, a topic she admitted derived from her own inadequate schooling. Although she had access to a good library as a child, Grand attended only two years of school, when she was in her teens. Almost immediately after leaving school in 1871, when she was only sixteen, she married Surgeon-Major David McFall, acquiring two stepsons, ten and eight years old, and giving birth to another son within a year of her wedding. As a military wife, Grand accompanied her husband to stations in Asia and Malta before returning to England, where part of her husband's work was in a quarantine hospital for prostitutes infected with venereal disease.

Modest income from publishing *Ideala* (1888) supported her decision in 1890, when she was thirty-six and her son grown, to leave her husband and change her name to Sarah Grand, the name under which her international bestseller, *The Heavenly Twins,* appeared in 1893. "I tried for many years to combine housekeeping and literary pursuits," she once wrote, "and managed both, but at infinite cost. My health, household, and literary work all suffered; and it was not until circumstances put it in my power to give myself up entirely to literature that I succeeded" ("Should Married Women Follow Professions?" 122). Between 1891 and 1901, she published five novels and a book of short stories; thereafter, her pace slowed considerably, as she devoted more time to politics and public speaking; in the 1920s she served as mayoress of Bath, a largely ceremonial position. Between 1908 and 1922 Grand published two story collections and the first two novels of a trilogy; the third novel was never published, though she lived until 1943.

Although her novels portray some of the most unpleasant households in literary history, and although Grand herself lacked any domestic skills other than needleworking, she celebrated domesticity in articles and interviews published throughout her life and emphasized that the New Woman could combine domesticity with public life. Grand claimed that "the really 'Advanced Woman' is the one who says little, and is constantly, yet unobtrusively, ameliorating the condition of her fellow mortals, be they men or women" ("Court Her with Respect," 103). Some of this rhetoric may be strategic, part of the same approach that inspired Grand to recommend that feminists dress becomingly in order to disarm critics who might otherwise accuse them of unwomanliness. Thus, in an interview with Helen C. Black, Grand commented that women "'should never let it be supposed that because they advocate the "higher education," it unfits them for domestic duties or renders them unable to handle a baby, or darn a stocking. As it happens,' she adds, with a smile, 'I can manage to do both, I think'" (280–81). As I will show in more detail in future chapters, Grand made much of the power of "doing both" housekeeping and politics.

Like Ward and Grand, Charlotte Perkins Gilman experienced a childhood of poverty and inferior education, though, like Ward, Gilman was born into a family with a distinguished literary and intellectual heritage. Born Charlotte Anna Perkins in 1860, she was great-granddaughter of the evangelist Lyman Beecher and grandniece of abolitionist Henry Ward Beecher, suffragist Isabella Beecher Hooker, novelist Harriet Beecher Stowe, and, perhaps most notably for the purposes of this study, educator Catherine Beecher, author of the advice manuals *A Treatise on Domestic Economy* and, with Stowe, of *The American Woman's Home.* Charlotte Perkins's father left her mother when Charlotte was nine; thereafter the mother and two children moved eighteen times in fourteen years, in fourteen different cities, frequently fleeing debts. Gilman's peripatetic childhood resulted in her attending seven different schools during her four years of formal education—which ended when she was fifteen—forcing her, like Ward and Grand, to autodidacticism. She also completed a two-year program at the Rhode Island School of Design. In 1884, at twenty-three, she rather reluctantly married artist Charles Walter Stetson, and she gave birth to her daughter after less than eleven months of marriage. During this marriage, she suffered from severe and debilitating depression, exacerbated by a "rest cure" prescribed by Silas Weir Mitchell—an ordeal fictionalized in "The Yellow Wall-Paper." Only when she separated from Stetson after little more than three years of marriage could she manage to combine motherhood with writing, completing "The Yellow Wall-Paper" and numerous essays and poems while her daughter was living with her. Nevertheless, her first major editorial work, for the weekly paper *The Impress,* and the writing of *Women and Economics* (1898), the book that brought her international acclaim, did not take place until after the Stetsons' divorce was finalized in 1894 and Charlotte made the difficult (and scandalous) decision to send her daughter to live with Walter Stetson and his new wife. Her much happier second marriage, to her cousin George Houghton Gilman, took place in 1900.

Although *Women and Economics* was translated into seven languages, Gilman never achieved the kind of financial success from her writing enjoyed by Ward and Grand; for many years, she depended on fees earned as she crisscrossed the country lecturing. Tremendously prolific, she published hundreds of poems, nearly two hundred short stories, five novels, three utopian romances, eleven book-length nonfiction works, and more than a thousand nonfiction articles; a significant proportion of this work appeared first (or only) in the *Forerunner,* the monthly magazine Gilman single-handedly wrote and edited from November 1909 to December 1916. After her last book publication (*His Religion and Hers*), in 1923, Gilman's pace slowed considerably, though she composed a mystery novel, *Unpunished* (posthumously published, 1997), and the bulk of her autobiography during the 1920s. Thus, although she lived until 1935, Gilman's active productive period, from the mid-1880s to the 1920s, corresponds very closely to Ward's (mid-1870s to 1920) and Grand's (mid-1870s to early 1920s).

As the grandniece of America's most famous domestic novelist and most famous purveyor of domestic advice, Gilman was fully cognizant of the ideas of mid-nineteenth-century domestic ideology. Moreover, as the daughter of an impoverished single mother, Gilman was, by necessity, a practiced housekeeper herself. For a time shortly before her divorce was finalized, Charlotte Stetson successfully ran a boardinghouse. But she did not share the idealization of housekeeping of her great-aunts, who had called housework "the most important, the most difficult, and the most sacred and interesting duties that can possibly employ the highest intellect" (Beecher and Beecher Stowe, 221). Gilman's discussions of housekeeping are marked by tremendous contrasts. On the one hand, such stories as "Through This," "An Extinct Angel," and especially "The Yellow Wall-Paper" vividly portray the suffering and wasted talents of women who find themselves trapped in uncongenial domestic roles and, frequently, highly unpleasant domestic spaces. On the other hand, many other stories, a number of which I will discuss in the pages of this book, offer sprightly accounts of devoted housekeepers who find economic and emotional fulfillment by transforming their domestic skills into successful businesses or their homes into miracles of comfort and efficiency. To overlook either extreme in Gilman's portrayals of housework would be to distort her views.

Despite the many biographical parallels and connections, these are not writers ordinarily discussed together. In part, this separation reflects the general tendency within English departments of studying American and British literature in separate courses, taught by different faculty, whose national specializations—and the practices of publishers—generate specialized books. Even the more transnational field of women's studies has tended to trace traditions and lineages along national lines. Yet to juxtapose these three writers is useful, not least so that the study of British women's writing of the Victorian era may benefit from the extensive scholarship about domesticity in the writings of their American contemporaries. Conversely, renewed interest in British fin-de-siècle literature has yielded exciting work on interrelationships between women's Aestheticism and the New Woman, insights that can be usefully applied to the American scene.

More to the point, perhaps, Ward, Grand, and Gilman stand together as anomalies among their contemporaries. Most discussions of women writers from this period identify four types: New Women, Aesthetes, domestic realists, and conservatives. Ward's, Grand's, and Gilman's writings, like those of the New Women and unlike those of the other types of writers, express overt commitments to public causes concerning issues of class and gender; yet their commitment to marriage and domestic concerns—including interior design—distinguish them from the New Women and ally them with the other women writers of their era. They represent, I contend, a distinct category. The strategy I have labeled "literary housekeeping" illuminates, even if it does not resolve, the tensions among these three writers' artistic and didactic aspirations and their sometimes radical, frequently domestic concerns. Ward's, Grand's, and Gilman's positions on women's issues, though obviously far from identical, share a paradoxical complexity. In all three, a feminist goal of equality with men competes with a valorization of gender difference—especially the values and concerns that each writer considers distinctively female. Thus, although there are important political differences among the three writers, these differences should not overshadow their shared commitment to solving major social and political problems, their shared belief that women should apply their distinctive domestic capabilities to solve these public dilemmas, and their commitment to engaging these issues in their writing.

In the chapters that follow, I explore these shared concerns, organizing the discussion around tasks the three writers ascribe to the "housework" of literature. In chapter 1, "Literature as Housekeeping," I examine the ways the three authors redefine literature itself as a form of housekeeping. Consciously rejecting turn-of-the-century Aestheticism and modernism, they favor a litera-

ture that, like housework, is practical, ostensibly even mundane—designed, as
Sarah Grand writes, to "set the human household in order." They embrace literature's "didactic" qualities. Thus, rather than attempting to fulfill masculine
definitions of "high art," these writers propose an alternative domestic aesthetic in which women "raise the dust," sweeping away boundaries between the
artistic and the practical, the public and private, the personal and political. In
the three writers I identify three main approaches to literature as housekeeping: the exemplary, the parabolic, and the dialogic. In exemplary fiction, which
is primarily Gilman's approach, the stories represent a kind of exemplum,
with fictional characters "modeling" how to change the world. The parabolic
approach, which Grand preferred, resembles a parable, teaching a moral in a
metaphorical, elusive way and promising spiritual evolution typified by her superior heroines. Finally, the dialogic approach, Ward's chosen method, embodies conflicting ideologies in the interactions both between characters and
between author and readers.

Subsequent chapters are organized around tasks one typically associates
with the traditional "housewife." Chapter 2, "'A Motherliness Which Dominated Society': Mothers in Literary Housekeeping," explores motherhood as a
means to effect social change. To varying degrees, Grand, Gilman, and Ward all
portray marriage and procreation not merely as private choices but as "racial"
decisions, in the broad sense of that term. Enthusiastic proponents of eugenics, like many turn-of-the-century feminists, they believed a woman's selection of a "fit" husband represented a responsibility to the nation and the human
race. Furthermore, motherhood, deployed metaphorically as "civic maternalism," becomes an assertion of power over an infantilized manhood. This ideal
is particularly problematic in Gilman's *Herland,* as maternal "surveillance" per-
meates a public sphere in which everywhere is home.

The practical and aesthetic questions of home design concern chapter 3,
"Making a Home: Literary House Makers." In literary housekeeping, analysis
of physical space involves interrogation not only of physical situation but of social and political territories and boundaries. In literary housekeeping, the need
for a private "room of one's own" balances uneasily with women's growing
power to redesign living spaces both within and beyond the family dwelling.

Chapter 4, "'Loaf Givers': Providing Food for the Human Family," argues
that Ward's, Grand's, and Gilman's portrayals of food provision fundamentally

challenge the separation between public and private spheres. Grand focuses on analogies between food and art; Gilman's utopian ideal of kitchenless homes forms the heart of her vision of socialized housekeeping, and Ward portrays androgynous "Land Girls" growing wheat to win the Great War.

Chapter 5, "Cleaning House: Sanitation and Social Purity," explores literary expressions of the growing domestic science and sanitation movements, with their emphasis on the germ theory of contagion, which demonstrated that disease passes invisibly between people of all classes and types, erasing the separation between the individual household and the public streets. Domestic science challenged the assumption that housecleaning is trivial, mindless drudgery for menials, within the purely private realm, arguing that sanitation represented a momentous civic responsibility best assigned to the experts: women. Grand, Gilman, and Ward portray cleaning and disease prevention both literally and metaphorically as treatments for fundamental cultural maladies.

In chapter 6, "The Needleworker Reworked," I show that although needlework appears to be antithetical to the work of public feminism, literary housekeeping writers—Sarah Grand especially—attempt in their writings to make needlework function as a means to reconcile women's distinctive domestic arts with their public aspirations, in both the aesthetic and economic realms. Like Thomas Carlyle, literary housekeeping looks to writers to retailor worn-out institutions.

Literature as Housekeeping

THE STATEMENT THAT LITERATURE is a form of housekeeping seems puzzling at the outset. Housekeeping, after all, is practical and mundane, while literature, especially literature of the late nineteenth and early twentieth centuries, has traditionally been considered purely aesthetic and frequently elitist. As Oscar Wilde, the prototypical figure of the fin de siècle, famously asserted in the preface to *The Picture of Dorian Gray,* "All art is quite useless." Traditionally, British literature of the 1890s—when Grand, Gilman, and Ward enjoyed their greatest success—has been identified with Wilde and his circle, the Decadents and Aesthetes, while the early twentieth century is linked to the rise of modernism, whose philosophy about the uses of art might be identified with W. H. Auden's observation, "poetry makes nothing happen."

Practitioners of "literary housekeeping," however, developed a literary aesthetic of their own, in conscious opposition to "art for art's sake." Writers of literary housekeeping texts not only discussed and portrayed domestic activities in their works but saw literature *as* a form of housekeeping, embracing the practical effects of art that the modernists and protomodernists denied. At the same time, recognizing that beauty and practicality need not represent mutually exclusive housekeeping goals—especially in the latter years of the nineteenth century, when household advice books cheerfully reconciled sanitary admonitions with guidance on "house beautiful" decor—Gilman, Grand, and

Ward endeavored to integrate the values of Aestheticism and "purpose." The advocates of literature-as-housekeeping articulated—sometimes explicitly, often indirectly—a goal of producing literature that takes the domestic world for its subject matter and attempts to effect change beyond the private home. More fundamentally, the literature itself functions as a type of housekeeping, taking care of the "human household" through literary means. Although not all the work of these writers embodies the goals I identify as "literature as house-keeping," this aesthetic nevertheless illuminates a significant portion of their writings.

To understand the goals of "literature as housekeeping," it is necessary to understand how Grand, Gilman, and Ward define their art in relation to that of their contemporaries. All three devote considerable energy to attacking naturalism and Aestheticism, though they do not always strictly differentiate the two movements, lumping them under the xenophobic label "French fic-tion." We can assume the target is naturalism when the literary housekeepers reject what Ward describes as books by "men of science" who "dissect" reality (*Life and Works of the Sisters Brontë,* 3:xxvi),[1] or when Grand's Colonel Colquhoun in *The Heavenly Twins* places French books in Evadne's bookshelves as a method of seduction, only to find that she suffers anguish over "*the awful, needless suffer-ing!*" (221; emphasis Grand's). Like the naturalists, the literary housekeepers, Grand and Gilman especially, build their philosophies of human nature around Darwinian theories, but unlike the naturalists, they reject scientific determin-ism. On the contrary, their reform Darwinism is built on the assumption that humans can actively intervene in human evolution; hence they stress the im-portance of exercising free will. Their fiction's overall emphasis on moral choices and on intervening in social problems to forward human progress like-wise assumes human freedom of ethical choice.

Another part of the insistence, especially by Grand, on creating a distance from "French fiction" must surely be a response to a general conflation by the literary housekeepers' contemporaries of French decadence with the New Woman novel. All three writers were linked to the New Woman genre, and Grand was credited with naming the New Woman.[2] In turn, the New Woman novel of the 1880s and 1890s, with its controversial subject matter, was linked in the public mind with writers who had challenged the control exerted by the circulating libraries like Mudie's over the content of fiction. These writers

included George Moore, in his pamphlet *Literature at Nurse,* and the participants in the *New Review*'s symposium on "Candour in English Fiction,"[3] who
contended that the libraries effectively censored the content of novels, especially the portrayal of sexuality. That is, books approved by the circulating libraries were insufficiently realistic. This was a critique with which Ward,
Gilman, and Grand all sympathized; Grand, in particular, gained notoriety as
one of the first writers to openly discuss venereal disease in fiction, and she
once praised Zola's aim of "giving true views of life" ("Illustrated Interview,"
214). Grand's contribution to the "Tree of Knowledge" symposium in the *New
Review,* the follow-up to "Candour in English Fiction," reiterates her advocacy
of educating girls about sexual matters. Even Grand's "purity school" of New
Woman writing, that is, shares the naturalists' insistence on describing "life as
it is." But the literary housekeepers express disapproval of naturalism's unflinching, unvarnished attention to the sordid side of poverty, crime, prostitution, disease, drug abuse, and so on. Indeed, Grand targets French writers for
some of her harshest attacks in *The Beth Book* and other novels, and she once
wrote the London *Daily Chronicle* to demand an apology for "coupling my
name with that of M. Zola in what amounts to a charge of indecency" ("A Case
for Apology"). The goal of Grand, Gilman, and Ward was not to produce the
dispassionate "science" of literary naturalism but to alert readers to problems
requiring solutions, or, in a domestic metaphor, messes to be cleaned up.

Moreover, although the literary housekeepers have important connections
with the "purity school" of the New Woman genre of the 1880s and 1890s,
none was terribly sympathetic to the other type of New Women, whom late-
Victorians identified as "neurotics" or "erotomaniacs" and Margaret Oliphant
dubbed the "Anti-Marriage League." A simple distinction between the two
schools is that whereas "neurotic" writers like George Egerton (Mary Chavelita
Dunne) or Iota (Kathleen Mannington Caffyn) sympathetically portray female
sexual desire, Grand, the best-known exemplar of the "purity school," celebrates female purity and condemns male sexual degeneracy.[4] Unlike many New
Woman writers, she calls marriage the "ideal" state, despite the fact that most
of the marriages she portrays are far from her ideal. Gilman and Ward share
Grand's firm approval of marriage, though Gilman, who advocates celibacy
even in marriage, takes the idea of purity further than Grand; Ward's novels
feature distinctly erotic passages, yet she consistently portrays extramarital

sexuality as a destructive force. Unlike many of the New Woman writers, the literary housekeepers are not so much concerned to abandon or revise traditional womanly roles as they are to expand them into the public sphere. In some ways, this approach is a descendent of the sentimental tradition of "domestic fiction," but whereas the sentimentalists remained content to produce literature that exerts the influence of "right feeling" and to envision women staying within the household and exerting a maternal "influence," the literary housekeepers wanted to take their brooms out of the parlor, even off the front stoop, and right into the street.

Less obvious allies of the literary housekeepers are the female Aesthetes, whose fin-de-siècle work is currently enjoying long-overdue attention. As in both the male and female Aesthetic traditions, "Aesthetic" domestic arts— home decor, clothing design, and needlework—play central roles in the housekeeping aesthetic of Gilman, Grand, and Ward; nor is it irrelevant that Grand was accomplished at lace making, a craft whose revival was taken up by the Aesthetic movement; that Gilman attended two years of art school and for a time supported herself with her art; and that Ward, whose husband was the *Times*'s art critic, commissioned an important London building from major Arts and Crafts architects and furnished a series of private and public buildings with "Art furniture," Morris papers, and blue pots. But while the female Aesthetes opted to participate in an apolitical high-art tradition and the New Women emphasized political reform, the literary housekeepers attempted to combine the goals of beauty and reform, the realms of private and public.

In their emphasis on ethical choice and even in their obvious "earnestness," the literary housekeepers participate in the traditions of high realism we associate with William Dean Howells and with George Eliot—whom all three writers admired, at least up to a point.[5] "Realism" is one of literary history's most slippery terms, having been claimed (and attacked) by exponents of a remarkable range of styles and approaches; nevertheless it seems safe to say that most of the writings I identify as participating in the project of literary housekeeping share traits that match classic definitions of "realism": portrayal of ordinary middle-class characters in everyday situations, with a plentiful supply of material detail to provide the illusion of verisimilitude. Of the three writers, Ward is the most consistently "realistic," and Gilman, with her utopias, parables, and allegorical sermons, the least. In any case, as we shall see, all three articulate an aesthetic of accurate representation of "real life."

At the same time, all three authors consciously wrote "with a purpose," producing fictions that range from the mildly to the overtly didactic. Susan Rubin Suleiman has argued that the *roman à thèse* "provides an extreme version of the didactic tendency at the origin of the novel—a tendency that theorists and practitioners of the modern 'text' have sought to suppress" (19). In their concern with "purpose," the literary housekeepers' refusal to embrace modernism could thus be seen as clinging to older traditions. In fact, the avowedly apolitical quality of Aestheticism and modernism is the primary reason the literary housekeepers repeatedly differentiate their work from "literature." Ironically, this tendency, too, allies them with much of the realist tradition. Howells in particular consistently distinguished interest in "style" from concern with "truth." The "persistent denigration of the 'literary,'" Michael Davitt Bell argues, is one of Howells's "principal tenets" of realism (21). George Levine, too, in his study of British realism, cites "the centrality to realism of a self-conscious rejection of literature" (9)—though the "literature" rejected by high realism is generally "the romance." Ironically, in American literary magazines at the end of the nineteenth century, realism (variously defined) was "sometimes denounced for being insufficiently literary, but it was more often praised for being supremely literary. Moreover, the controversies about realism took place within the most belletristic periodicals in the United States, whose attention guaranteed that realism was a literary issue" (Glazener, 2). For some late-nineteenth-century American women writers, like Sarah Orne Jewett, embracing literary realism offered a way to establish themselves as "'serious' artists," in contradistinction to seeking "wide moral influence" (Bell, 172); but Gilman, Ward, and Grand resisted this trend, seeking instead to reconcile the claims of literature and purpose.[6]

The private/public divide and its relationship with didactic purpose, which so concerned the literary housekeepers, is crucial to several recent studies of the novel in general and the Victorian realistic novel in particular. Critics like D. A. Miller, Joseph Allen Boone, Lennard J. Davis, Rosemarie Bodenheimer, and Catherine Gallagher have meditated on the novel's often unwitting complicity in maintaining the status quo, so that even novels ostensibly sympathetic to the powerless participate in their control, and novels concerned to define the domestic and private against the "disciplinary" world of institutional, public power implicitly undercut the very distinction, implicating the domestic world in social discipline. The novel, with its focus on the inner world of individuals and on personal ethical dilemmas, tends to reinforce contrasts between the private and public, the individual and the larger culture. In Miller's words, "the novel *belongs* to the disciplinary field that it portrays" (21; emphasis Miller's). Davis points out that because the novel as a genre embodies an individualist ideology and, therefore, "excludes any but the most individual solution" to social problems (119), even the "novel with a purpose" encourages passivity and withdrawal from social action. If nothing else, these studies, all published in 1987 and 1988, reveal their own era's fascination with the problem of the public/private dichotomy; yet, remarkably, their understandings of "private" and "public" run the full gamut: Marxist economic, Habermasian, Foucauldian, and feminist.

Gilman, Grand, and Ward seem remarkably cognizant of such narrative challenges, directly responding to the traditions of Aestheticism and naturalism that suggested, for different reasons, that artists either should not attempt to change the world—or could not if they tried. The three writers' fiction negotiates uneasily with the problems of traditional narrative structures that reinforce conservative ideologies, though if they were ambivalent about the marriage plot—as Gilman certainly was—it was not because they questioned matrimony itself: all three valued the institution of marriage and considered it fully compatible with fundamental social change. Perhaps it was because to some extent they recognized potential problems with fiction that all three writers became rather active public speakers, and that Ward devoted so much energy to translating *Robert Elsmere*'s fictional New Brotherhood into the bricks, mortar, and playgrounds of the Passmore Edwards Settlement. More to the point of this study, it may be the recognition of the fundamental inability of realist fiction to effect change that explains certain violations of realism, forays into the polemic, in their writing. Nevertheless, Ward, Grand, and Gilman all consciously continued the attempt to use writing, especially fiction, as a means of direct social action.

In their fiction we can identify three main approaches to portraying social messes and their domestic solutions: a parabolic approach, an exemplary approach, and a dialogic approach. The parabolic tale is, as the term suggests, a type of parable, an inspirational, rather metaphorical tale teaching a moral that is directly stated but ultimately somewhat elusive. Grand, who preferred this approach, tends in her parabolic stories to suggest the promise of a higher good in a vague future—and in a spiritual realm beyond the comprehension of ordinary mortals, if not of her gifted heroines. In fiction that teaches using what I am calling the "exemplary method," the stories represent a kind of exemplum or "modeling": readers learn pragmatic lessons in "how to change the world" by reading how fictional characters change theirs. This is primarily Gilman's approach, but Grand and Ward use it as well. Finally, the dialogic approach, embodying a clash of ideologies, might be said to characterize all successful fiction—indeed Mikhail Bakhtin has said just that. As a philosophy of style and plot and as a theory about the relation of writer and reader, the dialogic is most clearly what Ward strove to accomplish.

Sarah Grand's Parables of Domestic Genius

Probably the most effective articulations of the "literature-as-housekeeping" metaphor come from Sarah Grand, and yet Grand is the least systematic theorist of the three writers. Unlike Gilman and Ward, Grand wrote few essays or articles about the arts; rather, she embeds most of her comments about these subjects within her novels, particularly *The Beth Book* and *The Heavenly Twins*. Moreover, as John Kucich has demonstrated, Grand's discussions of truth telling in and by fiction are marked by contradictions and confusion. Nevertheless, one can extrapolate an aesthetic that claims for art the complementary traits of beauty and practicality, traits that Grand explicitly compares to the goals of housekeeping.

The challenge of clarifying Grand's aesthetic theories takes us to her paradigmatic statement about literary housekeeping in "The New Aspect of the Woman Question":

> Mirrors may be either a distorting or a flattering medium, but women do not care to see life any longer in a glass darkly. Let there be light. We suffer in the first shock of it. We shriek in horror at what we discover when it is turned on that which was hidden away in dark corners; but the first principle of good housekeeping is to have no dark corners, and as we recover ourselves we go to work with a will to sweep them out. It is for us to set the human household in order, to see to it that all is clean and sweet and comfortable for the men who are fit to help us to make a home in it. We are

> bound to raise the dust while we are at work, but only those who are in it
> will suffer any inconvenience from it. (276)

Although this passage does not refer directly to art or literature, it employs two
of Western culture's dominant metaphors for the human mind, metaphors
commonly adopted in turn by critical theorists from Plato to the present. M. H.
Abrams's framework for discussing critical theories, in *The Mirror and the Lamp*,
provides a helpful means for explicating the theoretical underpinnings of
Grand's passage. The passage refers both to the mirror, the common metaphor
for art's mimetic capacity accurately to represent objective reality, and to the
lamp, the staple metaphor of what Abrams terms "expressive" theories, ideas
that gained dominance in the Romantic era and hold that art expresses the
artist's thoughts, feelings, and perceptions. But perhaps most important in
Grand's passage is what Abrams calls the "pragmatic" theory, which focuses on
art's impact on its audience. Grand implies that writing is itself a form of
housekeeping that acts as the "broom" raising the dust, and offers "domestic"
solutions to the messes art identifies and sets out to clean up. Finally, what
Grand's passage leaves out, and what she explicitly rejects in many other passages, is the fourth approach to art identified by Abrams, that which concentrates on the artistic product itself, separate from the three other concerns, the
"objective" or "art-for-art's-sake" approach. Grand's "raising the dust" passage
and Abrams's categories offer a useful organizing principle for my discussion of
Grand's theory of the reality of art, her ideas about genius, her pronouncements about the functions of art, and her condemnation of the art-for-art's-
sake movement.

Complicating any attempt to define Grand's aesthetics, especially her
views of mimesis, is her own ambivalence about fiction, brilliantly explored in
John Kucich's important study. As Kucich notes, not only are Grand's portrayals of characters' honesty and lying inconsistent, but the representations of fiction itself are ambiguous. Beth Maclure in *The Beth Book* discusses the writing
of fiction, but the book she writes and publishes to great acclaim turns out not
to be a novel at all, and she ultimately discovers her "genius," the true vocation
that will serve humanity, is not writing but oratory. Well-educated Evadne, of
The Heavenly Twins, whose leading trait is that "[s]he wanted to know" (1), has
only biting criticisms to offer about the novels she reads as a young girl—
though to be sure, these are eighteenth-century novels by men. As an adult,

Evadne finds realistic fiction too depressing to read. Grand herself commented more than once that she rarely read fiction.[7] In a letter of 1 January 1895, she complained, "Fiction is of little or no value to those who wish to know the world they live in" (Heilmann and Forward, 2:46).

Yet Grand repeatedly insists on the "truth" of her writing, and on the importance of truth in literature. When Grand remarks, "Mirrors may be either a distorting or a flattering medium" and that "women do not care to see life any longer in a glass darkly," she is implicitly defending her own accuracy. The allusion to 1 Corinthians 13:12 subtly alters the passage as it appears in the King James translation: "For now we see *through* a glass, darkly; but then face to face." The Bible's sense of "glass" as a distorting lens becomes Grand's "looking-glass" providing a (potentially) distorting reflection of reality—distortions that women, she says, no longer care for. Accordingly she repeatedly insists on her own dedication to truth. "A Study from Life" is both the subtitle of *Ideala* and part of *The Beth Book*'s subtitle, and the preface to the collection *Our Manifold Nature* begins, "These stories are simply what they profess to be—studies from life of our manifold nature" (v); later Grand refers to the stories as "little essays" (vii).[8] Much of the preface to *Our Manifold Nature* addresses the problems of literary convention and the goal of truth telling: "Fiction has always been held to be at its best when it was true to life. To be true to life seems, therefore, to be the noblest ambition of an author; and this has led in our day to an effort to go beyond the mere semblance and to grasp the reality of life" (vi).

Even if an artist can avoid false convention, accuracy alone is insufficient, according to Grand. The portrayal of truth must have a "purpose." Specifically, says the artist who narrates the story "Eugenia," "if we would make [the world] lovely we must know exactly the nature of the diseases that disfigure it" (103). In *The Heavenly Twins,* Evadne, before she develops a morbid horror of reality, comments, "Social subjects seem to be forcing themselves on the attention of every thoughtful and right-minded person just now, and it would be culpable cowardice to shun them while there is the shadow of a hope that some means may be devised to put right what is so very wrong. Ignoring an evil is tantamount to giving it full licence to spread" (342). The purpose of describing evil is accuracy not for its own sake, but for the sake of reform, to know problems in order to solve them: "At one time, the subjects of vice and immorality were shunned altogether, now we are beginning to face them boldly, and to deal with them in fiction, not as the French do for love of them, but in order to expose the evils, mental, physical, and social, which they then entail both on individuals and the community at large" (Letter to Professor Viëtor, 190).

Fiction's job, therefore, is not simply to reflect but to interpret reality. Commenting on the future of the novel, Grand explains that a novelist must offer a reader more than "the life he is sick of, labelled 'real life,'" for the reader requires more than "the passing show." As to what, precisely, that something "more" entails Grand remains vague: it is "the bread of life" and will satisfy "the spirit's yearning to penetrate the mists that veil the goal" ("Future of the Novel," 204). To "penetrate the mists" generally requires bright light—here, some help with identifying "lessons." Dr. Galbraith, who acts as Grand's critical mouthpiece in *The Beth Book,* comments, "People can see life for themselves, but they cannot always see the meaning of it, the why and wherefore, whence things come and whither they are tending, so that the lessons of life are lost—or would be but for the efforts of the modern novelist" (375).[9] This strong statement attributes to novelists a unique interpretive capacity.

At the heart of Grand's views of art is what Abrams refers to as an "expressive" theory of genius, as a spontaneous overflow of a poet's imagination. Specifically, Grand develops a theory of domestic genius. The full title of her semiautobiographical *Künstlerroman* is *The Beth Book: Being a Study of the Life of Elizabeth Caldwell Maclure, a Woman of Genius.* Terry Lovell has pointed out that the recurrent trope of the "woman of genius" in New Woman fiction represents a double-edged strategy. A story of a gifted woman demonstrates that women can be men's equals and shows the injustice of suppressing women's talents through inadequate education or other barriers. However, "the woman of genius" story risks implying that the heroine is "exceptional," not representative of women generally; hence, it obliges authors to show that their exceptional heroines are nevertheless "true women," by portraying them in traditional roles, especially maternal or other self-sacrificing roles. As a result, says Lovell, "the net effect of such plot resolutions was to backhandedly confirm what feminism denied: the naturalness of gender" (122). However, Grand attempts to turn the potential conflict between domesticity and genius into an advantageous alliance in which art and housekeeping play complementary, not conflicting, roles.

She does this most explicitly in her "raising the dust" passage. When Grand proclaims, "Let there be light," the allusion to Genesis 1:3 paradoxically strengthens the connection between housework and literature, as Grand conflates the broom-wielding New Woman housekeeper with the traditionally masculine image of the godlike writer-creator, who separates light from darkness in order to "enlighten" the benighted masses, creating a universe out of chaos and humans out of dust—in Milton's phrase, "The Power . . . That rais'd us from the dust and plac't us here" (*Paradise Lost,* 4:412, 416). Grand's passage also employs an expressive trope for creativity revived in the Romantic era, that the mind in perception or creation resembles a lamp or radiating sun, actively contributing to the world rather than only passively reflecting like a mirror. Several places in *The Beth Book* allude to Wordsworthian ideas of the imagination. Grand frequently identifies Beth's "further faculty" as "the vision and the dream" (177, 338, 391, 434), and in one passage, Grand speculates on a kind of spiritual preexistence reminiscent of the ideas and imagery in Wordsworth's "Intimations Ode": Beth believes that "she possessed a power of some kind in her infancy which gradually lapsed as her intellectual faculties developed. She was conscious that the senses had come between her and some mysterious joy which was not of the senses, but of the spirit. There lingered what seemed to be the recollection of a condition anterior to this, a condition of which no tongue can tell, which is not to be put into words, or made evident to those who have no recollection" (28).

Like Wordsworth, Beth may have lost some "power" with distance from infancy, but she and many other Grand characters maintain a "further faculty" of perception. The further faculty is "some more perfect power to know than the intellect" (27). In part, it entails "heights of perception beyond the reach of the faculties of ordinary mortals" (*The Winged Victory,* 354), and a fuller understanding of an external truth. More important, perhaps, it is also active and collaborative, resembling Wordsworthian perceptions that "half create" ("Tintern Abbey," lines 105–7): "the union of sea and sky and shore, the light, the colour, absorbed her, and drew her out of herself. Her soul expanded, it spread its wings, it stretched out spiritual arms to meet and clasp the beloved nature of which it felt itself to be a part. It was her earliest recognition of their kinship, a glimpse of greatness, a moment of ecstasy never to be forgotten, the first stirring in herself of the creative faculty" (*Beth Book,* 15–16). Grand's "vision and the dream" also includes social and political power: "Great is the power of thought," says Lady Fulda, one of the feminist characters in *The Beth Book*: "By thinking these things the race is evolving them. Thought married to suggestion is a creative force. . . . I believe that the force which is carrying us along is the force that makes for righteousness. We women have in our minds now what will culminate in the recognition by future generations of the beauty of goodness. Woman is to be the mother of God in Man" (413, 414).

Despite her emphasis on genius, Grand suggests repeatedly that the further faculty is "a power lying latent in the whole race, which will eventually come into possession of it; but with which, at present, only some few rare beings are perfectly endowed" (27). Several of Grand's female characters have this extraordinary capacity for perception, a sort of second sense, though some seem more gifted than others. All are seen as precursors of humans with new capacities. The female characters thus endowed range from Evadne in *The Heavenly Twins,* whose occasional moments of insight include her recognition that Mosley Menteith is a "dreadful man" ("I feel—I have a consciousness which informs me of things my intellect cannot grasp" [232]), to Ella Banks, in *The Winged Victory,* whom we are to see as a highly advanced eugenic specimen, and who has moments of "Vision," in which the spirits of her ancestors send her warnings. The growth of Beth Caldwell's "further faculty" is a major plot of *The Beth Book,* which climaxes in her recognition of the nature of her "gift." In each case, the visionary capacity places its holder in the vanguard of human progress. Beth is described as "one of the first swallows of the woman's summer," and upon meeting her, Ideala remarks, "I suspect she is the genius for whom we are waiting" (527, 391).

One of the hallmarks of the further faculty that constitutes genius is a sensitivity to the Zeitgeist and extraordinary capacity to bring it to expression. Beth is one of the "people who collect and hold in themselves some knowledge of contemporary events as the air collects and holds moisture" (259). Grand emphasizes that this sensitivity is crucial for a novelist because it provides the spiritual means by which the public sphere "social atmosphere" charges the private individual/novelist, who in turn embodies this truth in fiction for the public's benefit. On numerous occasions Grand attributed *The Heavenly Twins* to this kind of sensitivity: "I am one of the people upon whom the ideas that are still in the air are apt to settle. I catch an idea as I might catch the measles, and it comes out in pen and ink" ("In the Days of My Youth," 204). Similarly, in the 1923 foreword to *The Heavenly Twins,* Grand claims, "The *Zeitgeist* determined my subject matter. . . . Sooner or later the thoughts and feelings of the inarticulate, seeking expression, select a medium, and I happened to be the medium on whom the ideas in the air laid hold" (ix).

One could argue that Grand's ascription of Beth's creative work to natural genius and her own to the Zeitgeist seems to depreciate the work involved. Here, once again, one of Grand's housekeeping analogies helps resolve the problem. When young Beth writes a poem for her childhood sweetheart, Sammy, she initially attributes its origin to her "further faculty": "Things come into my mind, but I don't think them, and I can't say them. They don't come in words. It's more like seeing them, you know, only you don't see them with your eyes, but with something inside yourself." This nonverbal mysticism suggests a kind of involuntary possession by some higher force beyond her control yet somehow "inside" her. But then she explains, "I didn't make it up, it just came to me. When I make it up it'll most likely be quite different. It's like the stuff for a dress, you know, when you buy it. You get it made up, and it's the same stuff, and it's quite different, too, in a way. You've got it put into shape, and it's good for something" (178). The analogy suggests that inspiration may come "whole cloth," but that effort must ensue to "make it up." The final results, moreover, will be "good for something." Like designing, cutting, and sewing a dress, writing a poem (or novel) may require considerable labor on the maker's part; and, as with a dress, the results will be more than pretty; they must also be functional, "good for something." This passage is one of several in which Grand, echoing Thomas Carlyle, directly connects sewing, including making a dress—or tailoring—to writing. As I will discuss in more detail in chapter 6, Grand, like Carlyle, looks to writers to "re-tailor" worn-out institutions. The mandate to make it "good for something" is at the core of her arguments about writing's housekeeping function.

Although Grand protested that *The Beth Book* was not autobiographical, she revealed just enough facts about her earlier years to fuel speculation to the contrary, for many events in the novel echo the little we know about Grand's life. Grand occasionally denied parallels between her mother and Beth's or her own husband and Dan Maclure, but she never publicly admitted the contrast between Beth's great domestic proficiency and her own domestic ignorance.

Rather, she wrote emphatically on the importance of domestic skills for middle-class girls, in "The Human Quest" and "The Case of the Modern Married Woman"; and she imparted the impression to her "devoted friend" Gladys Singers-Bigger that she always made her own bed. Yet Grand's biographer Gillian Kersley learned from Grand's former maid, Edna, that Grand never made her bed—it was made either by Edna or by the cook, Mrs. Tailor—and as for cooking, "Madame Grand couldn't do a thing for herself, couldn't even make a cup of coffee, never came to the kitchen" (Kersley, 349 n. 12; 133). Presumably Grand cultivated the fiction of her own domestic skills because she valued the *idea* that a feminist writer could cook, sew, dust, and make a bed. It therefore seems to me crucial that Grand's most sustained exploration of creativity, the story of "a woman of genius," should stress the character's housekeeping skills and frequently juxtapose them with literary skills: Beth learns cleaning and cooking from the same maid who impresses her with the joys of narrative; the young Beth makes both a poem and whiting on toast for her first boyfriend; and she alternately writes and embroiders in a hidden room of her own. Beth's "further faculty" is fostered in part through order, housekeeping. Loss of contact with the further faculty is signaled by lapsing of attention to such order. So the raising of dust and shining of light into dark corners is, to Grand's mind, more than metaphorical, for good housekeeping correlates with creativity. Whether or not Grand was familiar with the American use of the word "faculty" to describe housekeeping skill, in this part of *The Beth Book* she clearly connects the eclipse of Beth's "further faculty" with her inattention to household order.

This analogy between housework and art highlights Grand's fundamentally pragmatic aesthetic. Rejecting purely objectivist views of art, Grand describes Beth's foray into writing: "Art for art's sake she despised, but in art for man's sake she already discovered noble possibilities" (358). Beth articulates her goals in pragmatic terms: "[W]hat we want from the written word that reaches all of us is help and advice, comfort and encouragement. If art interferes with that, then art had better go. . . . I am speaking of art for art's sake, of course" (460). This is not to say that Grand is indifferent to beauty in art. We have already seen Lady Fulda's observation that, with women's help, future generations will recognize "the beauty of goodness"; and the analogy between making a dress and composing poetry suggests that the final product is "good for something" partly because it is beautiful. In *Adnam's Orchard,* Adnam Pratt, one of the few men in Grand's work graced with the mystical "further faculty," echoes John Ruskin's and William Morris's views of artisanship when he remarks, "I see no antagonism between use and beauty; they should be friends. In the old days, when men put heart into their work, they were friends" (254).

A number of critics have observed that Grand owed more debts to the Decadents and Aesthetes than she might have wanted to admit. She insisted on distancing herself from both groups, partly for political reasons, in an attempt to disassociate her message from theirs, especially as regards sexuality. Whatever her motives, she rather venomously attacked those she labeled the stylists, those who separate use and beauty. In *The Beth Book,* Ideala asserts, "The works of art for art's sake, and style for style's sake, end on the shelf much respected, while their authors end in the asylum, the prison, and the premature grave" (460). Ideala describes visiting a library where the "beautiful books" of the stylists had gone untouched, unlike the well-thumbed "instructive" books. No one reads them, she says, because "[t]here is no comfort in life in them. They are the mere mechanics of literature, and nobody cares about them except the mechanicians" (461).

If "art for art's sake" is mechanical, the works Grand approves do take advantage of beauty, but for the pragmatic purpose of appealing to human emotions, which in turn shape readers' ideas and actions. In "The Morals of Manner and Appearance," she declares that "it is not by arguments but by feelings that the world is swayed." She advises writers to "dress up" truth, "bedeck it with a touch of colour here, such as a little poetry would give it, or a shining jewel there, such as scintillates from a flash of wit; give them something to grasp in the shape of a brilliant epigram, a thing that they can commit to memory . . . ; let it be made musical to the ear by a soft voice, and appeal to the eye pleasantly in the shape of an attractive-looking person, and it is not only accepted with enthusiasm, but acted on eagerly" (24). This somewhat cynical analysis reflects the "performative" quality that John Kucich has pointed out in much of Grand's work, but it also reflects a maternalistic approach to a child-like reader, who requires songs and games to help him learn his lesson. Truth without pleasure, Grand argues, will be metaphorically left on the reader's plate, untouched: "Bare words uninformed with feeling are as insipid as meat without salt" ("Morals of Manner," 26). On the other hand, she compares pleasure without truth—even small "doses" of "inferior fiction"—to an "opiate, the effect of which is stupefying" ("On Clubs," 98)—not an appropriate way to deal with a child, however refractory.[10]

Despite these pragmatic comments about literature, and despite her novels' many discursive passages expressing strong "lessons" about everything from tight lacing to vivisection, Grand's fiction is, in its storytelling methods, the least overtly didactic of the literary housekeepers' work. Her novels feature experiments in point of view, unreliable narrators, dream sequences, and impressionistic descriptions that undermine doctrinal certainty. Because of the consistent mysticism at the heart of so many of Grand's stories, I have described them as "parabolic." In the spirit of her pronouncement, "Let there be light," Grand adopts a New Testament narrative stance, producing plots resembling biblical parables in that their didactic intent seems clear, their meaning frequently less so. Grand often employs fablelike plots, as in *The Heavenly Twins,* which contains three parallel plots about young women's marital decisions, only one of which turns out (relatively) well. Moreover, Grand's uncannily prescient heroines make unlikely role models, though, to be sure, their poor marital choices exemplify what Susan Suleiman calls "negative exemplary apprenticeships": models of what not to do. Grand premises much of her writing on eugenic ideas, but whereas Gilman, as we shall see, offers practical approaches for selecting better humans, Grand frequently starts with characters who already benefit from lucky breeding that has produced "further faculties" beyond the grasp of presumably less gifted readers. Beth may be "one of the first swallows of the woman's summer," but we follow her only into spring. In some ways, that is, the books focus less on sweeping out the dark corners than on "Let there be light." As Grand insists, however, "to have no dark corners" is the "first principle of good housekeeping."

Charlotte Perkins Gilman: Literature as Mothering

Despite her frequently reiterated denial that her writings are "literature" (the quotation marks are her own), Charlotte Perkins Gilman in fact develops and employs a consistent and well-articulated literary aesthetic. In sustained discussions of literature in chapters in *The Man-Made World* and *Human Work* and in numerous *Forerunner* essays, Gilman argues that genuine literary value is inseparable from "social" value. This social value corresponds in part to the aesthetic I have called "literature as housekeeping." Consistent with her approach to fiction as a motherly activity, Gilman shapes her fiction in "exemplary" plots that provide models of "Truth and Something Better Ahead" (*Moving the Mountain,* 116).

Critical discussions of Gilman's ideas about literature typically cite her self-deprecating denials that she wrote "literature."[11] One of the statements most frequently quoted is from the "Summary of Purpose" for the *Forerunner,* in which Gilman published the bulk of her fiction: "The subject matter, for the most part, is not to be regarded as 'literature,' but as an attempt to set forth certain views of life which seemed to the author of real importance to human welfare" (286). Similarly Gilman said of her successful collection of poetry, *In This Our World,* "I can't call it a book of poems. I call it a tool box. It was written to drive nails with."[12] Gilman even refused to identify her most respected literary production, "The Yellow Wall-Paper," as literary. When William Dean Howells wished to include the story in an anthology of *The Great Modern American Short Stories,* she "assured him that it was no more 'literature' than my other stuff, being definitely written 'with a purpose'" (*Living,* 121). She immediately follows this seeming demurrer, however, with the qualification, "In my judgment it is a pretty poor thing to write, to talk, without a purpose" (121). Thus she rejects not literature itself, nor the writing of literature, but "literature," that is, writing that calls itself literature but that is an exercise in either "art for art's sake" or "self-expression." By distancing her own work from so-called literature, Gilman explicitly distances herself from modernist and protomodernist aesthetic fashions. Her critical writings systematically reject these literary fashions and advocate an alternative literary aesthetic that would produce, in her view, authentic literature.

If an expressive concept of art was central to Grand's theories, Gilman seems to have had more mixed feelings about the idea of art as a form of self-expression. On the one hand, as numerous critics have observed, the journal kept by the narrator of "The Yellow Wall-Paper" embodies the character's compulsion to express herself somehow through writing; and similar therapeutic writing appears in *Moving the Mountain* and *Unpunished.*[13] In *Human Work* (1904) Gilman treats the idea of artistic self-expression with tolerant condescension, arguing in terms reminiscent of Grand's evocation of the Zeitgeist that artists who claim to be expressing themselves are in fact unwittingly expressing their time and their people. The artist's desire for "self-expression," Gilman writes, is indeed an "insistent force from within which will out through whatever medium is at hand," and the artist must "express that which is good in him quite regardless of whether the people around him want it or not; will pay him for it or not." The artist may even persist in the cliché that an "artist . . . must not consider social service in the least; he must express himself" (266). But unbeknownst to the artist, "that unfaltering expression *is* his social service," because "[w]hat he feels is the heart of his people" (267, 266). Gilman explains women's relatively small record of artistic expression by arguing that, for women, "the inner impulse demanding expression is considered 'selfish,' and a thing to resist; and their energies are forced into other lines because thereby they imagine they are best serving. If they recognised this inward propulsion as the call for social expression—not self's—it would stand differently in their scale of duty" (268). Not only does this reasoning justify the importance of women's writing, it also means that in "The Yellow Wall-Paper," John's forbidding the narrator to write—like Silas Weir Mitchell's orders that Gilman "never . . . touch pen, brush or pencil again"—not only represents a threat of "utter mental ruin" ("Why I Wrote 'The Yellow Wallpaper'?" 331) on an individual level, but also thwarts the public duty of the woman artist to answer the "call for social expression" through self-expression.

Yet elsewhere, especially in later writings, Gilman launches biting attacks on writing as "self-expression." In a 1913 review of the New York Armory Exhibition of Impressionist, Post-Impressionist, Cubist, and Futurist art, Gilman mocks the artists' "patter" about self-expression, dismissing the artists as "these poor morbid little ones suffering from elephantiasis of the soul": "Why should anyone on earth, unless some psychological specialist, care how these people feel?" ("On Some Recent 'Art,'" 112). Modernist artists and writers—for Gilman's discussion of the Armory exhibit includes an extended comparison to the writings of Gertrude Stein—represent an extreme case, but for Gilman the modernist emphasis on "self-expression" reflects a more pervasive, long-standing cultural problem of androcentrism. As she explains in the chapter on "The Effect of the Position of Woman on the Race Mind" in her serialized book *Our Brains and What Ails Them,* "The dominant masculine characteristics are Desire, Combat, and Self-Expression," and the cultural dominance of human males has created an overemphasis on these characteristics in the "race-mind" (249). At the heart of Gilman's recommendations for improving the arts is a belief in severely limiting "masculine art," specifically its focus on desire and combat and its aesthetic of self-expression. The change in Gilman's view of artistic self-expression from tolerant cooptation of the concept to scornful rejection may stem from the rise of modernist aesthetics, with their ever-greater resistance to the social service so central to Gilman's view of art. Moreover, the embrace of modernism by women writers like Stein belied Gilman's earlier optimism regarding the benefits of women's answering the "inward propulsion as the call for social expression—not self's."

Gilman's attacks on "art for art's sake" are even more scathing than those she makes on artistic self-expression. She dismisses the "assumption of the artist that his form of production is beyond all social responsibility or control, that 'there is no ethics in art,'" as an "instance of the ego concept at its most insane height" (*Human Work,* 270). To Gilman, as to Grand and Ward, the danger of the Aestheticist creed that "there is no ethics in art" is that it will produce immoral art. In discussing "The Effect of Literature upon the Mind" in *Our Brains and What Ails Them,* Gilman criticizes "Literature with a large L," which "seeks absolute divorce not only from fact but even from purpose. It must be Art pure and undefiled; . . . 'Never prostituted to any useful service'" (135). Gilman imagines her "pure" artist remarking, "I like to tell stories; the stories I tell are frankly objectionable—but what of that? . . . I can tell them in a supremely objectionable manner—it gives me pleasure, and I express myself thus!" To those who would object that by telling objectionable stories "he is deliberately coarsening and lowering the taste of the world," he scornfully replies, "Story-telling knows no ethics!" (138).

This is not to say that Gilman rejects beauty, which, theoretically, was the Aesthetic movement's central concern. Gilman insists, "To be surrounded by beautiful things has much influence upon the human creature: to make beautiful things has more" (*Women and Economics,* 66). Gilman frequently bemoans ugliness: of cities, of women's dress, of home decor. She praises technical proficiency in her reviews of fiction and poetry. In her utopian stories and novels, humanity is surrounded by beauty: lovely homes and forests in *Herland;* beautiful music in "Doctor Clair's Place" and by the end of "Making a Change." In the utopian *Moving the Mountain* one character exclaims, "There's more art in the world to make us happier" (73). But Gilman denies that contemporary "Literature with a large L" can add to human happiness, complaining, in a poem called "In Modern Verse," that

> *Time was when fearless heart and brain*
> *Used words as common as the rain,*
>> *And through that veil of lingual light*
>> *Shone Truth and Hope and Beauty bright;*
> *But weird, wild words small thoughts enchain,*
>> *In modern verse.* (10–15)

The "weird, wild words"—words for words' sake—and esoteric content of "modern verse" prevent it from fulfilling the function of genuine literature: to provide truth, hope, and, yes, beauty.

For Gilman, first and foremost, art is "social," and all her other ideas about the arts derive from this central premise. Gilman argues that human social evolution extends and surpasses biological evolution. As she explains in *Our Brains and What Ails Them,*

> We are a race of animals developing into Humanity. Humanity consists in its mind, of a group of emotions, a mass of knowledge, a flow of power; in its body, of the whole manufactured world about us. The social spirit; complex, highly intelligent, accumulating vast knowledge, is lodged in a social body of buildings, clothing, tools and implements of all sorts. The interaction of these gives the conduct of Society, the current of action which constitutes social life. That conduct is most modified by the brain, its character and contents; and that brain, in humanity, is mainly on paper. (137)

Humanity's "brain" on paper includes both the nonfiction cultural heritage—the scientific and technological information, the history and philosophy—and literature, whose advantage is its capacity to "enlarge our world of feeling," to "build up and tenderly develop" the human capacity for "higher perception and emotion" (*Our Brains,* 137). Accordingly, Gilman's definition of fiction combines the emphasis on knowledge that she associates with all written records, with literature's distinctive emotional contribution: "To feel and see some vital phase of human life; to throw that feeling, that perception, into such forms as to be easily assimilable to others—that is the art of fiction. It explains life. It translates the general into the particular and presents it to other minds; which, impressed by the particular instance, can re-generalize again in its own brain" (*Our Brains,* 138). A work of nonfiction, Gilman says, may "stir a nation to think more wisely," but "conduct is modified not only by what we know, but by how we feel." A book of fiction—and here Gilman cites her great-aunt's *Uncle Tom's Cabin*—can "rouse the nation to act" (137). At best, the literary artist has the power to "enlarge our world of feeling; to lift and carry less favored souls into a richer life." Because, Gilman says, "[w]e live, humanly, only through our power of communication," literature is humanity's "chief art" (*Man-Made,* 89). In literature, "the thought and feeling of all time stand bottled on our shelves" (*Human Work,* 192), so "[t]hose who make books make the race mind" (*Our Brains,* 135).

The creative expression of the "race mind" has been limited, in Gilman's view, by the standard generic conventions of fiction, which reflect men's disproportionate influence on human culture. In *The Man-Made World,* she claims that most fiction is of only two types: "the Story of Adventure, and the Love Story" (94), genres that reflect "the two essential features of masculinity—Desire and Combat—Love and War" (95). The story of adventure includes detective and picaresque stories, tales "of hunting and fishing and fighting, of robbing and murdering, catching and punishing" (94). The love story, which Gilman estimates to be 90 percent of all fiction, consists, Gilman says, of "Him in Pursuit of Her—and it stops when he gets her," in a "ceaseless repetition of the Preliminaries" (96). Gilman finds the "story of desire" no less androcentric than the story of adventure, because it is devoted to "the ceaseless outcry of the male for the female" (84), and because it ends rather than begins at marriage. Gilman faults traditional androcentric fiction on the grounds that these two types of story omit a whole raft of concerns.

Consequently, fiction, potentially so valuable, can actually cause harm when "a masculized literature" provides dangerous models of behavior (*Man-Made,* 88). In the story "A Mischievous Rudiment," the heroine's contention that "the caveman in modern literature [is] a mischievous rudiment" is confirmed by the behavior of a fan of the "Jack-Kipling school," who acts on the male writers' "note of brute force" by attempting to abduct a young woman and force her to marry him (281, 280). Gilman strongly suggests that Hugh

Wyndham's violence toward Ria Bland has been encouraged by writers who portray the "fact" that "man is stronger than woman and that in her heart she knows it and she likes it" (280). In the end, Ria marries a "new man" who also rejects "cave-man" literature, thus confirming that "'primevalism' in modern fiction" is a "rudiment"—an evolutionary throwback (280). But Wyndham's near success at overpowering Ria shows that such writing remains "mischievous."

In *The Man-Made World,* Gilman optimistically anticipates that as women writers begin to contribute more to the "race mind," literature will emerge from the limitations of androcentric plots, and writers will explore several "distinctly fresh fields of fiction":

> First, the position of the young woman who is called upon to give up her "career"—her humanness—for marriage, and who objects to it. Second, the middle-aged woman who at last discovers that her discontent is social starvation—that it is not more love that she wants, but more business in life: Third, the inter-relation of women with women . . . : Fourth, the interaction between mothers and children . . . : Fifth, the new attitude of the full-grown woman, who faces the demands of love with the high standards of conscious motherhood. (105)

Gilman's later writings on the subject add more "fields" for plots, especially what she calls "The Great Adventure: to find, to choose, to make one's place in human service and to fill it; Adventure of a lifetime, of many successful lifetimes; . . . nor limiting itself to the happiness of a few, but always opening before us, and carrying help and service to all the world" ("The Great Adventure," 251). Indeed, one could catalog a significant amount of Gilman's own fiction in light of the model plots she outlines in *The Man-Made World* and the essay "Coming Changes in Literature."[14] To be sure, Gilman ends her stories with marriage with surprising frequency, but generally speaking such stories subordinate the conventional marital "happy ending" to another, "fresher" triumph, thus illustrating the compatibility of personal happiness with "human service."

Like many proponents of realism, Gilman values fiction's capacity to expand readers' knowledge by vicariously experiencing the lives of others; Gilman's view of fiction adds the idea that this growth, in turn, expands the whole world's consciousness. In part, of course, this is because "[m]an's vast stretch of consciousness, made permanent and accessible to all by the arts, especially the art of literature, gives him the advantage of well-nigh limitless experience" (*Human Work*, 31). In her *Forerunner* essay "Class Consciousness, World Consciousness and Socialism," Gilman argues that fiction's value has grown with its increasing interest in "the lives and thoughts and interests of the working class," in the work of writers like Hugo, Dickens, Tolstoy, Gorky, and London (260). This writing contributes to social growth—and the growth of socialism—by extending the social consciousness of wealthy readers, and, even more important, as more members of the working class read, by arousing workers' "class consciousness." Thus for Gilman, fiction's mimetic capacity to help people see is intrinsic to its "social function," and literature's social function is the reason the "narcotic" quality of conventional fiction is so dangerous. If we recognize that creating art is (like all human productions) a "social process," then "[t]he value of an artist to the world is that he shall do as good work as he can for as many people as he can reach" (*Human Work*, 352). Simply by definition, then, art is not for art's sake, but "art for humanity's sake" (*Human Work*, 247).

Gilman espouses an aesthetic that values "realism" above other literary values. "Realism" is an ambiguous term, and Gilman's realism, as we shall see, is not simply documentary accuracy. Like Grand, Gilman employs the traditional metaphors of the mirror and lamp: "Literature is the most powerful and necessary of the arts, and fiction is its broadest form. If art 'holds the mirror up to nature' this art's mirror is the largest of all" (*Man-Made*, 93). Gilman insists, "Art is not great unless it is true" ("Coming Changes," 235), but the "truth" of fiction is inextricably joined to its appeal to the imagination. By imagination, Gilman means the "power of seeing over and under and around and through, of foreseeing, of constructing hypotheses." Through the use of the imagination, fostered by fiction, Gilman says, "our brains will stretch" (*Human Work*, 321). In a poem called "The Artist," Gilman compares the artist to a lens to "gather light." She concludes the poem, "The artist is the intermediate lens / Of God, and so best gives Him to the world, / Intensified, interpreted, to us." In *Our Brains and What Ails Them*, she praises the artist's power to "put his feeling into immortal form, and leave it pouring light and strength, peace, patience or courage, beauty or terror, down the ages" (137). Fiction gained its preeminent value "when the mind, specially sensitized to see and understand some part of life, began to use this fluent power to revisualize and interpret that life to others" (*Our Brains,* 138). The key word here is "interpret."

Because of literature's power to help readers "see" and interpret the world as it is and as it can be, Gilman valued it perhaps most for providing readers with models of behavior. Gilman, who partly supported herself through lecture tours, surely recognized the relationship between fiction and the exemplum of classical rhetoric. The exemplum provides "a concrete example from which a general conclusion (the 'moral of the story') can be drawn" (Suleiman, 27). Traditionally, an exemplum includes a narrative, an interpretation, and, distinctively, a "pragmatic discourse" that "derives from that meaning a rule of action" (Suleiman, 35). Several of Gilman's writings portray children's use of books as exempla. In *Unpunished,* Jack helps her young son endure his uncle's cruelty by reading him books that will "brace him up" (84), stories of "men who had been imprisoned by their enemies, enslaved, made galley slaves even, and yet survived, escaped in time. And we'd pretend that this was The Cruel Uncle, or an Ogre or an Enchanter, and that we were in his power for so many years" (83).

Similarly, In *Benigna Machiavelli,* the eponymous Benigna MacAvelly attempts to model her behavior on that in books. Indeed, *Benigna Machiavelli* is itself a model of how—and how not—to use books as exemplary models. Young Benigna's attempts to learn from fiction are not always successful, at least at first, and her failures provide an amusing commentary on realism—and didacticism—in fiction. Benigna discerns that her father is frequently drunk, based on observation and dedicated reading of temperance tracts: "Whiskey I had read about in Sunday School books, and drunkenness, and lovely little girls who had reformed their fathers, and a glorious ambition surged through me. I felt quite proud to have a Drunken Father like those heroes of fiction, and determined then and there to reform him" (18). Unfortunately, the fiction's suggestions for carrying out this mission are not terribly promising, for "on consulting the books I found that the literary variety of intoxicated parents either became violent and beat their families, in which case the angelic daughter took the blow and died like little Eva, or he lay breathing stertoriously [*sic*] on railroad tracks, and the angel daughter flagged the train with a flannel petticoat and again died gloriously—the agonized and repentant parent signing the pledge on the spot" (18).

This is patently the stuff of sentimental fiction—little Eva is the dead give-away—and suggests that Gilman had no illusions about solving life's problems through her great-aunt's sentimental methods of inspiring reform. Indeed, when Benigna attempts to model her behavior on temperance heroines, she fails ignominiously: "It usually said in the stories: 'She threw herself between them.' I never quite mastered the mechanics of this throwing oneself, but I just ran between them and put my arms around Mother's neck, and said, 'Talk to me, Father, not to Mother!'" (18). To this absurd request, her father responds not by reforming but by scolding Benigna for having "brains all addled with preposterous story books!" and by teasing her for "rescue work" (19). Benigna learns her lesson. Ironically, though, Benigna withstands the scolding by calling up other stories, exemplary accounts of Spartans and of savage "Ordeals" that make the sufferer stronger. She finds ordeal stories both "glorious" and "useful."

Having rejected the "sentimental power" approach, Benigna critically analyzes the behavior of fictional characters. Her plan to become a "good villain" derives from her observation that "the villains always went to work with their brains and accomplished something," whereas "[t]he heroes and middle ones were mostly very stupid. If bad things happened, they practised [sic] patience, endurance, resignation, and similar virtues; if good things happened they practised modesty and magnanimity and virtues like that, but it never seemed to occur to any of them to make things move their way." In other words, Benigna questions the dependence on "the special interposition of Providence" by heroes of sentimental fiction. She wonders, "Hadn't they ever read anything? Couldn't they learn anything from what they read—ever?" (12). Benigna does read, and from her reading infers that "what we wanted was good people with brains, not just negative, passive, good people, but positive, active ones, who gave their minds to it. A *good* villain" (13). Not finding a "good villain" in books—or real life—she sets about to become one. And thus Gilman sets about to create one in fiction, as a model for other readers. Throughout the novella and in several stories featuring the adult Mrs. MacAvelly, Benigna uses her brain to make things "move [her] way."[15] Appropriately, one of Mrs. MacAvelly's methods, illustrated in the story "Mrs. Elder's Idea," is to recommend reading material. Mrs. Elder decides to become a professional shopper and board in Boston after reading books recommended by Mrs. MacAvelly:

"She read, she was amazed, shocked, fascinated; she read more, and after a week of this inoculation, a strange light dawned upon her mind, quite suddenly and clearly" (196). Gilman offers Benigna's methods to her readers as models—so that they, too, may learn from reading.

Providing models is implicitly a maternal act. Gilman suggests in *Growth and Combat* that, for example, to teach children not to lie, teachers and parents should provide them with portrayals "in picture, drama, verse and prose, . . . such easy, vivid, appalling proofs of the mischief done by lying, that any child of five could see why it was wrong and older ones could learn the wide advantage of truth" (222). In *Moving the Mountain,* in a future world in which half the artists are mothers, the new children's literature concerns "Truth and Something Better Ahead," and "leaves the child with a sense that things are going to happen—and he, or she, can help" (116). Gilman calls *Moving the Mountain* itself a "baby utopia, a little one that can grow." She says the story "indicates what people might do, real people, now living, in thirty years—if they would" (37). Carol Farley Kessler, adopting a term coined by Riane Eisler, has described Gilman's exemplary stories as "pragmatopias," "realizable" scenarios, stories that subversively adapt the techniques of realism to describe how her "readers might go about realizing her utopian visions" through everyday changes (131).

Like that of a mother nurturing her child's growth, the "business" of the artist is therefore to "build up and tenderly develop [the world's] capacity for higher perception and emotion" (*Our Brains,* 137). A literature written by women will focus on growth, Gilman argues, not only as a topic but as a goal of the writing: that is, it will have a "purpose": to foster social growth. With the progress of the woman's movement, "we are beginning to look at [the world] as also woman's world, to be nursed and cared for, fed, protected, educated and improved, according to the cult of feminine productiveness" ("Coming Changes," 230).

Gilman pursues the analogy of the "world, to be . . . fed" in several other works. In *The Man-Made World,* she describes fiction as "world-food" (101). In "Apropos of Literature," Gilman plays on the dead metaphor of magazines' "catering" to the public, condemning popular literature as a kind of "disease" that is "fed" readers by publishers whose motive is profit. "Their living depends on selling; the more they sell the more they get, and how can you expect a man to consider peoples [*sic*] digestion when he keeps a restaurant. The caterer just cates—that is his business" (105). For Gilman, the publishing industry represents a major barrier to the production of genuine literature, because stories written solely for profit, "appealing to millions of low-grade intellects on their lower side," actively work against fiction's potential for good ("A Question of Conscience," 230). Sensationalist stories appeal only to "the universal taste for stimulants"; other potboilers cater to "the universal taste for narcotics" with "soothing sweetish stuff which lulls the weary mind and quiets pain" (230). Unlike the purveyor of fast-food literature, a true artist provides substantial, healthy fare, like a mother serving the balanced diet necessary for healthy growth despite her child's demands for nothing but candy. In a fable entitled "The World and the Three Artists," neither an "Artist Pure and Simple" nor an artist/merchant can provide a world adequate food, inspiration, or beauty, but "the third Artist, who was also a Citizen," asks, "How shall I feed the World?" The answer is that he "poured forth his very soul in Beauty," and the world's "taste improved continually under the influence of his Art." The artist is happy "[t]o be allowed to serve the World." Like a mother, this citizen artist "watched it grow; well-nourished now, full of sweet merriment, strong in steady inspiration, rich in unfolding beauty" (9).

It might therefore be more appropriate to call Gilman's writing "literature as mothering" than "literature as housekeeping." Gilman certainly would have rejected the type of "domestic" writing, discussed by critics such as Ann Romines and Josephine Donovan, that celebrates the rituals and recurring cycles of private housekeeping. In a poem called "Cycles," Gilman ascribes to plants "Little cycles, narrow, brief" and to animals "Little cycles, short and small," but ends each verse, "Not so, I." Because she is human, says the speaker, her existence is not cyclical but evolutionary:

> Building with immortal will,
> Rising through the ages slow
> On the generations grow—
> Upward still!

Writing that encourages growth is motherly, Gilman contends. Against the androcentric concerns of traditional literature, Gilman cheerfully juxtaposes "the coming changes in literature," changes to come about in literature written by women. Gilman says, "Combat is the essentially masculine principle"; but, because women are mothers, the "essentially feminine principle" is growth

("The Great Change," 324). As we have seen, Gilman expects the main "coming changes in literature" will be in its subject matter, the "fresh fields of fiction," but she also envisions a change of literature's purpose and approach. A world to which women writers fully contribute will be a maternal world of industry, creation, and growth.

Ward's Dialogic Approach to Literature as Housekeeping

Like both Grand and Gilman, Mary Ward frequently wrote about the nature and function of literature and the other arts. Like Grand and Gilman, Ward emphasizes literature's effects on its readers, and she unflinchingly admits to writing novels of ideas, but Ward, true to her Arnold family heritage, also unapologetically claims purely aesthetic value for literature, aside from its directly didactic impact. Indeed, even more than Grand and Gilman, Ward attempts to reconcile the didactic and the artistic, arguing the aesthetic legitimacy of the "novel of ideas."

Ward's most sustained defense of the novel of ideas appears in her preface to the one-volume cheap edition of *The History of David Grieve,* in which she answers reviewers in the quarterlies who are "especially intolerant of 'the novel with a purpose,' of any writing within the domain of art which, as the 'Quarterly' puts it, aims at 'reforming the world'" (xi). To strengthen her defense of "the novel with a purpose," Ward strategically changes the language of the debate:

> If one looks back over the fiction of the last fifty years, one comes again and again upon books that . . . have owed both their motive-power and their success to this desire, which the "Quarterly" finds so terrible and abominable, of "reforming the world," or, as I should put it, to the expression of "a criticism of life," which may advance, whether in the hearts of the many or the few, thoughts and causes dear to the writers. "Think with me!" "See with me!" "Let me persuade you!" they seem to say, and again and again the world, or rather the world which belonged to the book, has let itself be persuaded, gladly. (xiv)

Obviously, Ward's preferred phrase, "criticism of life," comes from Matthew Arnold's "The Study of Poetry," whose definition Ward pointedly quotes: "Poetry is a criticism of life under the conditions of poetic truth and poetic beauty."[16] Ward admits that Arnold's definition has "been roughly handled by the school which, in its zeal for certain elements and aspects of art, and under the influence of a narrow conception of criticism, would, if it could, divorce art from criticism and claim for it a divine and irresponsible isolation" (xiv). This "irresponsible" school, against which she gallantly leaps to her uncle's defense, surely is Aestheticism. Ward argues that to separate criticism from art is not only "irresponsible" but impossible: "Criticism lurks, and will always lurk, in the very holiest and secretest places of art" (xiv). Nor is this true only of poetry, for Ward identifies "criticism" with the greatest nineteenth-century English novelists—Austen, Scott, Thackeray, Dickens, Charlotte Brontë—reminding readers that "each of these writers, however objective and positive he may seem, has all the while an ethical and social ideal which he is trying to make prevail. Each delights, as every artist should and does delight, in the mere play of the imaginative gift; but through each and all throbs the wish 'to reform the world' in his or her measure." Then, echoing Gilman's statement, "it is a pretty poor thing to write, to talk, without a purpose," Ward rhetorically continues, "The question is, can you have lasting imaginative work without it?" (xv).

A further and more genuine question is "How far is the criticism to be carried?" To this Ward replies, "[T]here have always been two answers—the answer of those who wish to make of art a protection against life, and the answer of those who attempt to use it as the torch for exploring life" (xv). Ward's imagery here stacks the deck, for she articulates the distinction as not between the artistic and the didactic but between the escapist and the enlightening. With the "torch for exploring life," she has, like Gilman and Grand, adopted the metaphor of the lamp. When literature serves as "protection"—that is, escape—it becomes "an ark of refuge," and a "shrine for the common perennial passions and emotions of mankind, reared amid the clash of irreconcilable interests, and that surrounding darkness of the Unknown which neither philosophy nor religion, say what you will, can clear away" (xv). Of course Ward's point in this description is to indicate the insufficiency of literature as escape, for where those who use literature as protection see irremediable darkness, others supply a torch.

Somewhat ironically allying herself with George Moore's "Literature at Nurse" (which also cites Arnold) and with the participants in the symposium on "Candour in English Fiction," Ward proclaims: "Nay, let us have no lines, no exclusions! . . . Life divided into sections is life shorn of some of its fulness." However, the candor Ward recommends concerns not sexuality but ideas: "There are no hard and fast limits in reality; the great speculative motives everywhere play and melt into the great practical motives; each different life implies a different and a various thought-stuff; and there is nothing in art to forbid your dealing—if you can!—with the thought-stuff of the philosopher as freely as with the thought-stuff of the peasant or the maiden" (xvi). Ward, like Moore, wishes not to be limited to material suitable to "the maiden," and like both Moore and Arnold, Ward is concerned that literature deal with ideas, but Ward's primary concern is not only the "great speculative motives" but also the ensuing "great practical motives"—despite the fact that Arnold, in "The Function of Criticism at the Present Time," dismisses the "political and practical application" of ideas.

To be sure, Ward immediately concedes that ideas alone will not produce good art:

> For every artist of whatever type there is one inexorable law. Your "criticism of life" must be fashioned under the conditions of imaginative truth and imaginative beauty. If you, being a novelist, make a dull story, not all the religious argument in the world will or should save you. For your business is to make a novel, not a pamphlet, a reflection of human life, and not merely a record of intellectual conception. But under these conditions everything is open—try what you will—and the response of your fellows, and that only, will decide your success. (xvi–xvii)

In emphasizing the novel's role as "a reflection of human life," Ward, like Gilman, Grand, and any number of realists before and since, employs the mirror metaphor. Ward's version of realism transcends external realities, for, she says, once again using the language of the "real" and the "reflected," "I am so made that I cannot picture a human being's development without wanting to know the whole, his religion as well as his business, his thoughts as well as his actions. I cannot try to reflect my time without taking account of forces which are at least as real and living as any other forces, and have at least as much to do with the drama of human existence about me" (xvi). Ward also, more than do either Grand or Gilman, explicitly places "imaginative beauty" in the forefront of her aesthetic. Like Grand and Gilman, she disdains the attempt to separate art from "criticism of life," but Ward postulates an art that includes "great practical motives" and depends on "the response of your fellows." By substituting the Arnoldian phrase "criticism of life" for the phrase "reforming the world," Ward repackages her practical goals as aesthetic ideals, even as, for Ward, "criticism of life" includes a pragmatic agenda.

Like Gilman and Grand, Ward occasionally, if less frequently, adopts analogies between literature and housekeeping. Perhaps the strongest housekeeping analogy is not of Ward's own composing, but one describing her that she endorses enthusiastically. She reports with pride Thomas Henry Huxley's praise for her essay "The New Reformation," which she wrote in defense of the ideas in *Robert Elsmere:* "[T]he word of praise in which he compared my reply to Mr. Gladstone, to the work 'of a strong housemaid brushing away the cobwebs,' gave me a fearful joy!" (*A Writer's Recollections,* 2:172). Ward's joy over this praise obviously derived largely from its prestigious source, but the image of a public intellectual housecleaning seems to have delighted her as well. A housekeeping metaphor of her own, this time involving mothering, appears in *Robert Elsmere:* "There is so much of the artist in the maternal mind, of the artist who longs to see the work of his hand in fresh combinations and under all points of view" (125).[17] Here, of course, Ward reverses the metaphor, with the domestic activity as the tenor and art as the vehicle, and her point is to emphasize a mother's creative pride in her children. But, as often happens with metaphors, the analogy reverberates in the opposite direction to suggest that artistic creativity is maternal. Ward also employs analogies between writing and needlework. She often refers to "spinning a tale," as in her 1911 preface to *Lady Rose's Daughter* (11:xii), in which she says of Italy, "there is no happier lot for the weaver of tales than to be sheltered among your vines and olives while the web is spinning."[18] In *The History of David Grieve,* she compares textual scholarship of the Gospels to "the unravelling of a piece of fine and ancient needlework—and so discovering the secrets of its make and craftsmanship." Through the voice of her character, Ward marvels at "how close and fine a web" is to be found in the New Testament, as the scholar studies "the nature and quality of each thread, the purpose and the skill of each stitch" (555).[19]

Despite her embrace of figurative analogies between literature and domestic labor, Ward, like Gilman, recognized from painful personal experience that the more common, literal relationship between the domestic and artistic is that the private obligations of housework can thwart a woman's public artistic ambitions. Ward's father wrote her grandmother on the eve of the Wards' marriage, "Mary will have to look to her housekeeping very closely . . . [and] I have already warned her in the strongest words I could find, how absolutely it is her duty to postpone literature and everything else to the paramount duty of keeping a straight and unindebted household."[20] Ward's fiction features numerous women artists whose art must compete with household responsibilities. In *Robert Elsmere,* Rose Leyburn, a talented violinist, must postpone practicing to help with the sewing; the title character of *The Mating of Lydia* must take time from painting to do mending and other household chores. In *The History of David Grieve,* David's beautiful young French mistress, a promising painter, exclaims, "When I am with you . . . I must be a woman. You agitate me, you divide my mind, and my force goes. There are both capacities in me, and one destroys the other. And I want—I *want* my art!" (354). Elise, who has described art as her way to avoid becoming "one of the drudges that men make," tells David, "My life is imprisoned here with you—it beats its bars" (321, 358). Yet although Elise escapes the confinement of David's love, she later marries, and when her husband becomes disabled, she sacrifices her art. She tells her former lover, "I am no longer an artist but an artisan,—I have not painted a *picture* in years,—but what I paint sells for a trifle, and there is soup in the pot—of a sort." Elise paints only to put soup in the pot, and she explains, "I spend my life in making *tisane,* in lifting weights too heavy for me, and bargaining for things to eat," that is, in the minutiae of housekeeping (563). Art similarly becomes practical in the worst sense in Ward's very slight 1916 novel, *A Great Success,* whose protagonist had attended the prestigious Slade School of Art for two years; after Doris's "imprudent love-match with a literary man had plunged her into the practical work of a small household, run on a scanty and precarious income, she had been obliged, one after another, to let the old interests go. Except the drawing. That was good enough to bring her a little money, as an illustrator, designer of Christmas cards, etc.; and she filled most of her spare time with it" (27).[21] The end of the novel finds the Meadows' income less precarious, and the coming baby will certainly allow Doris less spare time: art is abandoned altogether.

In several of Ward's novels, women's subordination of art to love seems to meet with the author's approval. *The History of David Grieve*'s Elise Delaunay, for example, as she recounts the marriage for which she has sacrificed her art, "stood with her eyes on the ground, then she lifted them once more, and there was in them a faint beautiful gleam, which transformed the withered and sharpened face" (563). This "beautiful gleam" suggests a transformative love, but the "withered and sharpened face" equally suggests suffering. In other Ward novels portraying women artists, the heroine chooses love over art, in an apparently happy ending. But regarding a real author, Charlotte Brontë, Ward's response is less complacent. In *The History of David Grieve,* when David reads *Shirley* and learns about its author, Ward asserts that for Charlotte Brontë, "love did but open the gate of death" (78). In the introduction to *Shirley,* for the Haworth edition of *The Life and Work of the Sisters Brontë,* Ward writes with undisguised horror of Brontë's "marrying a country curate, without a tinge of letters, who encouraged his wife to give up the practice of novel-writing, and in return 'often found a little work for her to do' in his study or the parish; . . . submitting without a murmur, and finding in the quiet happiness of the simplest domestic life reward enough for the suppression of her gift and the taming of her soul" (2:xxv). If Charlotte Brontë or Elise Delaunay for a time finds "quiet happiness" in the "simplest domestic life," it seems clear from Ward's language that she considers that inadequate compensation for "suppression of her gift."

The woman's choice between love and art is a trope that appears throughout Ward's best fiction, in a dialogic pattern that reflects her description of reality as "the clash of irreconcilable interests." Ward's writing is dialogic in two ways: first, in her vision of the relationship between the writer and the reader; and second, in her structuring of stories that embody her "criticisms of life," in conflicts of ideas.

The relationship between writer and reader is crucial to Ward's ideas about women writers and readers. Specifically, Ward's discussions of the Brontës embody patterns identified by Patrocinio Schweickart as part of a female paradigm of reading. Schweickart sees in Adrienne Rich's essay on Emily Dickinson, "Vesuvius at Home," two different "settings," a "judicial" setting in which the feminist reader defends a woman writer against patriarchal misreadings and a "dialogic" setting in which the feminist reader engages the woman writer in a kind of "intimate conversation." Feminist readings, Schweickart argues, are "motivated by the need to 'connect,' to recuperate . . . the context, the tradition, that would link women writers to one another, to women readers and critics, and to the larger community of women" (41). To Schweickart, a "visiting" metaphor illustrates the feminist reader's (and I would add woman reader's) "tendency to construe the text not as an object, but as the manifestation of the subjectivity of the absent author—the 'voice' of another woman." Thus a writer's works become "doorways to the 'mind' of a 'woman of genius'" (47). Schweickart's paradigm illuminates Ward's response to the Brontë sisters, as Ward defends them against male *advocati diaboli* and describes visits to the Brontës' home at Haworth in both fiction and nonfiction. Ward insists that women authors must be studied as women, in their distinctive literary, social, and personal contexts—as Rich would say, "on their own premises."

We see the "judicial" stance when Ward's Haworth edition prefaces respond to Henry James, with whom Ward had debated in conversation and letters about literary matters from the beginning of their friendship in the mid-1880s. Ward explained in a letter to Charles Eliot Norton, "[T]he advocatus diaboli whose remarks in the *Jane Eyre* preface have displeased some, represents a long wrestle with Henry James on the sands of the Grange two years ago. He used most of the arguments I have reproduced and tried to meet" (qtd. in Peterson, "Henry James," 919). One of James's arguments that Ward answers is that the Brontës' popularity derives not from their novels but from their life stories. James scornfully calls the biographical response to their lives and work "the most complete intellectual muddle . . . ever achieved, on a literary question, by our wonderful public." Using a protomodernist argument emphasizing art's status as a discrete aesthetic "object," James continues, "The question has scarce indeed been accepted as belonging to literature at all. Literature is an objective, a projected result; it is life that is the unconscious, the agitated, the struggling, floundering cause. But the fashion has been, in looking at the Brontës, so to confound the cause with the result that we cease to know, in the presence of such ecstasies, what we have hold of or what we are talking about" (64).

In her own criticism, Mary Ward is clearly "guilty" of "confound[ing] the cause with the result" and not being "objective," as James defines it, but she sets out to demonstrate that her own approach, which combines expressive and pragmatic emphases, offers significant insights. Ward maintains that the Brontës produced "an art directed rather to expression than to form," so she begins with and always returns to the connection between the novels and the novelists—what James calls the "intellectual muddle" (*LW,* 1:xxii). Thus, in the *Jane Eyre* preface, Ward concedes technical flaws in plot, characterization, and style, crediting many of the criticisms to that *advocatus diaboli* she privately identified with Henry James. She quickly turns against her *advocatus diaboli,* however, asserting the insufficiency of treating literature as nothing but—as James called it—"an objective, a projected result":

> What is it that a critic of this type forgets—what item does he drop out of the reckoning which yet, in the addition, decides the sum?
>
> Simply, one might say, Charlotte Brontë herself. . . . The main secret of the charm that clings to Charlotte Brontë's books is, and always will be, the contact which they give us with her own fresh, indomitable, surprising personality. (*LW,* 1:xix, xx)

Ward turns, then, from discussing what James called the "objective result" to discussing the human "cause"—the "personality" that is "the sole but the sufficient spell of these books" (1:xxi).

Ward also defends the Brontës against arguments by Leslie Stephen. In the Haworth prefaces, Ward frequently cites Stephen's essay on the Brontës' books. Stephen had written, "Only a minority will thoroughly and unreservedly enjoy the writings which embody so peculiar an essence," and, "There is a primâ facie presumption against a writer who appeals only to a few" (Stephen, 3:414). Ward discusses problems of plot and characterization that Stephen examines, and Stephen (editor of the first twenty-one volumes of the *Dictionary of National Biography*) shares her biographical approach; but they reach different assessments. Stephen, like Ward, sees that Charlotte Brontë is "between the opposite poles of duty and happiness, and cannot see how to reconcile their claims," but Stephen concludes that "such a position speaks of a mind diseased" (3:422). Ward, whose own novels dialogically explore that very conflict, considers it intrinsic to "love as the woman understands it." The conflicting claims Stephen identifies recall Ward's praise of women writers' evocation of "the heart's defiance of the facts which crush it." In fact, Ward says, "It is precisely in and through [Charlotte Brontë's] treatment of passion,—mainly, no doubt, as it affects the woman's heart and life—that she has earned and still maintains her fame" (*LW,* 3:xxiv). Perhaps, then, the "minority" who enjoy the Brontës' "peculiar essence" is a minority of male readers, reflecting what Annette Kolodny has described as "the inaccessibility of female meaning to male interpretation" ("Map," 58).

Ward's attention to the Brontës as *women* writers is especially interesting coming from another woman writer. Ward devotes much of the *Villette* preface to analyzing women's success at novel writing, of which she considers Charlotte Brontë's case typical. Echoing both Gilman's complaints about androcentric conventions of art and situations in her own novels about ambitious women, Ward notes, "In other fields of art they are still either relatively amateurs, or their performance, however good, awakens a kindly surprise. Their position is hardly assured; they are still on sufferance. . . . [T]hey are comparatively novices and strangers, having still to find out the best way in which to appropriate traditions and methods not created by women" (*LW,* 3:xxiv–xxv). Ward's awareness of women's difficulties adapting to a masculine tradition and their need for female models anticipates Virginia Woolf and more recent feminist analyses of women's progress in formerly masculine activities, including, as Ward notes, the art of poetry. She recognizes that women poets are perceived "as though they had wrested something that did not belong to them" (3:xxv). The result of this attitude is that

> [a]s a rule, so far, women have been poets in and through the novel—Cowper-like poets of the common life like Miss Austen, or Mrs. Gaskell, or Mrs. Oliphant; Lucretian or Virgilian observers of the many-coloured web like George Eliot, or, in some phases, George Sand; romantic or lyrical artists like George Sand again, or like Charlotte and Emily Brontë. Here no one questions their citizenship; no one is astonished by the place they hold; they are here among the recognized "masters of those who know." (3:xxv–xxvi)

In this fascinating passage, Ward valorizes the novel by identifying it with male poets—Cowper, Lucretius, and Virgil—but cites only female novelists, whom she praises as "masters." Ward, as others have done, argues that women's "place" in the traditions of the novel grows out of "the art of speech, elegant, fitting, familiar speech," with which women "have long been at home" (3:xxv), and she briefly traces women's literary tradition from letter writing through early literary foremothers. In short, women novelists have not had to struggle as painfully as do other women artists with "traditions and methods not created by women," in part because the novel-writing tradition has developed from the private and domestic activities of women.

More important to Ward's point is her theory that women's success at novel writing derives from their distinctive experiences and perceptions. In a sonnet entitled "Charlotte and Emily Brontë," Ward stresses the Brontës' womanhood and its drawbacks—they were "tender women" whose time was devoted to "household arts"; yet therein also lay their power: a "strength in frailest weakness" (lines 7, 3, 6). Despite limits on what women may experience and what they may properly discuss, "one subject which they have eternally at command" is love. What women's novels have to offer is "love as the woman understands it"; Ward contends that women novelists' "peculiar vision, their omissions quite as much as their assertions, make them welcome" (*LW*, 3:xxvi). In Ward's view, most male English novelists write about subjects other than love—"manners, politics, adventure"—and their work reflects what she calls a "realistic masculine instinct" (3:xxvii); continental male novelists have other limits: they "dissect a complex reality . . . ; they are students, psychologists, men of science first, poets afterwards" (3:xxvi). Ward argues, echoing Grand's and Gilman's comments, "The modern mind craves for knowledge, and the modern novel reflects the craving. . . . But the craving for feeling is at least as strong, and above all for that feeling which expresses the heart's defiance of the facts which crush it" (3:xxvii). Responding naturally to that craving, woman writers "have thrown themselves on feeling, on Poetry. . . . It is as poets then, in the larger sense, and as poets of passion, properly so-called— that is, of exalted and transfiguring feeling—that writers like . . . Charlotte Brontë affect the world" (3:xxviii).

In discussing the Brontës and women novelists in general, Ward returns repeatedly to the concept of "poets in the larger sense." Ward uses "poetry" less as a generic marker than as an indicator of value, but it consistently applies to powerful emotions and to imagination, as opposed to pure observation—the "science" she finds so insufficient in male naturalist novelists. In a 1917 address to the Brontë Society, she says that "the poetic faculty can transform and transmute the detail it takes from reality" ("Some Thoughts," 26). To Mary Ward, Charlotte Brontë "lives precisely because of the mingling of these two strains in her—the power of poetry and the power of bringing the poetic faculty to bear on the truth nearest her, the facts of her own daily life" ("Some Thoughts,"

29). If women novelists are essentially poets, transmuting their private experiences, especially "love as woman understands it," into public art, then it follows that to study the novels is to confront those experiences. In identifying the Brontës as "lyric" poets, Ward further justifies her concern with their personalities. Thus, to treat the novel as merely an "objective, projected result," as James advises, is, to Ward, the true "intellectual muddle." In implicit answer to James's argument against "confound[ing] the cause with the result," Ward asserts, "The imagination is at least the fruit of the experience"; moreover, she adds, using a domestic metaphor, "the poet weaves with all that comes to his hand" (*LW,* 3:xvi).

The direct consequence of Mary Ward's personal criticism is her emphasis on how the Brontës' books affect her as a woman reader and writer. Here, Ward works in conscious opposition to the critical proscription of such personal response by Matthew Arnold. In "The Study of Poetry," Arnold warns that our "sense for the best," which is the only "true" estimate, may be undermined by two "fallacious" approaches, the historic estimate and the personal estimate. Of the latter, Arnold writes, "Our personal affinities, likings, and circumstances, have great power to sway our estimate of this or that poet's work, and to make us attach more importance to it as poetry than in itself it really possesses, because to us it is, or has been, of high importance. Here also we over-rate the object of our interest" (9:163–64). Perhaps Ward's sense that her uncle radically undervalued the Brontës' books confirmed in her the value of the "personal estimate." Arnold had found *Villette* "disagreeable" because "the writer's mind contains nothing but hunger, rebellion, and rage, and therefore that is all she can, in fact, put into her book" ("To Mrs. Forster," 1:34). Ward, who must have known this assessment, writes of *Villette,* in what seems a surprisingly irreverent response to "Uncle Matt," that many of its distinctive qualities "are repellent or tiring to the mind that has no energy of its own responsive to the energy of the writer" (*LW,* 3:xix). In contradistinction to her uncle, Ward contends that the personal response defines the Brontës' distinctive talents: "their vigorous effect upon the reader's sympathies and judgment has been always part of their ascendancy, and one great secret of their enduring fame" (5:xi).

Perhaps the most revealing of Ward's discussions of the Brontës' impact on their readers occurs in *The History of David Grieve,* in which the dialogic interaction between reader and novel offers a model for the uses of literature. While driving sheep across the moors, David, then an uneducated youth, stops one night at Haworth, where a friendly villager tells him the Brontë family story and lends him a copy of *Shirley,* along with *Nicholas Nickleby* and Benjamin Franklin's autobiography. In his first exposure to "novels of modern life," David encounters something that he "felt . . . in his veins like new wine," something "disturbing, personal, and stimulating," that instigates a "mental tumult," and leads to "a more intense self-consciousness than any he had yet known." As a result of his reading, "he began to realise the problem of his own life with a singular keenness and clearness. . . . An indescribable energy and exultation took possession of him. The tide of will for which he had been waiting all these months had risen; and for the first time he felt swelling within him the power to break with habit, to cut his way" (81–82). Fiction is here a liberating, even subversive force, encouraging David to break from his stifling existence—he leaves his home to seek education and independence. David is an active reader: in a metaphor reminiscent of Gilman's description of fiction as "world-food," Ward describes David's "voracious way of tearing the heart out of a book first of all, and then beginning it again with a different and tamer curiosity, lingering, tasting, and digesting" (81). David's reading is a "measuring himself with the world of 'Shirley'" and bringing the book to bear on his own life. He speculates that "if you had asked Miss Brontë what could be done with a creature like Louie [his worrisome sister] she would have had a notion or two" (82). The tribute both expresses admiration for Brontë's resourcefulness and asserts the value and use of fiction, in terms familiar from Gilman's exemplary stories: novels help readers confront their problems and examine their lives.

For Mary Ward, the experience of reading the Brontës to examine one's own life also involved the admiration of one writer for another. In her 1917 address to the Brontë Society, Ward claims Charlotte Brontë as a literary foremother, emphasizing her fondness for Elizabeth Gaskell's account of Brontë's literary success: the triumph of a shy, plain young woman who had written all her life—much like the young Mary Augusta Arnold.

[T]o one who had been from her childhood scribbling on her own account there was even greater fascination in the story of the memorable years— 1846 and 1847—which saw the publication of the *Poems* by Currer, Ellis,

and Acton Bell, of *Jane Eyre,* and *Wuthering Heights.* The sudden journey of
the two sisters to London; their meeting with their astonished publisher, to
whom their arrival first disclosed the identity of Currer Bell, the supposed
male author of *Jane Eyre*—that book of which all the world was talking—
with the shy, plainly dressed, tiny creature . . . : this too was a tale of which
I knew every turn. ("Some Thoughts," 31)

In her address on the Brontës, Ward delights, too, that "I little thought then
that twenty years later I should myself be in daily communication, as an author,
with the same Mr. George Smith" who served as Charlotte Brontë's editor and
friend. Clearly, Ward responds to the Brontës as one woman author to another,
with both shared professions and shared professional experiences.

According to Ward, the dialogic relationship between writer and audience
operates not only on an individual level but on a collective level as well. In her
1911 preface to the Westmoreland edition of *Robert Elsmere,* Ward says that the
book "possessed a certain representative and pioneering character; and . . . to
some extent at least the generation in which it appeared had spoken through
it" (xiv). Echoing Grand's crediting the Zeitgeist for *The Heavenly Twins* and
Gilman's argument that an artist's "self-expression" really expresses "the heart
of his people," Ward says that *Robert Elsmere* "belonged to a particular moment
both in my own life and in the life of my generation" (1:xliii). Ward emphasizes
this sense of a shared conversation between an author and her age in a remarkable passage:

> At a moment when the particular ideas put forward have a high degree of
> life and significance for a great many people, the public in a sense coöper-
> ates in the book. Such a novel as "Robert Elsmere" is entirely related to a
> particular time and *milieu;* and those who are drawn to read it, uncon-
> sciously lend it their own thoughts, the passion of their own assents and de-
> nials. Some happy chance bestows on a novel this suggestive, symbolic
> character; and the reader's eager sympathy, or antagonism, completes the
> effort of the writer." (1:xxix)

For Ward, a writer not only aims to affect readers; her "criticism of life" is not
"complete" without their response.

In addition to Ward's "collaborative" relationship to her readers, her books
are dialogic in a manner usefully illuminated by the theories of Mikhail

Bakhtin. Bakhtin argues that all utterances—written, spoken, even thought—are social. Each of us speaks many "languages"; that is, our speech and writing are permeated by many "voices," social dialects derived from our parents, class, ethnic group, religion, country, profession, and historical era. Furthermore, every utterance is inevitably shaped by the manifold, always-changing relations between the speaker (or writer), the listeners (or readers), and the topic (including fictional characters). Meaning emerges through these dialogic interactions. According to Bakhtin, the novel is by nature dialogic, reflecting the heteroglossia of the social world it portrays. All novels, though to varying degrees, challenge and subvert monologic thinking and other artificial constraints. Bakhtin considered Dostoevsky the greatest novelist because of his "polyphonic" qualities: in his novels, each character is a "person born of [an] idea"—not in that the idea "characterizes" the person but in that the idea is fully "incarnated" in the character (*Problems,* 85). Equally important, Bakhtin stresses that Dostoevsky's characters are not strictly defined objects or "types," but independent subjects. As a result, "Dostoevsky's novel is multi-accented and contradictory in its values; contradictory accents clash in every word of his creations" (15).

Obviously, Mary Ward's novels differ from Dostoevsky's in manifold ways, but at their best, they, too, feature fully realized, independent-voiced characters of the idea. Ward typically establishes a conflict between protagonists—frequently a man and a woman—with radically divergent opinions, whether about religion, politics, art, gender, or all of these matters at once. The characters in *Robert Elsmere,* for example, "incarnate" ideas of Roman Catholicism, Unitarianism, positivism, and many varieties of Anglicanism, Dissent, and religious doubt. Similarly, in *Marcella,* characters embody a range of political opinion, from radical socialism to deep conservatism. For Ward all these characters were very much alive. On finishing *Helbeck of Bannisdale* (1898), whose central characters embody the diametrically opposed ideologies of conservative Catholicism and atheism, Ward wrote her father, "I have alternately felt with Helbeck & with Laura, and have loved them both" (qtd. in Peterson, *Victorian Heretic,* 42).

Delia Blanchflower (1914) exemplifies Ward's dialogic "criticism of life." The novel portrays the shifting loyalties of the eponymous heroine, from Gertrude Marvell, leader of the militant suffrage Daughters of Revolt, to Mark Winnington, Delia's guardian with whom she gradually falls in love. At the novel's climax Gertrude and her collaborators burn down a historic mansion, killing the caretaker's handicapped daughter and Gertrude herself; a grieving Delia agrees to marry Winnington; and a suffrage bill is defeated by Parliament. Delia remains a feminist and a suffragist, but accepts the need for slower change and constitutional methods. Despite Ward's antisuffrage activism, the novel is not monologic. Throughout the book, suffragist arguments have a remarkable rhetorical effectiveness. In one speech, a fairly accurate rendering of suffragette positions, Gertrude eloquently justifies militant suffragists' breaking laws to call attention to women's grievances: "Slaves who have no part in making the law, are not bound by the law. Enforce it if you can! But while you refuse to free us, we despise both the law and the making of the law. Justice—which is a very different thing from law—Justice is our mistress!—and to her we appeal" (167).[22] Gertrude's powerful speeches shape the novel's discourse, giving the book, in Bakhtin's terms, "an orientation that is contested, contestable and contesting—for this discourse cannot forget or ignore, either through naiveté or by design, the heteroglossia that surrounds it" ("Discourse," 332).

Delia ultimately rejects the violent methods of the Daughters of Revolt, but she emphatically distinguishes strategy from substance, insisting, "I am just as much for *women*—I am just as rebellious against their wrongs—as I ever was. I shall be a Suffragist always" (356). Delia's unrepentant feminism challenges the assumption that Ward opposed feminism—or women's suffrage—in any simple way. Rather, Ward posits a multivocal feminism, in which being "for women" means different things to the novel's various feminist characters. Despite the novel's structural closure—with Gertrude's arson death, the defeat of the suffrage bill, and the marriage of Delia and Mark—it would oversimplify the book's ending to dismiss it as yet another instance in which the conventional resolution of the marriage plot upholds the status quo. More accurately, the "internal open-endedness of the characters and the dialogue" disrupts ideological closure (Bakhtin, *Problems,* 39).

On one matter the novel does seem unambiguous. Delia's love of Winnington "bring[s] her face to face with the deeper loves and duties and sorrows which she in her headstrong youth knew so little about, while they entered so profoundly into his own upright and humane character" (268)—by which Ward suggests that Delia will join Mark in charitable and educational projects and in local government. With or without the vote, a woman can apply domestic values to the public sphere to help her community. Civic housekeeping, that is, disrupts the supposed incompatibility between private, domestic happiness and public participation. Jessica Benjamin has pointed out, "The public world is conceived as a place in which direct recognition and care for others' needs is impossible—and this is tolerable as long as the private world 'cooperates'" (qtd. in Bauer and McKinstry, 1). Delia and Mark will not cooperate with this attitude of separation, nor, as we shall see, will characters like Marcella Boyce of *Marcella* and *Sir George Tressady,* Elizabeth Bremerton of *The War and Elizabeth,* or Rachel Henderson and Janet Leighton of *Harvest.*

Throughout her career, in her dialogic "criticisms of life," Ward attempted with varying degrees of success to reconcile the didactic and the artistic, the practical and the beautiful, the domestic and the public. When reviewers condemned *Sir George Tressady* as a "pamphlet & not a story," Ward commented to her editor, George Smith, "It seems to me the same would be said of any novel which introduced political & social matters at all, & it delights me to see that the book is being discussed as no mere pamphlet could be discussed." She insisted that her primary interest in the story had been its characters, but, she explained, "The fact is that I was brought up with people in whom the strongest emotions of life were generally combined with some intellectual end, & I suppose this reflects itself in the books."[23] For Ward, the dialogic interaction embodied in the clashes of such characters created the kind of "criticism of life" that she believed would enable readers to "think with [her]" and "See with [her]," and thus, as she said in her comments about the readers of *Robert Elsmere,* "complete the effort of the writer." For Ward, encouraging readers to think about religion, poverty, politics, gender—or housekeeping—was central to her fictional project, and hence reconciled the claims of the aesthetic and the practical.

$\sim$

Although Grand, Gilman, and Ward have somewhat different theories and approaches to fiction, their work and their theories show some remarkable parallels. They define their literary goals in conscious and explicit relation to other literary approaches of their era, rejecting naturalism and Aestheticism but embracing other versions of "realism," though in practice their styles and storytelling methods are not "real" in the same ways. They alternatively reject Aestheticism and make claims for the beautiful in their own work. Most important for the concerns of this study, they generally justify their theories of fiction on grounds having to do with literature's public "purposes," articulating these purposes, at least part of the time, using housekeeping metaphors: literature provides methods to nourish readers' minds, to sweep away their outmoded ideas, to nurture their futures.

Such concrete goals for literature seem unlikely to be realized in the real world. Certainly they have seemed unrealizable to those recent theorists who have argued that the novel's focus on the private individual undermines its ability to promote meaningful social change. Yet all three of the literary housekeepers believed with some justification that their own writings had indeed achieved real-world practical effects. Sarah Grand, looking back thirty years to the original publication of *The Heavenly Twins,* proudly claimed that it was largely responsible for raising public awareness of venereal disease, especially among women: "That this book accomplished the spade work it was designed to do is pretty generally acknowledged now by sociologists of its generation who knew what the work was that had to be done, if women were ever to be freed from oppression. It has been said of it (with a questionable juxtaposition of metaphors) that it 'set the ball rolling by breaking taboo'" ("Foreword, 1893–1923," xiv). Grand described the novel as an "allopathic pill" that had a "medicinal effect" on its readers. Gilman, likewise, firmly believed that "The Yellow Wall-Paper" had had its intended result: "But the real purpose of the story was to reach Dr. S. Weir Mitchell, and convince him of the error of his ways. I sent him a copy as soon as it came out, but got no response. However, many years later, I met some one who knew close friends of Dr. Mitchell's who said he had told them that he had changed his treatment of nervous prostration since reading 'The Yellow Wallpaper.' If that is a fact, I have not lived in vain" (*Living,* 121). There was also an attempt, ultimately unsuccessful but an attempt nevertheless, by Henrietta Rodman, a woman Dolores Hayden describes (197–202) as a "disciple" of Gilman, to build a Feminist Apartment House on the principles Gilman laid out in her writings.

Ward was more successful in a similar enterprise, for she was able to use some of the profits from her bestseller *Robert Elsmere* to establish a settlement house dedicated to carrying out the fictional Robert's ambitions in the real world. The settlement's mission was to change over the years, but the practical impact of Ward's fiction continued. Lady Sybil Lubbock, in her 1939 memoir, *The Child in the Crystal,* describes social service activities by young women in the 1890s and names them after the Ward heroine who leaves her wealthy country home to train and work as a nurse in London's slums: "It was what I may venture to call the 'Marcella period,' and Mrs. Humphry Ward's influence on the young, especially the female young, was widespread and almost irresistible. Before I knew where I was I found myself, the first time I met her . . . , promising to go to the Passmore Edwards Settlement every Saturday morning, to direct a group of children in what was really the first of the play-centres" (252–53). Today, the Mary Ward Centre offers adult education courses to thousands of students annually. Each of these practical consequences for fiction could be construed as a type of housekeeping, broadly defined, and for each writer, such concrete results were not ancillary effects but centrally important to her literary efforts.

The approach to literature as a form of housekeeping represents not a failure to understand the goals and methods of Aestheticism and modernism but an effort to provide an alternative, or, as Gilman puts it, "fresh fields for fiction." As we shall see, these "fresh fields" entail not only "domestic" goals for literature, explored in the present chapter, but also the portrayal of domestic activities traditionally associated with the private sphere, offering models for readers of women "raising the dust" in the public world.

"A Motherliness Which Dominated Society"

Mothers in Literary Housekeeping

Man, having no conception of himself as imperfect from the woman's point of view, will find this difficult to understand, but we know his weakness, and will be patient with him, and help him with his lesson. It is the woman's place and pride and pleasure to teach the child, and man is morally in his infancy. There have been times when there was a doubt as to whether he was to be raised or woman was to be lowered, but we have turned that corner at last; and now woman holds out a strong hand to the child-man, and insists, but with infinite tenderness and pity, upon helping him up.

Sarah Grand, "The New Aspect of the Woman Question"

USUALLY WE THINK OF MOTHERHOOD as an exceedingly private function. Not only does it take place outside the realms of politics and economics, but many of its important moments—sex, "confinement," and nursing—occur in the inner sanctum of a separate home housing a nuclear family. Yet discussion of motherhood is one way Ward, Grand, and Gilman confront broad public issues. They portray motherhood as a means to effect social change, and thus a means toward women's equal contribution, along with men's, in building a better world. But while motherhood represents a vehicle toward equal influence, it frequently also represents a claim to female superiority. Deployed metaphorically, as in the passage by Sarah Grand that I have chosen for an epigraph, motherhood becomes an assertion of power over an infantilized manhood, and even, at the most extreme, over childlike nations outside the "domestic"—national—sphere.

"Mothers of Men": *Eugenic Marriage and Literary Housekeeping*

Since the family is of course central to literary housekeeping, founding a family represents the obvious beginning place. Many stories by Gilman, Grand, and Ward seem to employ a simple, conventional marriage plot, ending happily in marriage. But in many cases, the writers define "happily ever after" in eugenic terms, or identify failed marriages as dysgenic. That is, they shift emphasis from the bridal pair to the children of the union. Literary housekeepers thus portray the private act of marriage as affecting the public welfare in the most fundamental manner possible, by influencing the development of the human species.

The embrace of eugenics by prominent American and British women writers like Mary Ward, Charlotte Perkins Gilman, and Sarah Grand is, to say the least, a troubling episode of intellectual history. How could these seemingly progressive authors have adopted social Darwinist ideas? After all, social Darwinist philosophy had been used primarily to justify the status quo. According to conservative applications of Darwin, civilization is masculine, demonstrating men's evolutionary fitness and superior intelligence relative to women; moreover, the "decadence" that horrified turn-of-the-century conservatives was considered effeminate, part of a racial "degeneration" blamed in part on the less-highly-evolved women. According to this theory, feminism's challenge to traditional gender roles both exemplified degeneration and threatened "race suicide," because women's education and employment supposedly diminished their reproductive fitness, thereby undermining their offspring's health and evolutionary fitness.

Actually, the Darwinism espoused by Gilman and Grand is reform Darwinism, which held that humans can and should consciously intervene in the evolutionary process. One of the primary means to intervene in evolution is eugenics, a movement founded by Francis Galton in 1883. Although eugenics acquired a well-deserved bad name in the subsequent century, at the turn into the twentieth century its pedigree was generally progressive rather than conservative, with such enthusiastic, reform-minded adherents as H. G. Wells,

George Bernard Shaw, Shaw's fellow Fabian socialists Beatrice and Sidney Webb, the economist John Maynard Keynes, and, in America, Margaret Sanger, W.E.B. DuBois, and socialist Emma Goldman. Both progressive and conservative eugenists worried about the population's "unfitness," especially among the poor. In England, high numbers of military recruits rejected as "unfit" during the Boer War fed anxieties about the empire's strength. Eugenists believed that this unfitness indicated "degeneracy," a reversal of evolution, and that national strength and human progress depended on encouraging reproduction by "fit" members of the population ("positive eugenics") and discouraging—in more extreme views, preventing—reproduction by the unfit or degenerate ("negative eugenics").

Social historians have proposed many explanations for the appeal of eugenics to turn-of-the-century feminists. Susan Kingsley Kent and Lucy Bland, for example, see connections between the eugenic and social purity movements, since "degeneracy" was associated with both physical ill health and moral decay. Teresa Mangum argues that Grand imagined a "super race" that would "transcend" power struggles between classes and genders; Patricia Murphy demonstrates that Grand's *Beth Book* reinterprets women's "innate" traits as "markers of human advancement" (222). Lois N. Manger notes that Gilman equated "evolution" with "progress" and optimistically proposed to accelerate social advancement by improving women's status. All these are useful explanations. What I propose to examine is the ways that feminists turned to eugenics as a means to resolve and transcend fundamental tensions within turn-of-the-century feminism: those involving the competing goals of achieving gender equality and appreciating women's distinctive attributes, and those involving tensions between the private and the public spheres.

"A New and Nobler Order": Ward and Eugenics

To be sure, social Darwinism was frequently used by conservatives to justify opposition to feminist goals. Indeed, when Mary Ward refers directly to Darwinist and evolutionary ideas, it is generally to bolster her more conservative positions. In a 1908 article, "Why I Do Not Believe in Woman Suffrage," Ward uses a Darwinist phrase—rather loosely—in arguing that only men can develop the "trained knowledge of the world" on which international diplomacy depends: "It is their natural business to get it; they are not held back from getting it by the cares of the home and family; and, as far as we can see, it must always remain their business, by virtue of a *natural selection*, against which it is childish to fight" (15; emphasis added). Here, men's "natural" fitness for international politics is biologically determined and therefore scientific "fact." Yet Ward also recognizes exceptions. Describing women (like herself) who played a "consultative" role in politics, she self-consciously uses Darwin's phrase to distinguish the influence of a few knowledgeable women from the votes of the many: "At present in politics there is cooperation between men candidates and men electors and *some* women; a 'natural selection' of women, in all classes" ("Mrs. Humphry Ward and the Suffrage," 8c). Here, in comparing women to other women, "natural selection" implies "more highly evolved"—though it is evolution through education. However, Ward generally resists the implication that men are more highly evolved than women. Quoting Tennyson in *The Princess,* she insists that "women are 'not undeveloped men but diverse,' and the more complex the development of any State, the more diverse. Difference, not inferiority—it is on that we take our stand" ("Women's Anti-Suffrage Movement," 348). Here, then, Ward attempts to claim both difference and equality, on the basis of the ways the sexes have supposedly evolved.

A core assumption of social Darwinism as developed by Herbert Spencer (and endorsed, as we shall see, by Gilman), is that evolution is a movement from homogeneity to heterogeneity, of increasing "specialization." To conservatives this doctrine justified "separate spheres" for the sexes. "Progress," Ward writes, "depends on 'specialization'; not on men and women doing precisely the same things, but on the full development of the functions of each" ("Discussions," 400). This argument justifies antisuffragism by linking it to a "progressive," "scientific" idea: "We have to show that neither sentimentalism nor reaction has anything to do with our opposition to the suffrage; that it is we who in these days of differentiation and division of labour are the scientific and modern party" (qtd. in "Anti-Suffrage Campaign," 14c). At the same time, however, Ward calls for the "full development" of women's "functions," and Ward's life and works show that she held women's "functions" to be remarkably varied.

Despite her comment about "a natural selection, against which it is childish to fight," in her fiction Ward resists the rigid determinism associated with conservative social Darwinism. In two of her novels, *Marcella* and *The Testing of Diana Mallory,* prospective in-laws question the heroine's "fitness" to marry into the family, but each novel rejects such views.[1] In *Marcella,* when Aldous Raeburn announces his hope of marrying Marcella Boyce, his grandfather attempts to explain "the reasons why no daughter of Richard Boyce could ever be, in the true sense, *fit* wife for a Raeburn" (83;[2] emphasis added). The term "fit" suggests a eugenic agenda, though other aspects of Lord Maxwell's thinking, as Aldous interprets them, are more traditional:

> [W]hen it came to *marriage,* then it behoved him to see that "the family"— that carefully grafted and selected stock to which he owed so much— should suffer no loss or deterioration through him. Marriage with a fit woman meant for a Raeburn the preservation of a pure blood, of a dignified and honourable family habit, and moreover the securing to his children such an atmosphere of self-respect within, and of consideration from without, as he had himself grown up in. And a woman could not be fit, in this sense, who came either of an insignificant stock, untrained to large uses and opportunities, or of a stock which had degenerated, and lost its right of equal mating with the vigorous owners of unblemished names. (83–84)

While the class-based tradition of "pure blood" and the concept of breeding "stock" have long histories, these concepts are grafted, so to speak, onto more recent concepts like the opposition between "fitness" and "degeneracy" or "deterioration." Richard Boyce's scandalous misbehavior is not merely unforgivable personally but also ominous genetically: does Marcella carry a hereditary taint? Marcella, it turns out, is not yet "fit" to marry Aldous, but not on account of biological destiny. The novel, a bildungsroman, recounts Marcella's intellectual, interpersonal, and spiritual growth; all talk of hereditary taint is dropped after the scene with Lord Maxwell. In short, Ward hints briefly at eugenic issues, but ultimately subordinates them to a story of personal growth. Similarly, in *The Testing of Diana Mallory,* the autocratic Lady Lucy Markham insists that her son break his engagement to Diana when Diana is revealed to be the daughter of a notorious murderess. Diana is not "fit" because, Lady Lucy dreads, "inherited lawlessness and passion" will "reappear in the descendents" (282, 251). Other characters condemn Lady Lucy for "lack . . . of heart, of generosity, of imagination" and argue, "Nobody is responsible for their mothers and fathers. We make ourselves" (254, 264). But the strongest argument against Lady Lucy's fear of "criminal taint"—a standard eugenic phrase—is the character of Diana herself: far from lawless or violent, she is generous, honest, and gentle. Both *The Testing of Diana Mallory* and *Marcella* "settle" the eugenic question by portraying the protagonists' marriages as fully satisfactory, not only for the lovers themselves, but for those around them, including, in *Marcella*'s case, England's political future.

The political implications of eugenic marriage also arise in *Delia Blanchflower*. Ward slyly attributes to a witty and wise suffragist, Lady Tonbridge, the view that love is the chief consequence of the naturally evolved differences between the sexes. Speculating on a possible romance between Delia and her guardian, Mark Winnington, Madeleine Tonbridge observes, "Men are men, and women are women—in spite of all these 'isms,' and 'causes'" (107). Similarly, when the love-smitten Delia begins to find her interest in suffragist politics overcome by "the thirst for individual happiness, personal joy," Ward assures us that "she was thereby best serving her sex and her race in the fore-ordained ways of destiny" (350). This imperative to "serve the race" applies not only to women. Lady Tonbridge, reflecting on her old friend Mark's long loyalty to his dead fiancée, muses, "It was positively anti-social—bad citizenship—that such a man as Mark Winnington should not produce sons and daughters for the State, when all the wastrels and cheats in creation were so active in the business" (264). Here two manifestations of social Darwinism come together: belief that young people feel a biologically determined urgency to marry and reproduce, and nationalist arguments from eugenics. For a couple like Delia and Mark, then, parenthood is a gesture of good "citizenship."

These passages suggest eugenic conceptions of marriage that might be used to advocate a retreat from the public sphere into the private: Delia should abandon attending public rallies and retire to make healthy babies with Mark; the babies will be all the healthier for her permanent withdrawal from public life. That, to be sure, was a common conservative argument, but it was not exactly Ward's position. In the same paragraph in which she asserts that Delia's loss of interest in suffrage is "best serving her sex and her race," Ward calls Delia's "altruistic" devotion to women's rights "premature," and writes, "Her time would come again—with fuller knowledge—for bitter loathing of the tyrannies of sex and lust" (350). Upon her marriage, Delia does not abandon politics; she only postpones her activism until greater maturity and "fuller knowledge" better qualify her to serve her sex and her race. Indeed, the novel's most positive female characters are mature suffragists: Lady Tonbridge and the rescue worker Miss Dempsey. Delia's husband-to-be feels a deep conviction of the "need for women in the home tasks—the national house-keeping of this our England," a country he hears "crying out for the work of women, the help of women" (331). The novel ends on a promise of inevitable evolutionary progress: with the "vast and ceaseless tide of human efforts towards a new and nobler order . . . , generations more patient and more wise" (396) will determine how to "evolve new forms out of the old to fit new needs" (331). Ward's attempts to invoke Darwinist language to claim both public and private remain muddled, but they seem to suggest that biology—and national interest—demand that young women "serve the race" through biological motherhood. Then, "with fuller knowledge," the Mothers of England will be prepared to perform the public "home tasks—the national house-keeping of this our England." In Ward's worldview, personal maturation and knowledge, manifested in the performance of "tasks," including "national house-keeping," matter more, in the final analysis, than biology.

"The Perfecting of Life": Grand and Eugenics

The tensions between public and private, gender difference and gender equality also characterize Grand's use of Darwinist and eugenic ideas in narratives of marriage and motherhood. Angelique Richardson has argued that "Grand's enthusiasm for eugenics perpetuates biological essentialism in its most powerful form" ("Eugenization," 228). Richardson provides a useful corrective to those interpretations of Grand's writing that focus on the equal education of "heavenly twins" Angelica and Diavolo as evidence of Grand's feminist emphasis on the impact of nurture over nature,[3] and Grand certainly believed in fundamental differences between the sexes, but Richardson's discussion seems to me to err too far to the opposite extreme. As I will argue, Grand's approach to eugenics represents a paradoxical attempt to embrace both "biological essentialism" and a vision of feminist progress founded on equal education and on the human capacity to exercise free will to overcome biology.

Both Grand and Gilman believed in the inheritance of acquired traits. A century of research in genetics has exploded this theory, but when Grand, Gilman, and Ward were writing, Lamarckianism, the theory associated with the eighteenth-century biologist Jean-Baptiste Lamarck, remained highly influential.[4] Lamarckians believed that acquired characteristics such as education or "moral courage" would be inherited by one's offspring. Grand, for example, says that Ella Banks of *Adnam's Orchard* and *The Winged Victory* has inherited "a lace-maker's hand" (*Adnam,* 88). Because "she came of generations of lacemakers," Grand explains, Ella "must have made lace as the birds build and the beavers make their dams" (*Winged,* 42). By the same token, young Adnam was brought up on a farm and is unaware that he descends from German royalty on his mother's side; nevertheless, upon meeting his uncle, Prince Aubon Strelletzen, the surprised young man does "the right thing automatically" and makes "his ancestral bow." As Grand explains, "Race tells in an emergency. Adnam did not come of a long line of courtiers and diplomats for nothing" (512–13). Thus, according to Grand's theory, learned, chosen, and habitual behaviors become "biological" in the sense that they are inherent in, rather than learned by, future generations.

Inherited behaviors are subject to modification and are not necessarily sex-linked. Grand takes pains to argue, "There are cases of natural depravity, of course, but they are not peculiar to either sex; and as the girl may inherit the father's vices, so may the boy have his mother to thank for his virtues." After all, acquired traits must first *be* acquired to be inheritable. Significantly, however, men and boys more frequently acquire negative traits than do women and girls. As Grand explains, "Depravity is oftener acquired than inherited. As a rule, the girl's surroundings safeguard her from the acquisition; but when they do not, she becomes as bad as the boy. The boy, on the contrary, especially if he is sent to a public school, is systematically trained to be vicious" (*Beth,* 249). Both sexes equally pass along acquired traits, to both sons and daughters; therefore, in Grand's version of eugenics, women must receive education equal to men's (without systematic training in vice), to pass along the advantages to their children of both sexes, while men must attain levels of virtue formerly reserved for women, to further moral progress.

Consequently, one must exercise great care in selecting one's marriage partner, the parent of one's future offspring. Eugenics transforms the seemingly private satisfactions of love and marriage into public responsibilities, as Grand's discussions of marriage, particularly in the later novels, invoke terms like "moral progress," "good patriots," and "public spirit." Grand rarely takes the next step, advocated by many eugenists, of proposing state interference in reproduction, though she did remark in an interview, "I hope that we shall soon see the marriage of certain men made a criminal offence" in order "to protect the married women from contagion" ("The Woman's Question," 162). Generally speaking, however, Grand mainly emphasized individuals' making responsible private decisions in a "public spirit."

In Grand's view, the eugenic form of "public spirit" is primarily, though by no means exclusively, women's responsibility. In *The Descent of Man,* Darwin describes human reproduction as differing from that of other species in that "the males, instead of having been selected, have been the selectors" (2:371). Feminist proponents of eugenics—including Grand and Gilman—argue that in the interest of human advancement, women should reclaim the female prerogative of sexual selection. Grand explained in an interview her view that "women are the proper people to decide on matters of population" because they, unlike men, have learned self-restraint ("The Woman's Question," 168). Women's control over sexual selection will benefit humanity because, as Angelica Kilroy asserts in *The Beth Book,* "Now women want husbands of a nobler nature, strong in all the attributes, moral and physical, of the perfect man, that their children may be noble too, and thus the ascent of man to higher planes of being become assured" (413). If women choose "husbands of a nobler nature," these highly evolved mates will pass their traits to more highly evolved children. This responsibility—a social responsibility—is at the center of Grand's versions of the marriage plot.

The pointedly titled story "Eugenia" (1894) centers on the eponymous heroine's choice of husband—between a "used-up" society man of her own class and a "yeoman" of less wealth and "lower" social position, who possesses "moral courage" and education—he was "wrangler of his year" (109, 175, 129). Eugenia is the sole heiress in a noble family whose weak sons, for many generations, have died before reaching maturity—and producing heirs—so that family inheritance has descended through the female line (116). The yeoman Saxon Wake is Eugenia's "ideal" because "[b]it by bit his family have been developing every quality in which my own was deficient, . . . by their virtues"

(172). In other words, virtuous behavior has, according to Lamarckian principles, become an inherited Wake family trait. Eugenia removes the "curse" on her own family by marrying Saxon. She explains, "I believe I see the mistake we women have all made in the choice of our husbands. It is a universal mistake. We admired mere animal courage in a man, which is only one form of courage, instead of requiring moral courage, which includes every other kind—until I came. But I chose my husband for his moral qualities. . . . I have removed the curse unawares" (175). Eugenia removes an ancient curse on one family, but she also describes her situation as "universal." The future is for men with "moral courage," for women wise enough to choose them, and for their healthy, courageous descendants. As Grand comments, "With such women for the mothers of men, the English-speaking races should rule the world" (140). The racial and imperialist aspects of this statement, not to mention the name "Saxon Wake," ironically underline the importance Grand placed on marital choice. A purely private, "domestic" choice, in the narrow sense, implicitly opposes the "domestic," in the national sense, to the "foreign" and inferior.[5]

Such paragons as Saxon Wake are all too rare, however, at least in Sarah Grand's fiction. Grand's marriage plots only rarely hinge on "positive eugenics"—selecting "husbands of a nobler nature"—tending more to cautionary tales than utopias. These cautionary tales inform readers of the causes and manifestations of degeneration, in order that future mothers may avoid matches with "degenerate" men, that is, in order that they can practice "negative eugenics." A woman must investigate a prospective mate's family tree and his own past actions (knowledge that her male family members should help to provide), and observe his character and physiognomy—and perhaps that of his parents. To evaluate this information, Grand's novels and stories indicate the conditions that she considers causes of hereditary degeneration: environmental pollutants, venereal disease, "vice," inbreeding, and faulty education.

Grand links the environmental causes of degeneration primarily to urban poverty. In *Adnam's Orchard,* Seraph Pratt's "mongrel" qualities are blamed on degenerate traits handed down by his mother, who "had been an anaemic girl of a town stock, the child of tradespeople with impoverished blood, bred in the days [of] municipal ignorance, mismanagement, and neglect of interest in the health of the community generally" (21). As a result of this inheritance, Seraph Pratt is a "weedy specimen, ill-proportioned, neutral-tinted, with a small insignificant head" (2). Grand here emphasizes the crucial importance of intelligent municipal management, to safeguard the "blood" and breeding of the entire country, in the "interest in the health of the community generally." More immediately, the passages suggest the need to be circumspect in selecting a mate from among the urban poor, because those with "blood" weakened by urban conditions will likely produce degenerate offspring.

Much of Grand's concern with "degeneration" involves inherited disease, but in an era that knew little about genetic disorders and that thus was unable to distinguish viral or bacterial infection from genetic predisposition or, say, fetal alcohol syndrome, Grand lumped together all afflictions in which ante-natal factors might play some role.[6] Chief among these in her early work was syphilis—the topic with which Grand became identified as a result of her open discussion in *The Heavenly Twins* of the effects of venereal disease on the wives and children of infected men. In *The Heavenly Twins*, Grand creates a character, Evadne, whose unsupervised girlhood reading has provided her with knowledge unusual for an unmarried girl (or any woman of her era): "After studying anatomy and physiology, she took up pathology as a matter of course, and naturally went on from thence to prophylactics and therapeutics" (23). Thus, when she is about to depart for her wedding journey and receives a warning as to the "character and past life" of her new husband, Major Colquhoun, she understands the potential significance. Upon investigating the allegations, she refuses to consummate the marriage because, she explains, "'marrying a man like that, allowing him an assured position in society, is countenancing vice, and'—she glanced round apprehensively, then added in a fearful whisper—'*helping to spread it*'" (79). "Vice," here, is clearly (though, as we shall see, not exclusively) a euphemism for syphilis, as Evadne continues, "you must know that there is no past in the matter of vice. The consequences become hereditary, and continue from generation to generation" (80). Evadne's medical knowledge, Grand thus assures us, enables her to protect her own health, as well as that of future generations and "society."

Nevertheless, in case readers have not fully understood, Grand vividly illustrates the consequences of "countenancing vice," in the story of Edith Beale, the pure and naive daughter of a bishop, who marries dissolute soldier Sir Mosley Menteith. The more discerning Evadne, apparently attuned to the "science" of physiognomy by her reading, instantly "noticed something repellent about the expression of Sir Mosley's mouth." She observes, too, the obviously atavistic trait that "his head shelved backwards like an ape's" (178). Thus, when Edith announces her engagement, Evadne's visceral and immediate response, is "Edith! You are not going to marry that dreadful man?" (232). She explains that her conviction that "he is bad—thoroughly bad" comes partly from her husband's hints but even more from "a consciousness which informs me of things my intellect cannot grasp" (232–33). This "consciousness" arises from Evadne's own superior evolutionary development, a spiritual gift that distinguishes Grand's "advanced" heroines and further distances them from "atavistic" specimens like Menteith. Edith, however, ignores Evadne's warnings, instead following her equally naive mother's theory that "[l]ove is a great purifier" (234).

When next we see Edith, a year into her marriage, Evadne's warnings have proven justified, for Edith and her child are dying from syphilis:

> [F]rom the first the marriage had been a miserable example of the result of uniting the spiritual or better part of human nature with the essentially animal or most degraded side of it. In that position there was just one hope of happiness left for Edith, and that was in her children. If such a woman so situated can be happy anywhere it will be in her nursery. But Edith's child, which arrived pretty promptly, only proved to be another whip to scourge her. Although of an unmistakable type, he was apparently healthy when he was born, but had rapidly degenerated, and Edith herself was a wreck. (277)

The passage emphasizes a number of crucial points. First among them is degeneration: Sir Mosley himself represents the "animal or degraded" part of humanity, which should never have been matched with Edith's spirituality, and the result is not only that the marriage is unsuccessful but, more concretely, that his child's health has "degenerated." Second is the mother who would find her only potential satisfaction in a healthy infant—a joy that is denied her—and the child who is "an unmistakable type." Both are innocent victims. Third is of course the syphilis itself, never explicitly named, but hinted at yet again as Grand describes Edith's symptoms: her senses are "rendered morbidly active by disease," as she is dogged by "the shadow of an awful form of insanity" that is described as "mental torture" and a "fury of the rage within," concealed beneath an outward "dull apathy" and a "puzzled, pathetic expression" (280–81, 288).

The greatest horror, carefully withheld from readers, is the baby himself, whom we see for the first time through the eyes of the young girl Angelica: at a few months old, the child is "old, old already, and exhausted with suffering, and as his gaze wandered from one to the other it was easy to believe that he was asking each dumbly why had he ever been born?" (289). The question is precisely Grand's point: the poor sufferer should never have been born because Edith should have had the knowledge to protect herself and her offspring, knowledge that Grand is, accordingly, purveying in *The Heavenly Twins*. Indeed, Edith might have avoided marrying Menteith had she and her mother not actively avoided "unpleasant" contact with a beggar woman and her baby a few months before Menteith's proposal. Edith's eyes are opened when she meets the young mother again, and sees her baby, which "should have been running about by that time, but . . . was small and rickety, with bones that bent beneath its weight, slight as it was." She learns the baby's name is "Mosley Menteith, . . . after his father" (290); the child's mother then tells how Menteith paid her sister to help him seduce and abandon her. The child is double to Edith's, not only in name but in his diseased condition. Thus, by implication, Edith is no less than the other young mother a victim of a conspiracy to seduce an innocent young girl.

While the most dramatic evidence of inherited consequences in *The Heavenly Twins* is Edith's child's congenital syphilis, Grand's Lamarckianism holds that bad behavior has hereditary consequences, even in the absence of organic disease. One of her spokesmen in *The Heavenly Twins* remarks, "Will [repentance] prevent a drunkard's children from being weakly vicious? or the daughters of a licentious man from being foredoomed to destruction by an inherited appetite for . . . vices? . . . [T]he once vicious man becomes the father of vicious children and the grandfather of criminals" (186). "Decadence" and "degeneracy" thus acquire connotations beyond current licentious behavior to denote decline in one's descendants. Moreover, private behavior or misbehavior, by affecting family lines for generations, acquires a broader public implication, a point stressed by Prince Aubon Strelletzen in *Adnam's Orchard,* who warns of

> "the predestination which men are making every day for each other and for
> their own descendants; the predestination which, because it is the outcome
> of their own acts, they certainly have it in their power to control. If men
> would but realise how far-reaching the effects of their habits are, habits of

mind as well as habits of life, those at least who are public spirited, in the best sense we attach to that term at present, would certainly see that the responsibility of making provision for the future of the race begins earlier and extends further than they are wont to suppose." (547–48)

The obligation to maintain appropriate "habits of mind as well as habits of life" is thus a matter not only of personal conscience but of "public spirit," for individuals possess free will, the "power to control" their own "habits of mind as well as habits of life" and thus to create "predestination" for their descendants. This Calvinist language conflates religion, morality, genetics, and fate.

If syphilis and vice are the primary causes of degeneration in Grand's novels of the 1890s, inbreeding takes on increasing importance in Grand's twentieth-century pathology. According to Grand, inbreeding within the aristocracy has fostered negative (dysgenic) traits. In *The Winged Victory,* the Duke of Castlefield Saye observes that negative traits have intensified through the generations of his own family: "Heredity was a pet study of his, and he had observed that bad traits came out worse in the next generation. His wife was foolish, his daughter a fool. He hesitated in his speech, Eustace stuttered; he had direct intentions but procrastinated, Melton, the hope of his house, was a drifter" (232). The explanation: the duke's family is "exhausted stock" (*Adnam,* 22), whose "blood" has been "much thinned in the course of ages by marriages with cousins, and vitiated by alcohol and other excesses" (309). In other words, the duke's (and Grand's) eugenic ideas challenge traditional definitions of "good blood" or "breeding." The duke advises his son, when thinking of a wife, to avoid "noble dames with hereditary disease in their families. Degenerate specimens. . . . Contaminated blood contaminates the character, and comes out in bad conduct. Vice." (*Winged,* 242). While vicious conduct creates hereditary disease, by the same token, aristocratic inbreeding "comes out in bad conduct," in a cycle of dysgenic dangers.

The solution, naturally, is to avoid inbreeding. The duke has come to believe that "noble" blood needs an infusion of "new" blood. In *Adnam's Orchard* and *The Winged Victory,* Grand endorses the duke's advocacy of careful "cross breeding" to solve the problem of "exhausted stock." In these works, young women's avoiding degenerate mates is less at issue than young men's selecting "healthy young mothers" (*Adnam,* 519). In Grand's view, women are both more highly evolved than men and less prone to degeneration. This theory also explains the long line of "dominant women" and weak men in Eugenia's family in the story named for her. Although inheritance generally follows the male line, the "dominance" of women—from whatever class—challenges traditional class-based understandings of "good breeding." Early in *Adnam's Orchard* Grand explains, "It is probable that in the days to come high-born and low-born will have changed in significance: low-born being applied to the degenerate offspring of an exhausted stock, regardless of social position; and high-born to the inheritors of health and strength, mental, moral, and physical" (22). The duke observes that his own natural child—Ella Banks—by a nonaristocratic mother is stronger, healthier, brighter, and generally superior to his acknowledged children by his aristocratic parasitic duchess; this is why he tells his heir to seek a "fine, intelligent country girl, of good sound stock, that's the thing for a wife. . . . Educated, refined, straight" (*Winged*, 242). Marrying a healthy working woman will yield healthy children, and, says the duke, "What the nation wants is health. The parents of healthy children are good patriots" (243).

These parents are "good patriots" because, as *Adnam's Orchard* illustrates, one's choice of wife may affect not only one's family but the economic and social development of an entire community. Squire Pointz, having married an "ill-bred" and "vulgar" woman, finds that his son is an irresponsible "mongrel." Only his daughter retains the energy or capacity to manage the family property and the tenants whose welfare depends on it. Emory Pratt's first marriage likewise produces a "mongrel" son who grows up to be selfish, underhanded, unoriginal, and inclined to "secret drinking" (354), a behavior commonly identified as "hereditary vice" by eugenists. Emory's second marriage, to the penniless German Countess Ursula, engenders the eponymous Adnam, creative, enterprising, handsome—and, significantly, full of ideas for agricultural innovations that rejuvenate an ailing rural economy.

The broader social significance of intermarriage is underlined by another curious theory: Grand's blaming aristocratic inbreeding for the "rapacity and hardheartedness" of the wealthy that so infuriates lace maker Ella Banks. Of one unsympathetic aristocrat, Lord Terry De Beach, Grand explains, "It was hereditarily inherent in him to require others to suffer for his good" (*Winged*, 477). Naturally, Ella has no conception that heredity underlies selfishness, and she vows to make the wealthy "pay" for their cruelty, but Grand insists: "She made no allowance for adverse circumstances, for custom, for the pressure of hereditary predisposition, for the unarmed state of those who have not been educated to do as they would be done by" (603–4).

As this passage illustrates, however, Grand wishes us to understand that degeneration derives not solely from physical "hereditary predispositions": poor upbringing and education are also significant causes, for, like other attitudes and behaviors, education has "genetic" effects, for good or ill, on future generations. Moreover, these effects are transmitted equally by and to members of both sexes. In a letter written 16 November 1897, Grand justifies the women's movement as an effort "to strengthen ourselves in all womanly attributes by developing our intelligence, by enlarging our sympathies"; the result of this effort, she writes, is that "the woman movement seems to be evolutionary—an effort of the human race to advance a step higher in its development, a result which can only be attained by making the mothers finer creatures than they have been heretofore" (Heilmann and Forward, 2:61–62). It is not just women who must develop their intelligence and enlarge their sympathies; men, too, need better training. Seraph Pratt's "mongrel" traits emerged because his mother damaged her son not only through physical inheritance but also through his early childhood training. An "idle, self-indulgent sloven," Seraph's mother "lived long enough to infect him, her only child, with her innate defects of character and of manner" (*Adnam*, 22, 21). These combined influences, significantly conflating education with contagion and genetics, were enough to overcome his father's hereditary gifts.

The emphasis on early childhood education creates a quandary for Grand, leading her to propose positions seemingly contrary to her advocacy of womanly independence, professionalism, and self-development. In an essay called "Should Married Women Follow Professions?" Grand asserts, "The influences brought to bear upon a child in the first few years of its life are so all-important that no woman worthy of her sex would leave it to the care of others except under pressure of cruel necessity" (121). Grand's focus on education as a means to control heredity also reflects her attempt to bridge the feminist gap between the idea that gender difference is learned (so the sexes are fundamentally similar) and the idea of inherent gender differences. Since acquired traits may be transmitted to one's offspring, according to Grand's theory, not only a woman's moral behavior but her education will benefit her descendants and thus the entire race. Because motherhood is so important, Grand argues, feminism is important: "moral progress has been checked for ages by the criminal repression of women" (*Twins*, 193).

If women's repression has checked human evolution, nevertheless women represent the evolutionary vanguard. A character in *The Heavenly Twins* speculates that "all this unrest and rebellion against the old established abuses amongst women is simply an effort of nature to improve the race" (219). As a character in *The Beth Book* explains, "[T]his woman moment is towards the perfecting of life. . . . I am sure it is evolutionary. It is an effort of the race to raise itself a step higher in the scale of being" (412–13). Grand's heroines represent the forefront of the forefront. Evadne in *The Heavenly Twins* is part of a "seventh wave" carrying the "tide of human progress" a stage higher; the eponymous feminist, gender-bending twins are "signs of the times"; and Beth McClure of *The Beth Book* is "one of the first swallows of the woman's summer" (527). Grand conveys a sense of inevitability to the evolutionary process, associated as it is with a worldwide women's movement described as "evolutionary. It is the outcome of a great involuntary effort of the human race to lift itself up a step higher in the scale of its development" (*Adnam*, 345).

Evolution may be portrayed at times as an inevitable natural process led by women, but even in *Adnam's Orchard* and *The Winged Victory*, with their almost obsessive focus on eugenics, Grand resists simple biological determinism, insisting that humans have free will, not only to change themselves individually but to shape the future race. Even as she explains the causes of Seraph Pratt's "mongrel" qualities, she insists that "such differences of character do not prove that qualities good or bad are inherent in the blood, things neither to be acquired nor eradicated. In childhood heredity may be successfully combated by training and environment; and in later life by knowledge and determination" (*Adnam*, 22). In the Lamarckian view of heredity, the acquired traits that one's children inherit are not accidental features like a limp, but habits, attitudes, and intellectual capacities, traits developed over time and in many cases as a result of conscious decisions and considerable effort. This is the kind of effort that Ursula Pratt recommends to Lena Kedlock, who, as the daughter of the duke's alcoholic cousin/agent, must contend with an extremely degenerate bloodline. Ursula tells Lena, "You can save yourself . . . By resistance. . . . Map out your own nature, and mark the dangerous places, the rocks and shoals that you must avoid. Don't drift. Steer straight for the Happy Haven—you know the way. You know, too, where you are apt to go wrong" (452). A young woman with knowledge of heredity—like Lena—who will combine self-examination with the "valuable cargo" of "ideas, opinions, principles," and who will exert the effort and concentration to "steer straight," can triumph over her inheritance. Thus, for all her insistence on the power of heredity, Grand insists repeatedly on her characters' free will to resist all but the most severe congenital defects—such as syphilis.

Unfortunately, by the end of *The Winged Victory,* the second book of a planned trilogy, its heroine, Ella Banks, has failed to take Ursula's advice and has drifted into a fate caused largely by the combined effects of her heredity, her training, and her ignorance of her actual bloodline: her unawareness of her father's true identity leads to her marrying her half brother, who then rides his horse off a cliff. Whether Ella would then move forward, armed with more knowledge, to a happier ending in the third book, Grand never revealed, for the trilogy that promised to embody her eugenic feminism remained unfinished.

Why? Some explanations are relatively mundane: writer's block, the destruction of Grand's manuscripts in a fire, her claim that "the War had then intervened and altered everything" (Kersley, 158).[7] Teresa Mangum has suggested that "Ella herself personifies the most vehement condemnation of the eugenists' scheme. All unknown to her, the conflicting anger of the working classes and pride of the upper classes are her 'hereditary' inheritance. Adnam's mixed heredity produced a heroic New Man; in Ella eugenic hybridization breeds disaster" (218). Perhaps, but Ella's failures have less to do with "inherent" flaws, since her superiorities are repeatedly insisted on, and more to do with her embittered maternal grandmother's training, her father's withholding the truth—always a problem in Grand's world view—and her being poor and female. It may be that another of Grand's theories rendered the third novel impossible. She had long held that close proximity in marriage to a degenerate man could corrupt even a superior woman—ideas raised in *The Heavenly Twins* and *The Beth Book*—and that corruption was hereditary. So once she carried out the "doom" of the Castlefield Saye family and involved the Duke's children in an incestuous union, she had also rendered Ella an unfit mother of a new race.

Grand offers foreshadowings of eventual marriage between Adnam and Ella, protagonists of the first and second books, each a healthy representative of "new blood." But while Adnam leaves his orchard for the wide world, he never joins hands with his Eve. In a world that stifles women's opportunities, Grand's ideal "mother of men" remains only hypothetical. Grand's eugenic feminism, which, to her, seemed to promise so much hope—combining women's supposed innate superiority with the Lamarckian benefits of equal access to education—runs up against recalcitrant realities of class- and sex-based oppression. This last trilogy, in which public benefit and private joy promise to merge in a perfect eugenic marriage plot, never gets to its happy ending—or any ending at all. And Grand, though she lived another twenty years, never wrote another novel.

Gilman, Eugenics, and the "Beautiful Work" of "Right Marriage"

Gilman, too, uses eugenic ideas to resolve tensions between feminist ideas about private and public, equality and difference. Reform Darwinism provides Gilman a way to explain who we are and how we got this way, while promising both insight into and control over our future. As with Grand, eugenics impinge on Gilman's thoughts about marriage, with wise selection of a healthy mate playing a role in her thinking. However, for Gilman, as we shall see, mere biological evolution represents too slow a form of progress to satisfy her social ambitions.

Gilman insists that the sexes are fundamentally—and naturally—equal. In *With Her in Ourland,* the Herland visitor to Ourland concludes, "They are born equal, your boys and girls; they have to be. It is the tremendous difference in cultural conditions that divides them" (185). Gilman delights in analogies with other species: the equal strength of migrating birds, grazing herds, or breeding salmon, and hunters' fear of the greater ferocity of protective mothers (*Women and Economics,* 45). Nevertheless, while assuming that the sexes inherit shared traits, Gilman, like Grand and Ward, also assumes "inherent" gender differences. Many of the differences are dysgenic. In *Women and Economics,* Gilman argues that human courtship and marriage customs are the primary causes of differences between the sexes. Humans, she says, are "the only animal species in which the female depends on the male for food, the only animal species in which the sex-relation is also an economic relation" (5). This "abnormal sexuo-economic relation" has "morbid" effects (23): women are overfeminine, or, in Gilman's terms, "over sexed" (40). Because the human female's survival depends on her attracting a mate to support her, humans' "secondary sex-characteristics," differences whose sole function is to attract a mate (analogous to a peacock's plumage), have become exaggerated. Because human males have preferred small women, "Little creatures, undersized and generally feeble" (*Ourland,* 174), women have indeed evolved into "the weaker sex." Gilman identifies the "feebleness and clumsiness common to women, the comparative inability to stand, walk, run, jump, climb, and perform other race-functions common to both sexes" as "an excessive sex-distinction" that harms both women and their offspring of *both* sexes, and "the ensuing trans-mission of this relative feebleness . . . retards human development" (*Women and Economics,* 46).

Moreover, Gilman, who, like Grand, accepted Lamarckian theories about inheritance of acquired traits, argues that due to the human "sexuo-economic relation," women have remained economically dependent, serving only their immediate families, and this situation has, in turn, developed in women behaviors that retard the species' development, including an "intense self-consciousness, born of the ceaseless contact of close personal relation; an in-ordinate self-interest, bred by the constant personal attention and service of this relation; . . . a thwarted will, used to meek surrender, cunning evasion, or futile rebellion; a childish, wavering, short-range judgment, handicapped by emotion" (336–37). Because of the widespread and long-continuing nature of women's dependence, these behavioral traits have become hereditary. Like such "secondary sex characteristics" as smallness, dependence, and "meek sur-render" that have been considered "natural" for women, they are counterevo-lutionary for humanity in general.

Gilman's argument brilliantly co-opts and reverses standard fin-de-siècle "degeneration" theories. Her terminology exploits those fears but subversively redefines the terms. In Gilman's revisionist parlance, "To be over-feminine is to be over-sexed" (40). To traditionalists on both sides of the Atlantic, the "masculine" New Woman was "un-sexed," and represented both evidence and cause of racial degeneration, but the promiscuous "over-sexed" or "fallen" woman was even more thoroughly degenerate. Gilman has reversed the terms, showing that the less feminine—or, in standard parlance, "un-sexed"—woman is the more healthy, eugenically fit woman and explaining that the traits of the "over-sexed" (feminine) woman are indeed dysgenic: "In the human species we find sex-distinction carried to an excessive degree. Sex-distinction in humanity is so marked as to retard and confuse race-distinction, to check individual distinction, seriously to injure the race" (31–32).

But Gilman wants things both ways, arguing that women "inherently" possess traits superior to men's. She says, for example, "The constructive tendency is essentially feminine; the destructive masculine. Male energy tends to scatter and destroy, female to gather and construct" (*The Home,* 127). It is therefore racially disadvantageous that men have heretofore been responsible for developing government, industry, art, religion, and science. These being areas of women's "inherent" strength, they have not evolved as quickly or as well as they might have with more contributions from women. In order to make that point and to explore what might happen if women alone—rather than men alone—had responsibility for major cultural institutions, Gilman created her all-woman utopia in *Herland.* In Herland, "[b]eing women, we had all the constructive and organizing tendencies of motherhood to urge us on and, having no men, we missed all that greediness and quarreling your history is so sadly full of" (*Ourland,* 190). Ourland's history has seen women evolving primarily vis-à-vis sex distinction, with disastrous effects on children, boys and girls alike. Again, Gilman has matters both ways: gender difference is simultaneously "morbid" and natural, resulting from both cultural practice and evolutionary pressure.

Like Grand, Gilman believed that wise marriage can advance human evolution—and prevent racial degeneration. Adopting the animal model wherein males compete for the attentions of a female who then selects her mate, Gilman asserts that "woman's beautiful work is to improve the race by right marriage" (*Women and Economics,* 92). A significant aspect of that "work" is knowing how to avoid "wrong marriage." When Herland native Ellador visits Ourland, she is appalled that the women of Ourland understand "their duty as mothers" so poorly that they "do not even know enough about motherhood to demand a healthy father. Why, a—a—sheep would know better than to mate with such creatures as some of your women marry." Echoing Grand, she continues, "They are only just beginning to learn that there are such diseases as they have been suffering and dying from for all these centuries" (*Ourland*, 185). For humanity in general to attain Herland's perfection, we must similarly attend to reproductive fitness and avoid diseased mates.

Gilman's 1911 novella *The Crux* models such a negative eugenic choice, always focused on a potential mother's responsibility to her children. Young Morton Elder, who "never was taught anything to protect him" growing up with his maiden aunt in a tiny New England village, has done "a lot of things he shouldn't" in the nine years since he was expelled from college and became a salesman. Reunited with Vivian Lane, the young woman who has loved him since childhood, he now has a "coarsened complexion," a sore throat, and cold sores (141, 143, 145). Eventually, he proposes to Vivian, but her friend, Dr. Jane Bellair, warns her that Morton has syphilis and probably gonorrhea as well. Vivian proclaims herself willing to sacrifice herself for the man she loves, but Dr. Bellair replies, "Will you tell that to your crippled children? . . . Will they understand it if they are idiots? Will they see it if they are blind? Will it satisfy you when they are dead?" (225).

Dr. Bellair's fundamental argument is "Marriage is for motherhood," and Vivian must consider that her children "may be deformed and twisted, have all manner of terrible and loathsome afflictions, they and their children after them, if they have any. And many do!" (224, 226). Dr. Bellair is the appropriate source of this information, not only as a woman doctor—for the male doctor in the novel has refused to violate confidentiality (patient "privacy") despite the potential consequences—but also because she herself contracted gonorrhea from her ex-husband. As she explains to Vivian, "When I found I could not be a mother I determined to be a doctor, and save other women" from, as the narrator puts it, "that worse than deadly peril, because of which she had no daughter" (221, 213). Protecting young Vivian as if she were her own daughter, and protecting Vivian's children, is now Dr. Bellair's motherly mission. Though crushed by the news of Morton's condition and the doctor's advice, Vivian has "a fair and reasoning mind" and a love of children (228). She does the only thing she can—breaks her engagement—applauded by her grandmother, Mrs. Pettigrew.

Mrs. Pettigrew, by far the book's cleverest character, advises Vivian—and the reader—as to the wider implications of her situation: eugenic implications. Vivian is shocked (as well she might be) to hear that three-quarters of men are diseased, but, Mrs. Pettigrew points out, "Our girls are mostly clean, and they save the race, I guess" (244). She commends some states' laws requiring a medical certificate to obtain a marriage license, but mainly she looks to the future:

> "And that's in the hands of woman, my dear—as soon as we know enough. Don't be afraid of knowledge. When we all know about this we can stop it! Think of that. We can religiously rid the world of all these—'undesirable citizens.'"
>
> "How, Grandma?"
>
> "Easy enough, my dear. By not marrying them." (246–47)

With 75 percent of men diseased and most women "clean," removing the "undesirable citizens" and producing the clean children of tomorrow naturally falls to women. Their responsibility is to spread knowledge that will save future young people from "biological sin" and its consequences. If "marriage is for motherhood," motherhood is for citizenship. The private decision of selecting a husband has become the public responsibility to "save the race."

These moderate methods represent a far milder form of negative eugenics than that described in *Moving the Mountain,* the novella serialized in the *Forerunner* concurrently with *The Crux.* In *Moving the Mountain,* a traveler returns to America in 1940, after a thirty-year absence (and amnesia), to find its culture and attitudes changed utterly. In contrast to the centuries-long development in the later and gentler *Herland,* the alterations in Gilman's "short-distance utopia" required radical methods, including a negative eugenics in which, at first, its inhabitants "killed many hopeless degenerates, insane, idiots, and real perverts, after trying our best powers of cure" (136). The "perverts" who were not "promptly and mercifully removed" were "incapacitated for parentage and placed where they could do no harm" (98). Because "[c]ertain classes of criminals and perverts were rendered incapable of reproducing their kind," the society could "check the birth of defectives and degenerates" (86). As a second step, births to those with "infectious diseases"—venereal diseases—were prevented, by two methods. First, the changes recorded in *Moving the Mountain* involved a nationwide social purity movement: when "health" became a cultural "ideal," the "young women learned the proportion of men with syphilis and gonorrhoea and decided that it was wrong to marry them. That was enough" (77). Laws made unwitting transmission of venereal disease to a wife or child a misdemeanor, and conscious infection a felony (86–87). Furthermore, they "passed laws in every State requiring a clean bill of health with every marriage license. Diseased men had to die bachelors—that's all. . . . A man who has one of those diseases is so reported—just like small-pox." The information is registered at the "Department of Eugenics," accessible by any potential wife (77–78).

Gilman's Herland has not needed to legislate against unhealthy or unsuitable fathers—for there have been no men for centuries. In *Herland,* the focus is on positive eugenics—the hallmark of an entire civilization, albeit a small one. Starting from Lester Ward's premise that "throughout nature the female is the race-type, being in reality the earlier organism; the male developing later in the interests of cross fertilization" ("Feminism," 186), Gilman imagines in Herland a parthenogenetic race, who have developed a culture far superior to ours—cleaner, more beautiful, without poverty, crime, or conflict. In Herland, every growing thing is bred for maximum utility and beauty, including, of course, the Herlanders themselves. They are strong, daring, and athletic, but graceful and "womanly": in short, admirably built to bear healthy daughters. To avoid overcrowding and to ensure continuing racial progress, most Herlanders give birth to only one child; a few superior "Over Mothers" are encouraged to have more than one, a "positive eugenic" practice that reproduces the most valuable traits. As a result, the Herland race has been "steadily developing in mental capacity, in will power, in social devotion" (*Herland,* 72). On the other hand, "atavistic" women "forgo motherhood" for the good of the country (92, 69). Herlanders have made it their "first business" to "breed out, when possible, the lowest types" (82).

Despite the progress attributed to Herland's eugenic methods, even Herlanders consider what they call "bisexual reproduction" superior to parthenogenesis, the evidence deriving, naturally, from evolution: "two sexes, working together, must be better than one. . . . It *must* be best or it would not have been evolved in all the higher animals" (*Ourland,* 88). As Gilman writes in an essay, "Superfluous Women," "Neither sex does its best alone; each needs the influence of the other" (123–24). The arrival of three eligible males in Herland affords an opportunity to, as we would say today, strengthen the Herland gene pool. Herlanders see their visitors as potential fathers, and of course not just any man will do for that function. Accordingly, Gilman shows us the kind of man approved by citizens in a highly evolved female culture that places eugenic motherhood above all other values. The three visitors to Herland, Jeff, Terry, and Van, represent a range of male "types": Jeff is the chivalrous idealist who wants to "worship" and "protect" women; Terry is an athletic "ladies man" who likes to "master" women, and Van, the narrator, is a sociologist who wants to understand and befriend the women he meets in Herland.

According to standard social Darwinism, Terry, the most aggressive, would most likely win a battle of "survival of the fittest," but Gilman pointedly rejects that view. Van, as a sociologist, attempts to explain to his hostesses that "the laws of nature require a struggle for existence, and . . . in the struggle the fittest survive, and the unfit perish" (63), but in Herland he realizes that an evolutionary theory premised on competition is an androcentric construct. Herland's history teaches Van that when the country faced "the pressure of population," Herlanders resisted the kinds of responses Thomas Malthus—and, influenced by Malthus's theories, Darwin and his followers—would have predicted. They did not engage in "a 'struggle for existence' which would result in an everlasting writhing mass of underbred people trying to get ahead of one another," with "no possibility for really noble qualities among the people at large" (68). Instead, Herlanders, cooperatively, as mothers, analyzed the best interests of future generations—the children of the future—as a basis for selecting parthenogenetic mothers. When the time comes to involve men, Herlanders have no concept of choosing a "lover," but instead select fathers in "the highest social service" to their nation (88). Van is the most popular among the Herlanders, who see him as "more like us—more like People" (89), and his and Ellador's marriage proves the most successful because it becomes the most companionate and cooperative. They are the couple who first produce a son, a "new Hope" for Herland (*Ourland*, 193).

By contrast, masterful, competitive Terry, who wants sex, not fatherhood, is expelled from Herland for attempted marital rape. Indeed, Terry represents atavistic traits that Gilman would breed out through negative eugenics; she explicitly deploys the language of "degeneration" when Terry is imprisoned for his crime: "Moadine, grave and strong, as sadly patient as a mother with a degenerate child, kept steady watch on him" (*Herland,* 135). Terry's intense sexual drive and probable past "success" at fathering illegitimate children suggest that in a Darwinian evolutionary sense he is among the "fittest" to reproduce. That he is the only one of the three explorers who fails to father a child by a Herland woman indicates, however, that by "enlightened" eugenic standards, this "degenerate child" has traits that are not promising for racial progress. Thus, while clearly endorsing an evolutionary philosophy, Gilman rejects the underlying premise of competition as "underbred," substituting a vision of eugenics through cooperation.

In fact, Gilman argues that controlling human evolution through eugenic reproduction is a small and inefficient aspect of the evolutionary project. Partly because she believed in the inheritance of acquired characteristics and partly because she believed, like Grand, that human evolution has progressed to a stage beyond the individual, Gilman put her primary emphasis on "social evolution." In her theory, society is simply the most complex system of cells: "The evolution of organic life goes on in geometrical progression: cells combine, and form organs; organs combine, and form organisms; organisms combine, and form organizations. Society is an organization. Society is the fourth power of the cell. . . . The course of social evolution is the gradual establishment of organic relation between individuals" (*Women and Economics,* 101–2). In an 1892 essay, "The Labor Movement," Gilman cites Spencer's theory that evolution is "progress from indefinite, incoherent, homogeneity, to definite, coherent, heterogeneity, by a series of differentiations" (62). That is, just as the evolution of organisms has entailed increasing specialization of each cell and organ, so, as society evolves, individuals become more specialized, each contributing something different to the "social body" and each depending on the others for existence. Gilman argues, "The more perfectly this specialization is carried out, the more powerful is our collective existence" (64). It is for this reason that women's lack of specialization in the home—in which each woman is an amateur cook, cleaner, decorator, child-care worker, teacher, and so on—retards human progress; and that the professionalization of household tasks—including child care—represents evolutionary progress. With specialization comes greater interdependence, greater social cohesion, and greater altruism—a more highly evolved society.

According to Gilman, motherhood was the original source of altruism, for the mother's unselfish love for her baby is the first social bond, but it is only the first step in social evolution: "Love began with the mother; but it should not stop with her" (*The Home,* 165). In Herland, motherhood extends well beyond the individual mother and baby. Here, the visitors are told, is a country in which "'we have Human Motherhood—in full working use. . . . The children in this country are the one center and focus of all our thoughts. Every step of our advance is always considered in its effect on them—on the race. You see, we are *Mothers,*' she repeated, as if in that she had said it all" (66). A society in which what Sara Ruddick has called "maternal thinking" is the shaping ideology of the culture is one, according to Gilman, governed by forward thinking, an emphasis on the future: one's daughters and granddaughters. In Herland, motherhood is not a retreat from the public sphere, but one's most important civic contribution, for "motherhood [is] exalted above a mere personal function, looked forward to as the highest social service, as the sacrament of a lifetime" (88).

In an androcentric culture, the "struggle for existence" governs life, and women and children are peripheral, functioning perhaps as beneficiaries of (a man's) successful struggles—or perhaps as the booty—and the home functions as a private retreat from the public world of competition. In a "gynaeocentric" culture, by contrast, the "private" world of mother and child is not contrary to the public world but constitutive of it: maternal values shape public values. In *Herland,* Gilman describes an entire culture with a vision of motherhood completely antithetical to our own: "A motherliness which dominated society, which influenced every art and industry, which absolutely protected all childhood, and gave to it the most perfect care and training" (73). Such a value system is more than the simple role reversal on which Gilman bases much of the humor and commentary of the novel; it is a complete paradigm shift, a revolution—or evolution—in thinking.

Social Motherhood and Literary Housekeeping

For all our cultural idealizing of motherhood, the portrayal of mothers as positive figures is surprisingly uncommon in women's fiction and even in feminist fiction. In the bulk of women's novels about women, the protagonist's mother is ineffectual—or dead. The heroine must find her own way in the world, relatively unaided, or struggling against conservative ideologies epitomized by her own stupid or smothering or suffering mother. Thus Jane Eyre's, Dorothea Brooke's, Mary Barton's, and Aurora Leigh's mothers are dead; Elizabeth Bennett's is foolish; Maggie Tulliver's is unsupportive; Margaret Gale's (in Gaskell's *North and South*) is sickly; and Hadria's (in Mona Caird's *The Daughters of Danaus*) is downtrodden. This pattern is repeated in much of the fiction by Ward, Grand, and Gilman. But for every dead mother (the mothers of Ward's Delia Blanchflower, of Diana Mallory, and of Laura Fountain in *Helbeck of Bannisdale;* her Lady Rose of *Lady Rose's Daughter;* the mother of Grand's Ella Banks), and for every querulous, weak, or stupid mother (Beth McClure's in Grand's *The Beth Book,* or Grand's Duchess of Castlefield Saye, or Benigna MacAvelly's mother in Gilman's *Benigna Machiavelli*), there are also a few more complicated mothers and, at best, mothers whose nurturance typifies a feminism that brings maternal influence into the public sphere. All three writers, to varying degrees, look directly at mothers of the present in their writings, addressing motherhood not merely as a private relationship but as a public responsibility.

Sarah Grand's Disciplinary Motherhood

In Sarah Grand's books, especially the well-known New Woman novels of the 1890s, mothers tend to be either powerless or hampering. They have their occasional good moments, as when Evadne Frayling Colquhoun's mother finally stands up to Mr. Frayling, defending Evadne in the name of every "mother in the country from her Majesty downward" (*Twins,* 120), but this defense comes long after it could help Evadne in any meaningful way. For the most part, Grand's fictional mothers are weak, either exacerbating the challenges faced by strong but impressionable characters like Evadne and Beth or producing daughters who are as weak as themselves—and thus fatally weak—like Edith Beale and like Ann Brabant, daughter of the Duke and Duchess of Castlefield Saye. Angelica of *The Heavenly Twins* is only marginally luckier, for her mother, though ineffectual, is sensible, allowing the twins to take control in ways that allow them to develop themselves, but here the best we can say is that she is not a bad mother.

As we have seen, Grand contended that "moral progress has been checked for ages by the criminal repression of women" (*Twins,* 193). In "The New Aspect of the Woman Question," Grand addresses the implications of a motherhood that has evaded or transcended this repression, the metaphorical motherhood that she calls "the new woman." According to Grand, "The man of the future will be better, while the woman will be stronger and wiser," because the New Woman will raise the new man up to her level (272). Grand here manages both to insist on equally shared traits and to suggest that woman is currently "better," since the women will bring about the changes—and will do so in maternal fashion. In the past, she says, woman has "allowed [man] to arrange the whole social system and manage or mismanage it all these ages without . . . considering whether his abilities and his motives were sufficiently good to qualify him for the task" (271). Obviously, they were not; therefore, maternal woman should take over, and furthermore, she should end the habit whereby she has indulged faulty man like a spoiled child, and "screened him when we should have exposed him and had him punished" (271). Grand continues this disciplinary metaphor a few pages later, when she explains that New Women will no longer stoop to men's level: "Heaven help the child to perceive with what travail and sorrow we submit to the heavy obligation, when it is forced upon us by our sense of right, of showing him how things ought to be done" (274). The passage has a quality of "this hurts me more than it hurts you," a matriarchal condescension. Grand relishes the prospect of taking the naughty boys by the ear and teaching them a lesson. Motherhood thus provides a convenient and vivid justification for women's stepping outside the private "Home-is-the-Woman's-Sphere" to metaphorically take charge of a public sphere redefined as the "human household."

Mary Ward's Civic Maternalism:
Individualistic Experiments and Collective Action

Like Grand, Mary Ward places more emphasis on metaphorical motherhood than on fictional portrayals of mothering itself, for most of her protagonists are unmarried women, and frequently they are orphaned. As we have seen, in some of her antisuffrage writings, Ward invokes motherhood as a reason women should not vote. Yet Ward's advocacy of women's service in local politics is also premised on valuing women's unique family experiences. Women working locally could draw on their experiences and concerns as mothers to rectify public problems affecting mothers and children. This is the "civic maternalism" that historian Seth Koven has found at the heart of Ward's social welfare activities. Moreover, Ward argues, motherhood can exert a positive influence on public behavior. In *Delia Blanchflower,* the spokeswoman for the importance of motherhood is not a literal mother but a maternal woman who exemplifies the principle of civic motherhood. Miss Dempsey, rescuer of prostitutes (and also a suffragist), argues that men's reformation is their mothers' responsibility: "[M]en are what their mothers make them! . . . And when women are what God intended them to be, they will have killed the ape and the tiger in men" (332). That is, women, as mothers of men, have the capacity and responsibility to help society evolve, to raise its moral tone.

Ward's most important contribution to civic motherhood was not in fiction but in the development of Invalid Children's Schools and the Play Centre Movement. Building on the success of informal Saturday play times that had begun serendipitously at the London settlement house Ward founded, the first play center—day care center—in England opened in the Passmore Edwards Settlement within a week of the building's 1897 opening. Ward, credited by her daughter as the "motive force" guiding the movement, followed the Saturday "play room" with after-school activities—the Recreation School—to accommodate children of working mothers. Within a year, 650 children were attending per week; three or four years later, 1,200 (Trevelyan, 124, 125). In 1899, Ward obtained funding from the London School Board to open an Invalid Children's School, the first opportunity for London's physically handicapped children to obtain formal schooling. She envisioned it from the start as a first-of-its-kind endeavor that, though begun as a private experiment, would eventually expand throughout England under state funding. In August 1902, a Vacation School opened for children otherwise unsupervised during the summer. With these innovations, Ward solved one particularly vexing problem facing working mothers—balancing the need for work in the public sphere with responsibilities for children—and of course began a child-care arrangement crucial to women's economic independence. Pleased but not content with her successes, Ward promoted the establishment of similar centers throughout London, to be supported by the school board. She lobbied actively for what the *Times* dubbed the "Mary Ward Clause" of the 1906 Education Act, which gave permission to local education authorities to provide play centers; then, in

a move that pitted her against organizations that opposed any but private support based on "merit" rather than financial need, Ward campaigned for financial support of play centers and invalid schools by the national government.
Thanks to her lobbying, support for physically disabled children was written
into the 1918 Education Act.

Ward once explained that she valued settlements like hers because such
private efforts "prepare . . . the way for the steady advance of the collective and
legal methods of social reform. . . . These irregular and individualistic experiments are the necessary pioneers and accompaniments with us of all collective
action."[8] That is, her individual efforts to help children and their mothers in
the public/domestic settlement house fulfilled the literary housekeeping
function of gradually moving maternal care into the public sphere. The play
centers were not as ambitious in their aims as Gilman's baby gardens, for Ward
saw them not as socialized motherhood to improve the nurturing of infants but
as a stopgap for school-age children. Nevertheless, one cannot overstate the
play centers' practical benefit of providing supervised activities for the children of the working poor. For Ward, this civic maternalism demonstrated that
a woman need not vote in parliamentary elections to make a significant maternal contribution to the public good. Ironically, her successful lobbying to gain
public funding for these services contributed to the shift in the government's
role in maternal and child welfare that rendered obsolete Ward's distinction
between women's appropriate participation in local government and their
supposedly inappropriate demand to participate in national government.

State Motherhood in Gilman's Herland

Of course, of the three authors, the one known for placing motherhood at the
center of her philosophy is Charlotte Perkins Gilman. Gilman's portrayal of
civic-minded motherhood in *Herland* represents an attempt to reconcile the irreconcilable, to smooth away conflicts between equality and difference, public
and private. Gilman's Herlanders have consciously created a social system in
which the most fundamentally private relationships—between mothers and
babies, between sisters—are the foundation for all public decisions and social
structures. *Herland* meditates on several different versions of the public/pri-
vate dichotomy. It describes a land whose citizens possess "the highest, keen-

est, most delicate sense of personal privacy" (125), yet who observe and regulate the most minute details of their "guests'" lives; it considers a world in which the usually private maternal domestic sphere provides the organizing principle of the public sphere—its political, economic, and even spiritual realms; and it gives us a world in which there are no significant differences, and all are equal—because everything about the country is different from our androcentric culture.

By the end of the novel, Van describes his relationship with Herland women as "like—coming home to mother" (142), but the initial emphasis is on Herland as different and alien, an idea created largely by the exploration trope that *Herland* shares with other utopian novels. First described in the "legends and folk myths" of "savages" encountered during an expedition to the "enormous hinterland of a great river, up where the maps had to be made, [and] savage dialects studied" (2), Herland promises to be a site for colonial conquest or for Kurtzian horror. The native guides agree in characterizing the unknown land (which none of them has actually seen); it is "dangerous, deadly, . . . for any man to go there" (3). The young explorers quickly dub it "Amazonian." Gilman thus prepares her characters—and readers—for a primitive, savage world, drawing on the ideological assumption that difference implies hierarchy, and that to Western male explorers a world of women is by definition both inferior and threatening.

These expectations are strengthened by the novel's narrative point of view, as Van, the male narrator, and his two male companions, Jeff and Terry, dominate the first chapter. These aren't just men but "manly men": a sociologist, a doctor, and a pilot/engineer—intrepid explorers all. There are many advantages to Gilman's telling her tale through men's eyes. First, to identify the differences—and the similarities—between a woman's world and a man's world (that is, our world, "the Man-Made World; or, Our Androcentric Culture" as Gilman phrased it in her 1911 book title), she needed to present the views of men who know what that man's world is. These are young men of privileged backgrounds and professional educations, "rich enough to do as [they] pleased" (1). An upper-class white male point of view is the best way to get a full sense of differences between the perspectives of powerful men from a male-dominated culture and that of Herland's woman-only culture. Furthermore, when the men find themselves in the role of outsiders—the Other—

they experience for the first time the position that women are accustomed to hold in a male-dominated culture: powerless, economically dependent, defined almost exclusively by their reproductive function.

By having men encounter Herland, Gilman takes full advantage of readers' expectations. The characters articulate stereotypical expectations of an all-woman world: primitive, sex-starved, incompetent, full of catty conflict, and so on. She then lets us follow the characters' thinking as they (or at least Van) gradually change views, inviting readers to change too. Moreover, because the men carry their androcentric values with them, those values become as much the subject of analysis as Herland values and behaviors. The Herlanders are as much anthropologists as the "explorers," for, like the men, the Herlanders confront, observe, analyze, and evaluate, frequently without the men even realizing that they're being studied. And the Herlanders are horrified, when they're not merely amused, by the culture that the men—and we—take for granted. In other words, even as cultural differences are emphasized by the two groups' simultaneous study of one another, the cultural differences and gender differences are collapsed, showing that Ourland is as much a "man-made world" as Herland is a "woman-made world."

From the outset the women respond to the male travelers much as the men respond to Herland: as representing the Other, threatening and fascinating, subject to investigation and control. Late in the novel, we learn that "first contact" carried much the same meaning for the women residents as for the male explorers. On the sighting of the airplane, a Herland council meets and issues a terse bulletin: "From another country. Probably men. Evidently highly civilized. Doubtless possessed of much valuable knowledge. May be dangerous. Catch them if possible; tame and train them if necessary. This may be a chance to re-establish a bi-sexual state for our people" (87–88). Just as the men analyze "well-woven fabric" (4), "clean, well-built roads" and "a land in a state of perfect cultivation" to determine, "[W]hy, this is a *civilized* country!" (11), so too, the women observe a technological artifact—a biplane—and conclude, "Evidently highly civilized." The women's "May be dangerous" echoes the men's prejudices, and the Herlanders' plan to "Catch them if possible" provides ironic comment on Terry's effort to use "bait" to tempt and grab the girls in the tree. Members of both sexes adopt an anthropological stance because both assume the fundamental otherness of the "dangerous" race they are about to encounter. This immediate wariness reflects the question of whether men and women can in fact understand one another, or whether they belong to alien races speaking different languages.

One of the most notable manifestations of the mutual sense of fundamental difference between the Herlanders and the Ourlanders is their mutual—and amusingly similar—surveillance activities. As Foucault has taught us, to examine or observe someone is to exercise power over them. Initially, the men, in their panoptical position in the airplane, enjoy power over the Herland landscape. Gilman's language in describing their encounter with this landscape is highly sexualized, suggesting the men's taking "possession"—or, as Terry will later say, "mastering"—the female body politic. After "poking" along the side of a river, they find a tributary of pure mountain water leading to a lake: "When we reached that and slid out on its broad glistening bosom, with that high gray promontory running out toward us, and the straight white fall clearly visible, it began to be really exciting" (9). They discuss "skirting" the rock wall to find a path up the mountain, but return to their original plan, and fly over the country "to get 'the lay of the land,'" a process that entails "a long skirting voyage" "up one side of the triangle" (10). This narrative, which humorously echoes the language of colonialism identified by Annette Kolodny in her classic study of metaphors of male conquest in American exploration narratives, treats the Herland landscape as a female body that the men penetrate and that the phallic mountains overshadow. Upon landing their "airship," in the second chapter, whose title, "Rash Advances," punningly combines military and sexual metaphors, the men's "ardor" takes them in quest of the imagined "national harem," and their first "objects of pursuit" are three young women in a tree, who are alternately said to resemble "peaches" and "so many big bright birds on their precarious perches" (13, 15). Although Terry, in his "ardor," attempts to snare this prey, they outsmart him and escape, at which Van dryly observes, "Inhabitants evidently arboreal" (17). The men's anthropological impulse is thus firmly associated with sexual predation, exploitation of natural and human resources—and mild incompetence.

The women of Herland are no less anthropological in their responses to the men—but their maternal methods prove more skillful, despite lacking the "expertise" that might be thought to arise from Euro-American culture's long imperialist tradition. From the time the plane is sighted, the Herlanders maintain constant surveillance, with three complementary purposes: to control the men's movements, to study them, and to teach them. Control is maintained by a guard of five "stalwarts" per man, "unobtrusively watching" (27). Van remarks to his companions, "One or another pair of eyes is on us every minute except at night" (34). After six months in captivity, the men are considered "tamed" but remain "under surveillance for three [months] more" (53). After Terry attempts to rape Alima, he is imprisoned again, under even sharper surveillance: "They watched him like lynxes. (Do lynxes watch any better than mousing cats, I wonder!)" (143).

After the men's initial capture and imprisonment, they are interrogated. To be sure, the overt intent is scientific and civic: to understand the culture of the outside world these visitors represent. But there remains a somewhat coercive or, at the very least, objectifying stance toward the men, who are, in Van's words, "[s]tudied as curiosities": "All that time we were in training they studied us, analyzed us, prepared reports about us, and this information was widely disseminated all about the land" (27, 88). It is only when the men are preparing to leave Herland that they recognize that the Herlanders "had been extracting the evidence without our knowing it all this time" (144). The effect is panoptical in reverse: an entire country watching three men.

The situation also provides a somewhat pointed commentary on the nature of celebrity. As the only men in the country, Van, Jeff, and Terry become the center of attention, celebrities whose only "achievement" is being male. Then, as the three couples begin their courtships, they undergo the scrutiny of movie stars:

> "It is beautiful to see," [Somel] told me, "this new wonderful love between you. The whole country is interested, you know—how can we help it!"
>
> I had not thought of that. We say: "All the world loves a lover," but to have a couple of million people watching one's courtship—and that a difficult one—was rather embarrassing. (104)

To be sure, this "whole country" watches not out of idle curiosity but out of civic concern for the future of their race: ultimately, the triple wedding takes place in the country's largest temple, before thousands of spectators celebrating "the dawn of a new era" (119–20). Nevertheless, to have the progress of a private relationship carry the weight of an entire civilization's future—and to have it scrutinized accordingly—seems remarkably uncomfortable. Despite Van's expressions of discomfort, Gilman actually seems content with the situation, a surprising attitude considering her own unhappy experience when her divorce became fodder for newspaper accounts, producing a lifelong distaste for newspaper reporters that Gilman expresses in her stories.

The men are studied and ultimately displayed like captive animals, for mating purposes. Terry, the explorer most unlike the women, seems most subject to examination as another species: "At first he used to storm and flourish quite a good deal, but nothing seemed to amuse them more; they would gather around and watch him as if it was an exhibition, politely, but with evident interest. So he learned to check himself, and was almost reasonable in his bearing—but not quite" (65). These male "specimens" are "at last brought out and—exhibited" (88) as potential "mates," rather like bulls at auction, while young women coolly examine the merchandise: "all with keen appraising eye, studying us" (88). In part, of course, this parodies male objectification of young women. The grandniece of Harriet Beecher Stowe must also have considered the analogy with a slave auction, thus suggesting that the sexual exploitation of these men—and by further analogy of Ourland women—resembles the auction and breeding of slaves.

Most of all the treatment the men receive is compared to the educating of children. The analogies between the explorers and children are relentless, beginning with the first encounter with the "aunts," the women who are in charge of Herland.[9] Early on, Van compares his response to the aunts to "that sense of being hopelessly in the wrong that I had so often felt in early youth when my short legs' utmost effort failed to overcome the fact that I was late to school. . . . We felt like small boys, very small boys, caught doing mischief in some gracious lady's house" (19). The three adult men are reduced to naughty truants thoughtlessly committing "mischief." As punishment, they are unceremoniously hauled off: "Instantly each of us was seized by five women, each holding arm or leg or head; we were lifted like children, straddling helpless children, and borne onward, wriggling indeed, but most ineffectually" (23). In a land other than Herland, this treatment would precede punishment—a paddling at the very least—but here they are, metaphorically, sent to their rooms, bathed, and put to bed without supper: "We have been stripped and washed and put to bed like so many yearling babies" (25). That they are first chloroformed and that these adult men are bathed, while unconscious, by adult women, adds to the sense of their absolute helplessness. Jeff's embarrassment at this treatment lightly hints at the idea of sexual servitude—like the very young girl drugged, kidnapped, imprisoned, and possibly brainwashed, as a prelude to a life in "white slavery." Gilman thus suggests that the status of sexual minority might not be so appealing after all—yet another role reversal the book plays with.

But this is merely suggested, while the comparisons between the men and children are unambiguously emphasized. Among the captors' first acts is to give each man a schoolbook like that from which Herland's own children learn to read, that the men might learn the language (27–28). Terry objects to the compulsory education for its "disciplinary" qualities, in Foucault's rich sense of the term: "Here we are cooped up as helpless as a bunch of three-year-old orphans, and being taught what they think is necessary—whether we like it or not" (33). Van's countering advice, though meant to placate, only confirms Terry's interpretation of the situation as one in which "education" includes socialization: "If we are good boys and learn our lessons well, . . . [i]f we are quiet and respectful and polite and they are not afraid of us—then perhaps they will let us out" (31). Terry keeps insisting on the unacceptability of this option, always in terms of their infantilization: "'*Let* out!' he stormed. '*Let* out—like children kept after school. I want to Get Out, and I'm going to'" (33). Children require permission from Mama; Terry not unreasonably wishes to be treated like a free adult.

Ironically, of course, when the men do escape, their situation remains that of wayward children. Word is sent out to the Herlanders to "keep an eye on our movements," and the men remain under surveillance by "careful ladies sitting snugly in big trees by the riverbed, or up among the rocks," indicating that the "great escape" is no more dangerous than the exploits of boys playing hide-and-seek: "it struck me as extremely funny. Here we had been risking our lives, hiding and prowling like outlaws, living on nuts and fruit, getting wet and cold at night, and dry and hot by day, and all the while these estimable women had just been waiting for us to come out" (44), for when they are captured, their guards express "a mild triumph as of winning some simple game; and even that they politely suppressed" (42–43). This passage is reminiscent of Grand's indulgent observation in "The New Aspect of the Woman Question":

"O man! man! you are a very funny fellow now we know you!" (274). Men, generally, are children to be treated patiently by wise and motherly women. The men's childlike quality in comparison to the Herlanders extends more generally to their "man-made world," in that Herland boasts a "social consciousness besides which our nations looked like quarreling children—feeble-minded ones at that" (81).

The infantilization of the men, Herland's sexual minority, is an obvious comment on the infantilization of women that Gilman describes in *Women and Economics*. It also resembles Grand's comments, "It is the woman's place and pride and pleasure to teach the child, and man morally is in his infancy. . . . [A]nd now woman holds out a strong hand to the child-man, and insists, but with infinite tenderness and pity, upon helping him up" ("New Aspect," 273). This way of thinking presupposes not gender equality but difference: the superiority of the woman over the man, and thus a reversal rather than denial of traditional assumptions about gender differences. On the other hand, it at least presupposes the educability of men—and thus assumes that men's—and women's—flaws are learned rather than innate, which, in turn, suggests that their differences are learned as well. Certainly Gilman allows Van the capacity to learn, though Jeff and Terry prove less able to acquire an idealized androgyny.

Furthering the analogy between the men and children, the explorers are "protected," guarded not only because they are presumed dangerous, but, ironically, for their own safety: "If, by any accident, you did harm any one of us, you would have to face a million mothers" (66). Being educated in a protected environment once again resembles the circumstances of young Herlanders, who begin in "baby gardens" specially designed with "nothing to hurt—no stairs, no corners, no small loose objects to swallow, no fire—just a babies' paradise" (107). Furthermore, Herland children (and adults) have "no shame—no knowledge of anything to be ashamed of" (101). This level of protectiveness is simultaneously ideally nurturing and stifling, a bit like Mark Twain's Hadleyburg, where no one is led into temptation. In many ways the Herland system runs counter to that Gilman describes, somewhat autobiographically, in *Benigna Machiavelli*, in which the heroine observes the errors and successes of those around her and of the characters in books, and accordingly makes well-informed decisions about the way she will live her own life.

In the men's case, of course, such freely knowledgeable choice is available, since they have had access to Ourland's worldview prior to being educated about Herland's. That Van and Jeff adopt the Herland life demonstrates their greater wisdom than Terry, but all freely choose. Nevertheless, the coercive quality of the men's education, modeled as it is on the education of Herland's children, suggests equal coercion in the way the children themselves are raised. The resulting sameness of the women—the three young women whom the explorers marry are virtually identical, their most distinctive traits being, ironically, the different kind of man each likes—suggests the type of frightening uniformity we associate with education in a totalitarian state.

The men's imprisonment high in an old fortified castle, whose origins stretch back to the era when men still lived in the country that is now Herland, is also reminiscent of the situation of the narrator of "The Yellow Wall-Paper," enclosed in an "ancestral mansion," where she is controlled and observed. "The Yellow Wall-Paper"'s narrator is relegated to a former nursery with barred windows and treated like a child, even put to bed, by her husband, and later reverts to "creeping" around the room like a baby. Like the Herland captors, John apparently believes he is acting in his captive's best interest, based on his supposedly greater knowledge. This is in part yet another reversal: the men's imprisonment teaches them the frustrations of imprisonment in the domestic role. Observing the parallels, one is forced to conclude that Terry's determination to escape is the healthy response, with Jeff's and Van's contentment to remain imprisoned at their captors' will resembling all too much the willingness of the narrator in "The Yellow Wall-Paper" to tie a rope around her waist and throw the key out the window. Yet it is Terry who, by implication, is mentally unstable: in the latter stages of the group's imprisonment he is "irritable," suffering from "nerves"—another reversal of gender roles. As in the "The Yellow Wall-Paper," conflict arises between individual desires and the culture's expectations of appropriate behavior. While Terry's violation of Herland norms leads him to be imprisoned as a criminal, he has the implicit support of an entire culture, to which he is allowed to return. By implication, Ourland's culture, therefore, is degenerate and criminally insane.

Although Terry receives humane punishment, exiled rather than executed or imprisoned for life, his treatment also inspires fundamental questions about Herland culture. Terry's crime is that he is too "personal," as evidenced by his sex drive, his competitiveness, and his strong desire for Alima to take his last name when they marry—as a "sign of possession." He is not sufficiently focused on the national "we" (126). Although an unappealing character in many ways, Terry nevertheless raises some legitimate objections to Herland.

Herland, for one thing, is surprisingly authoritarian. Theoretically, all Herland citizens are equal "sisters." Differences among citizens supposedly concern only their professions—some are foresters and some are cooks, and so on—and thus represent the "specialization" that, according to social Darwinist thinking, characterizes any highly evolved organism / culture. Of course, prior to the explorers' arrival, there are no hierarchies based on gender. Nevertheless, in Herland a kind of hierarchy remains. There is a leader, chosen on the basis of her wisdom, to be sure, but a leader. The institution of "Over Mothers" reflects another hierarchical differentiation. Because "to be encouraged to bear more than one child is the very highest reward and honor in the power of the state," in Herland "the nearest approach to an aristocracy . . . was to come of a line of 'Over Mothers'—those who had been so honored" (69). That they are called "Over Mothers," with the hierarchical adjective "over," rather than being called, say, "multi-mothers," shows that this is a type of class hierarchy based as much on "birth" as Ourland's. Theoretically, of course, it is no arbitrary bloodline, but based on rational standards of eugenic superiority, but then aristocrats—and men—have always assumed themselves superior according to rational rather than arbitrary standards. In short, the "Over Mother" system builds inequality into Herland. More fundamentally, perhaps, the relationship between children and mothers is inherently unequal, with the worship of motherhood producing in Herlanders "a deep, tender reverence for one's own mother—too deep for them to speak of freely" (96), a reverence that endures past childhood.

One problem with Gilman's theory of a society based on mothering seems patently obvious to anyone with an adolescent daughter: girls rebel, inevitably withdrawing to discover and claim their independent, private, autonomous space. Gilman might have accepted Nancy Chodorow's theory that girls have less need than boys to assert their difference from their mother as part of achieving a sense of adult personhood, since girls continue gender-role identification with the mother. In the absence of fathers in Herland, mother-daughter identification would presumably be all the stronger. In the absence of male genes, conflict is suppressed and collaboration fostered. Nevertheless, that in two thousand years the country has avoided any revolution against its motherly social structure or any major conflict caused by a national form of sibling rivalry seems remarkable indeed.

To be sure, Gilman acknowledges the development of separate personhood in adolescence when she says that "from earliest childhood each had a separate bedroom with toilet conveniences, and one of the marks of coming of age was the addition of an outer room in which to receive friends" (125). But the emphasis on privacy is belied by Herland's group dynamic, in which all agree, share the same values, have no shame—and seem to know the whereabouts and behavior of everyone else. This is a world in which there is little differentiation between public and private, because the private is here identified solely with the family unit, and in Herland, the family unit—both emotionally and economically—is the entire civilization. Gilman's attempt to have things both ways doesn't hold up here, perhaps because of the very slipperiness of the concepts of public and private she is attempting to reconcile. Indeed, as we shall see in the next chapter, the creation of domestic spaces that successfully balance the claims of public and private—in all senses—would be a continuing challenge of feminist literary housekeeping.

∾

Grand, Ward, and Gilman all posit a kind of civic maternalism as an alternative to traditional forms of power. Ironically, although Gilman's and Grand's ideas are far more radical than Ward's, with Gilman's theories in particular challenging the most basic assumptions of androcentric culture, Grand's and Gilman's matriarchal ideas inadvertently reproduce some of the worst flaws of patriarchy. Both Grand's mockery of the "child-man" and Gilman's coercive utopia, not to mention the horrifying implications of state-sponsored eugenics, suggest that "a motherliness which dominated society" could have as many drawbacks and dangers as "the man-made world" each writer intended to reform. Rejecting versions of a private-public dichotomy that overlooked state interest in protecting mothers and children, Grand and especially Gilman envisioned a disciplinary state that inadvertently reproduced the worst stereotypes of the smothering mother. In this case, surprisingly, Ward, despite her conservative justifications for her positions, performed practical work that, by breaking barriers to public funding for child care and education, had more progressive implications for mothers and children than Grand's or Gilman's grander plans.

3

Making a Home

Literary House Makers

Have nothing in your houses that you do not know to be useful, or believe
to be beautiful.

William Morris, The Beauty of Life

BY THE 1880S, THE DECADE when Grand, Gilman, and Ward launched
their writing careers, the fashion of "The House Beautiful," as Oscar Wilde had
titled one of his successful American lectures, was at its height. Exponents of
this movement, inspired by John Ruskin and William Morris and popularized
by such advice writers as Charles Eastlake, Clarence Cook, Mary Eliza Haweis,
Jane Ellen Panton, and Rhoda and Agnes Garrett, held that art was no longer
exclusively the province of painters and sculptors, nor was it to be displayed
exclusively in public galleries. Instead, the home itself and all its furnishings
could be, indeed ought to be, works of fine art. Urging "the beauty of simplicity,"[1] advocates of the house beautiful told readers how to create "a room which
makes a harmonious whole" (Garrett and Garrett, 6). They praised "art" col-
ors, eighteenth-century furniture, and (although artistic decoration advocated
"reduction of ornament") accessories such as peacock feathers, blue and white
china pots, and Japanese fans.

At the same time the house beautiful movement was shaping middle-class
home decorating, the "domestic science" movement also exerted a major in-

fluence on home design. Interest in sanitation had begun in the 1840s, when men like Edwin Chadwick in England and Lemuel Shattuck in the United States called public attention to relationships between disease and unsanitary urban living conditions. Their findings and recommendations inspired a series of public health measures, including the building of sewers and public water supplies, and efforts to replace urban slums with sanitary housing. These reform measures progressed slowly: in America, only 24 percent of homes had running water in 1890; by the 1930s running water was available to virtually the entire urban population, but it remained unavailable to most rural dwellers until after 1945 (Lebergott, 263). As late as 1934, half of the working-class residents of London had no running water within their dwellings; as late as 1951, 21 percent of households in England and Wales lacked a water closet (Caroline Davidson, 31, 20). Understanding of the causes and prevention of disease also lagged. The nature of contagion was poorly understood despite the early findings by Oliver Wendell Holmes (1843), Ignaz Semmelweis (1860), and Louis Pasteur (1862), and even after the turn of the century publications still warned against "sewer gas," a lingering version of the "zygmotic" or "miasma" theory that diseases generate spontaneously in "bad air." Even once bacterial explanations for disease had gained wide acceptance, around 1900, antibiotics to cure communicable diseases had yet to be discovered. Clearly, so long as cures remained unavailable, the best way to save lives from disease was prevention. From the outset of the sanitary science movement, even before the advent of germ theory, the emphasis was not merely on removing dirt but on selecting, redesigning, and building sanitary working and, especially, living conditions.

The sanitary science movement and the house beautiful movement did not, however, coexist comfortably. Beginning in the 1860s, physicians and sanitary inspectors waged an often successful effort to discredit plumbers and architects, whom they blamed for endangering the public's health with "unscientific" housing designs. Architects, who had introduced such innovations as running water to the middle-class home and who brought kitchens out of the basement and onto the ground floor, were assailed for poisoning interior air with sewer gas that entered through improperly trapped or badly located drains and lingered on account of inadequate ventilation; architects were also faulted for concealing pipes within walls, hanging arsenic-laced wallpapers, and laying carpets that harbored lethal dust. Claiming the exclusive ability to inspect houses, "building doctors" redefined the house as itself a form of "preventative medicine" (Adams, 42). Some sanitarians took the next step, designing houses using "scientific principles" of space, materials, ventilation, lighting, and especially the placement and fitting of pipes. Annmarie Adams argues that architects increasingly concentrated on "the decoration of houses" to compensate for their decreased authority over the building of houses.

Ironically, the conflict between Aestheticism and sanitary science encouraged greater appreciation of women's responsibilities for home design. While the male professionals—the doctors, plumbers, and architects—competed among themselves, the woman homemaker claimed an authority of her own, as a sort of independent contractor, drawing on the expertise of each professional. The responsibility for creating healthy living spaces had been claimed by women as early as Catherine Beecher's highly influential 1841 advice book, *A Treatise on Domestic Economy,* and Florence Nightingale's pioneering work *Notes on Nursing* (1860). By the turn of the century, numerous "books on home architecture" argued, like E. C. Gardiner's *The House That Jill Built, after Jack's Had Proved a Failure,* that because women spend their days in the house, they are better qualified than men to design convenient kitchens and comfortable bedrooms, fireplaces with chimneys that "draw" properly, and bathrooms with up-to-date, sanitary drains. It was a clever way to claim an equality (or superiority) based on difference.

Moreover, these guides explicitly or implicitly extended women's responsibility beyond the individual home to the public sphere. Most guides assumed a direct relationship between the private dwelling and the public street, reinforced by the pipes and wires physically joining each house to civic networks of water, sewers, gas, and electricity. On the one hand, sanitary scientists warned women to be vigilant of dangers from an encroaching outside world—adulterated foods, corrupt plumbers and architects, unsanitary air and water—but, on the other hand, many also suggested that women's work to create clean homes for their separate families might appropriately reach outward, since one's own family could be assured a healthy home only if one's neighborhood and community enjoyed the cleanliness appropriate to a well-designed city. If a "scientifically" designed private dwelling could provide preventative medicine for one family, neighborhoods full of healthy homes or healthy model tenements could not only improve a city's mortality rate but produce healthy generations of citizens for a free and powerful nation. Responsibility for creating a sanitary home and a sanitary nation was ascribed to—and claimed by—women.

Women were also empowered by the house beautiful movement. Although the "well-known artistic houses" celebrated in Mary Eliza Haweis's book *Beautiful Houses* were identified by their male owners and their beauty credited almost exclusively to male designers, nevertheless, by the end of the century, a few women were emerging as architects.[2] To be sure, as Talia Schaffer and Kathy Psomiades have pointed out, male Aesthetes attempted—frequently successfully—to co-opt crafts that had formerly been associated exclusively with women, but at least the Aesthetic movement lifted the status of interior decoration. "The Decoration of Houses," as Haweis titled her most successful book, represented an art form readily available to women, as individual homemakers and as professionals whose manuals were eagerly consulted by householders of both sexes. Advice books like Jane Ellen Panton's *From Kitchen to Garret: Hints for Young Householders* and Helen Campbell's *Household Economics* draw on both artistic and medical discourse, as well as a good measure of practical experience, in their advice for creating a home that is beautiful, healthy, and convenient. Discussions of Liberty art serges and "art pots," and celebrations of William Morris, rub shoulders with admonitions about the location of the kitchen, directions for account keeping, and disquisitions about the value of fresh air in a bedchamber.

The writings of Gilman, Grand, and Ward embrace this free-ranging eclecticism in their portrayals of homemaking, but the similarity between homemaking guides and works of literary housekeeping also indicates an important difference between literary housekeeping texts and other New Woman writings of the era: their portrayal of their heroines' relationships to domestic spaces. From Ibsen's *Doll's House* forward, New Women famously slammed the door on confining private home spaces, seeking more fulfilling experiences in the public sphere. As middle-class women gained new opportunities to work or study away from their parents' homes, late-Victorian women's fiction frequently explored young women's first experiences with independent living. Ann Heilmann has observed, "Many New Woman writers, especially when they recreated their own quest for artistic voice and individual space in their novels, saw the reclaiming of privacy as being the necessary precondition for their characters' occupation of public spaces" (178). This was an individual privacy separate from a domestic "private sphere." In the works Heilmann studies, success in the public sphere is inextricably bound with women's possessing a room of their own, for "[i]f, as a result of parental interference or romantic attachments, they exchange their rooms (signifying independence) for domesticity and marriage, they almost inevitably lose their foothold in public life" (179).

While the works of Gilman, Grand, and Ward similarly portray the New Woman's foray into independent living, they depart from the pattern Heilmann describes, by attempting to reconcile the public and the domestic. The literary housekeeping tradition radically complicates the standard narrative of the New Woman's competing quests for personal and domestic privacy and aspirations for public success. Neither stereotypical New Women fleeing domestic confinement nor apolitical female Aesthetes exhibiting their delicate connoisseurship in their taste for antique china nor domestic drudges immersed in what Gilman calls "kitchen-mindedness" to the exclusion of all else, the heroines of literary housekeeping hold a unique place in literary history, as their authors identify the designing of a beautiful and sanitary living space as an implicitly or explicitly political act. Because literary housekeeping envisioned women's contribution to society in familial terms, creating livable space emerged as a crucially important public activity.

In the works of Gilman, Grand, and Ward, when women characters cannot or will not design their own living space in ways comfortable to them, the results are nearly always bad.[3] On the other hand, to take charge of one's home decor is linked to a broader sense of empowerment, both individually and socially. Like literary housekeeping itself, homemaking in these novels entails a reimagining of the relations between the aesthetic and the practical, the individual and the familial, the private and the public, the traditional and the innovative, the scientific and the artistic. In the texts examined in this chapter, literary homemakers attempt to build edifices that reconcile these competing claims.

Grand's Liminal Spaces

In an interview with Sarah Grand for the magazine *Woman at Home,* Jane T. Stoddart describes Grand's Kensington flat, praising its "Chippendale bureaux and book-cases, Rose du Barri curtains and restful lounges and armchairs." The article is illustrated with photographs of the flat's entrance hall, sitting room, and drawing room, revealing a relatively "artistic" interior, with its eighteenth-century furnishings and a large pot of the approved style in the entrance hall. Stoddart gushes, "It would be difficult to imagine a more delightful home for a literary worker" ("Illustrated Interview," 211). Yet whatever her interviewer might have thought, Grand herself remarked during the conversation that "although she finds a top flat an excellent workshop, she much prefers to write in the country"—a preference she repeatedly voiced elsewhere. On the occasion of Stoddart's interview, she was in London for only a few days following some weeks in the country and en route to the Continent (211).

The interview highlights several elements that figure in the portrayal of dwelling places in Grand's writings. The flat reflects fundamental contradictions, especially as a public-private space. It functions as Grand's private dwelling, of course, but also as a public place—a perch from which she can conduct her London business. Stoddart's interview ostensibly emphasizes the private life of a public figure, going so far as to turn the home into an object of photographic spectacle, rather than preserving the "sanctity of the home," as one might expect in a magazine called *Woman at Home*. Yet Grand takes pains to distance her primary public work, her writing, from this particular domestic space. The room, aestheticized by the interviewer and the camera, is to be understood as decorated by Grand herself—she points out that "she does not consider her rooms fully decorated as yet"—and thus an expression of herself (211). But it is also, professedly, a flat with a function, a place for the business of publishing and promoting (the public, in the economic sense), and the business of novel writing, for Grand always emphasized the practical functions of her art (the public, in a political sense).

Even in the public interview, Grand insists on her privacy. She comments on her writing, but not too much: she refuses to talk about her next book, "the name of which," Stoddart admits, "I tried in vain to discover." The writing, Grand's public work, remains concealed until she's ready to reveal it, not only from "her public," but also from those in her domestic circle. Grand explains, "I keep my work a close secret even from my own family" (213). To her current interviewer, Grand complains of "how few so-called interviews with me are really genuine," and can't seem to decide whether she's more annoyed by the guest who "published an account of her visit" that was full of errors or by the woman whom Grand never actually met, who, in a completely fabricated visit "abused my hospitality by trying to pry into my private life, and afterwards selling the information she collected and invented for a few pieces of silver" (217). Grand prefers accurate, but controlled, publicity that exploits her domestic space, but not the domestic space where she actually works. These issues recur in portrayals in Grand's fiction of domestic sites, which frequently act as liminal spaces, poised on the threshold between the visible and the concealed, the commercial and the domestic, the functional and the aestheticized.

In both *The Heavenly Twins* and *The Beth Book,* domestic spaces function at least part of the time somewhat as Heilmann describes: either a character has a room of her own, from which to escape from the demands of parents or husband, or she is trapped within an oppressive domestic environment. Thus Evadne, as a girl, tells her aunt, "Having a room of my own always has been a great advantage," because it has allowed her a place to do the reading— anatomy and physiology, Mill and Galton—that has made her into a New Woman (*Twins,* 36). After she marries Colonel Colquhoun and discovers his dissolute past, she agrees to "keep up appearances" only on condition that he will "allow [her] to live in his house quite independently, like brother and sister" (108); she has two connected rooms of her own and for a time is relatively happy, combining physical inviolability with domestic harmony.

Similarly, in *The Beth Book,* Beth's self-discovery and self-development are closely tied to privacy, beginning in early childhood, when only Kitty, Beth's beloved Irish Catholic nurse, objects to Beth and her sisters' sharing a room with their ten-year-old, "thoroughly corrupted" brother Jim (38). Later, Beth thrives during the hours spent in the feminine room inhabited by Great-Aunt Victoria Bench, where Beth learns her great-aunt's "dainty fastidious ways" (203). When Aunt Victoria dies, she stipulates in her will that Beth "have her room when she was gone, in order that Beth might, as she grew up, have proper privacy in her life, with undisturbed leisure for study, reflection, and prayer" (222), and Beth cherishes the room, where she dreams and reads but also develops domestic skills like dressmaking.

With her marriage to Doctor Dan Maclure, Beth loses touch with "the vision and the dream" that constitute her spiritual and creative gifts, in part because she lacks private space: "It was a positive hardship—never to be sure of a moment alone" (345). Searching desperately for "some corner where she would be safe from intrusion" (345), she discovers a forgotten tower room, a "secret chamber" that becomes Beth's "secret spot, sacred to herself" (347). Beth's new private space is one of a series of attics where she seeks refuge, starting with the attic through which, as a child, she climbs out onto the roof (132, 135–38) and culminating with the attic rooms where she befriends Arthur Brock.[4] Like Grand's top-floor London flat, these attics are liminal spaces, both a part of and apart from their buildings, rendered inaccessible and a little superior, if only by their height. As I will discuss in the examination of needlework in chapter 5, Grand associates Beth's tower room, like Evadne's in *The Heavenly Twins,* with the towers in Tennyson's "Lancelot and Elaine" and "The Lady of Shalott." Beth's room is no island prison like the lady's dwelling, nor does it have the dismal aspect of Shalott's "four gray walls and four gray towers," but instead it offers a homey space that Beth can decorate with personal "treasures," including books, curtains, and a rug, that her husband has dismissed as "rubbish" (347).

Like the book's other attic rooms, Beth's secret chamber becomes a site of creative work, identified with the "sacred": Beth decorates it, explores her own ideas, and designs an embroidery pattern, which in turn becomes a money-making project she can complete in concealment, without exciting Dan's suspicion. Thus, while a "room of one's own" has undeniable value, its relationship to the private-public dichotomy is complex, for Beth's private (concealed) room is an explicitly domestic space whose value is inextricably bound to public purposes. The room facilitates Beth's public independence—in the economic sense—which in turn allows her to discover her public—in the sense of political—vocation as an orator on the woman question.

The Heavenly Twins features similarly ambiguous relationships between issues of public and private in its portrayal of Evadne's living space. Evadne's retreat to sexual, or rather sexless, privacy quite literally saves her life, as she avoids contracting a sexually transmitted disease. But Grand, who considered celibacy unnatural and unhealthy, shows that Evadne ultimately suffers from her extreme bodily privacy. Her depression is exacerbated by isolation in a small, dark house ironically called "As You Like It." Doctor Galbraith speculates that "Colonel Colquhoun took it to suit his own convenience without consulting his wife's tastes or requirements" (*Twins,* 566). As with Beth, inability to control her own physical space represents a "positive hardship." According to

Doctor Galbraith's diagnosis, Evadne "is a fragile little creature, for whose health and well-being generally I should say that bright rooms and fresh air are essential" (566). Doctor Galbraith's prescription of sunshine and ventilation echoes those of numerous turn-of-the-century "house doctors," and he may be correct up to a point concerning the ill effects of damp and lack of sun, but Evadne's problems are more fundamental. The primary cause of her mental instability is her promise, exacted by Colonel Colquhoun, to "never take part publicly in any question of the day" (345). Rather than suffering too little privacy, Evadne has too much, both because she is isolated and celibate and because she has removed herself from the political arena for which she has such a natural aptitude.

Grand's fascination with liminal spaces is highlighted by her recurring image of women sitting in windows. Doctor Galbraith, when he sees Evadne sewing in the west window of "As You Like It," calls to mind "The Lady of Shalott" (586): a woman trapped in a private domestic space and no longer capable of surviving outside her tower walls.[5] The Tennyson allusion has more promising qualities in *The Beth Book.* Unlike Tennyson's lady, seeing only shadows of the world, Beth in her tower attains economic freedom by the sewing she does there and also a power of surveillance. While Beth is sewing in her hidden room, she witnesses her husband kissing and giving a bracelet to his "patient"—really a nonpaying house guest—Bertha Petterick: "From where she sat she could see Bertha on a seat just below . . . , but Bertha could not see her because of the curtain of creepers that covered the iron rail which formed a little balcony round the window. Besides, it was supposed that that was a blank window" (402–3). Her empowering knowledge allows Beth to recognize her actual situation, deny Dan's claims to her income, send Bertha packing, remove herself from Dan's home, and embark on her public career.

Ella Banks, of *Adnam's Orchard,* like Evadne and Beth, works in a window, though in her case primarily to catch the light necessary for her lace making. Ella does occasionally look out, and, like the Lady of Shalott, she might have been wiser keeping her eye on her work, for the horseman who catches her eye is Ninian Brabant, Lord Melton, who, unbeknownst to either of them, is Ella's half brother. More to the point, however, like Tennyson's lady and Grand's Beth, Ella is not content to remain in her high room, even though, unlike the other two, she can both see and be seen. Ella's motivations are primarily economic, and she neither leaves her needlework, like the Lady, nor uses it buy the opportunity to discover her true gifts, like Beth; she takes it with her to London in order to better pursue the art that for her provides both economic career and political tool.

In *Adnam's Orchard,* the window imagery once again suggests the power of the gaze, this time to highlight the aestheticizing of poverty. Here, attempts by the wealthy to blur the line between a working farmhouse and a picture for their own leisure-time enjoyment are condemned as illegitimate impositions rather than a legitimate creation of liminal space. As Ella works at her window, she involuntarily becomes a piece of aesthetic spectacle, for the Banks' home, Red Rose Farm, "was such a picturesque little place no one of any taste could have had the heart to alter it"—even though in fact it has a leaking roof, provides too little light and ventilation for health, and is "ill-adapted to the rearing of a large family" (38). The aesthetic and the practical clash, as the landlord forbids the Banks family to alter the house they rent because it is "a pretty object for a drive for London guests, who loved to sketch it, and photograph it, and sentimentalise about it and the Simple Life, when the Simple Life became the last luxury of fashionable talk" (38).

By showing how wealthy outsiders and an indifferent landlord aestheticize the labors and discomforts of the working-class Banks family, Grand foregrounds class issues that are crucial to the novel and to Ella's motivations. The Duchess of Castlefield Saye, for example, imagines she need not pay Ella well for the lace she has created by the window, because "surely you live with your father in that lovely little farmhouse which always looks so sweet. . . . And they say, when they see you sitting in the window making lace, that you give the necessary touch of life which just completes the picture" (*Adnam,* 79). But Ella refuses to be turned into a "picture," defacing the picturesque image by bluntly retorting that her father has expenses. Like Beth and Evadne, Ella and her family require the freedom to create a living space appropriate to their needs.

The most liminal spaces in Grand's books are those Ella creates in *The Winged Victory,* the second book of the unfinished trilogy that *Adnam's Orchard* begins. Ella establishes her London showroom in a setting that uneasily combines the domestic with the aesthetic and commercial. Her natural father, the Duke of Castlefield Saye, unwilling that his daughter set herself up in the London "shop" with a "shop-window full of lace" that she had envisioned for herself (*Winged*, 13), places Ella in the "Corner House," for generations the Dower House of the Brabants and thus home to generations of Brabant women (he hides behind the pretense that the duchess is Ella's patroness). Not only is the "handsome Family Mansion" distinctly unlike a shop, it can never become one, for the Corner House is to be Ella's on the single condition that it "must not be made to look like a shop, or in any way be advertised as a shop" (13). But because Ella will nevertheless use the house as a base from which to sell lace and run her lace cooperative, the Corner House represents a radical intermingling of the domestic and the public.

In some respects the house that functions as a shop resembles situations in Gaskell's *Cranford* and Hawthorne's *House of the Seven Gables;* in those cases, however, a lady in reduced circumstances maintains illusions of sweet gentility despite her modest commercial enterprise. Here, the mix of a not-at-all-modest domestic setting with Ella's apparent upward mobility—and actual illegitimacy—creates a much edgier situation. Furthermore, Ella aspires to more than mere genteel survival. Better even than an ordinary shop, Ella's exclusive ducal "showroom" allows her to create a "fashion" in "Society" and command greater prestige and therefore higher prices. While functioning as (and unknowingly being) part of wealthy society, Ella can better fulfill her vengeful vow to "make them pay" for the sufferings of the poor.

Ella is given carte blanche to redecorate the Corner House, but she elects not to "alter," but to "preserve." Her decisions reflect Grand's own tastes, manifested in the "artistic" rooms featured in *Woman at Home*. Late-Victorian architects, under the influence of Ruskin and Morris, revived architectural traditions from the medieval Gothic (primarily in civic architecture) to the "vernacular" and the "Queen Anne" style. Each of these styles, in a different way, aimed at counteracting the mechanistic anonymity, sameness, and ugliness that the architects and their clients associated with the modern world, while expressing reverence for what they saw as traditional building styles. Of course this traditionalism easily shaded into mockery of early-Victorian taste and smug assurance that theirs were more up-to-date styles of building and decorating. As Mark Girouard observes, regarding the popularity of the Queen Anne style, "artistically, it became progressive to be old-fashioned" (5). Thus, Ella shows "innate" taste in her decision not to alter the house, including the ballroom's eighteenth-century trappings.

Ella also adopts her era's fondness for clean surfaces, plenty of light, and healthy air, a fashion representing common ground between sanitarians and artistic decorators: "My idea is to have the best conditions for work—air, and light, and space. . . . My room must look healthy and fresh. Everything in it must be cleanable. It must be clean before everything. And not made stuffy and enervating with a surplus of cushions and curtains and easy chairs" (15). Generally speaking, Grand advocates simplicity of decoration yet, despite her adoption of several "artistic" decorating fashions, rejects what she apparently perceived to be "Aesthetic" decoration. For example, Ursula Pratt's room impresses the duchess because

> there was something eminently restful in the cloistral atmosphere of the room. The restfulness came of the severity, the sparseness of the furniture and the form; the satisfying purity of design, and the spaciousness. The general effect could not have been called either old-fashioned or modern. Restful was the only word for it, especially to the duchess, who had subjected herself in some of the rooms she occupied to the restless discomfort of Morris papers, and suffered like one who is hit, but does not know where." (*Adnam*, 114)

Similar condemnation of "Aesthetic" clutter appears in *The Winged Victory*, in which Grand's criticism of the rooms of the Oscar Wilde figure, Col Drindon/Joyday Flowers, reflects a gendered theory of decorating, influenced by the backlash against Aestheticism following the Wilde trial. Col, who has fallen in love with Ella, invites her to see his rooms, a "man's rooms, you know." Ella's idea of an appropriate room for a man is actually not so different from her own morning room: "Spacious, airy; polished floors; no curtains, no cushions, frills, or fripperies. Books, of course, and pictures—a few—no crowding. Fresh, clean, plain—that is my idea of a man's rooms" (311). Having heard Ella's pronouncements about a man's rooms and seen her own rooms, Col perceives his flat and himself—and by implication, the "Aesthetic" interior—with new eyes:

> He felt now that there were too many cushions in it, too many curtains; it was too softly carpeted, too crowded with fripperies and nicknacks of all kinds. He was lodged like a *prima donna*, he acknowledged it. The general effect suggested a feminine absence of backbone. . . . The deep, springy,

> softly padded easy-chairs were made to recline in; the broad divan piled high with big down cushions covered with soft satin, to loll upon. And the exquisitely sensuous colouring, womanish again. (312–13)

This parodic Wildean decor in the rooms of an Aesthete poet is condemned for "effeminacy," but of course the decor is not so much gendered feminine—since the ladylike Ella's room resembles "a man's room"—as condemned for its sensuality and especially for its associations with "lolling" and useless "fripperies." As we have seen, the environments that Grand approves combine beauty with usefulness. Thus, the difference between Col's rooms and those of women Grand sees as true artists, like Ella or Beth of *The Beth Book,* is an objective correlative for the difference between Col's philosophy of art for art's sake and art, as Beth says, "for man's sake" (358). To Grand, a genuinely artistic interior, like a genuinely artistic novel, will have "backbone," will be "of use," "something that appeals to the best part of us" (*Beth,* 375). And a "useful" place in Grand's writing is a liminal space that commingles personal privacy and public function.

"It's a woman's business to make a home": Gilman's Literary Houses

Charlotte Perkins Gilman's views about houses are at the center of her work; indeed, Gilman's "architectural feminism," to use Polly Wynn Allen's term, provides one of the clearest illustrations of the phenomenon that I have called "literary housekeeping." By moving many "domestic" activities outside the home into the public sphere—where female entrepreneurs professionalize the private activities of homemaking—and redesigning living space accordingly, Gilman's theories of homemaking and home designing express her effort fundamentally to rethink the categories of the public and the private. Gilman's theories about housing design epitomize a housekeeping philosophy that attempts to have things both ways: she advocates "the passing of the home," as she titled one of her essays, arguing that the traditional home, by stifling women, has held back human evolution; yet she also celebrates a new type of home in utopian stories such as *Moving the Mountain* and *Herland,* extolling the privacy and family love that a more "home-like" world might bring. At the core of her ideas is a vexed relationship between the individual and the community. On the one hand, Gilman places a premium on personal privacy; on the other, she envisions supposedly "home-like" worlds in which enlightened communal decision making displaces private choice.

In *Women and Economics,* Gilman writes, "The progressive individuation of human beings requires a personal home, one room at least for each person" (258). That is, access to private space correlates with evolutionary progress. In a statement that would seem to confirm Heilmann's description of the New Woman's rejection of domesticity, Gilman argues that the home as now constituted does not provide the necessary privacy, especially for women: "To women, especially, a private room is the luxury of the rich alone. . . . The home is the one place on earth where no one of the component individuals can have any privacy" (258–59). To this problem Gilman offers a revolutionary solution:

> If there should be built and opened in any of our large cities to-day a commodious and well-served apartment house for professional women with families, it would be filled at once. The apartments would be without kitchens; but there would be a kitchen belonging to the house from which meals could be served to the families in their rooms or in a common dining-room, as preferred. It would be a home where the cleaning was done by efficient workers, not hired separately by the families, but engaged by the manager of the establishment; and a roof-garden, day nursery, and kindergarten, under well-trained professional nurses and teachers, would insure proper care of the children. (242)

Gilman makes a special point of insisting that these apartments would provide "family privacy with collective advantage" (242) and that "[t]he privacy of the home could be as well maintained in such a building as described as in any house in a block, any room, flat, or apartment, under present methods" (243). Moreover, though she is less detailed in her plans for a suburban arrangement of detached—and thus more private—homes, she does mention "a grouping of adjacent houses, each distinct and having its own yard, but all kitchenless, and connected by covered ways with the eating-house" (243).

Having thus laid out her theory of home design in her first book—the book that brought her international renown—Gilman refined the idea throughout her career. In her utopian novel *Herland,* each citizen, beginning in childhood, has her own room and bath, along with a receiving room once she comes of age. In consequence, Herlanders possess "the highest, keenest, most delicate sense of personal privacy" (125). More important to Gilman, however, is that although they "had no exact analogue for our word *home*," the women of Herland "loved their country because it was their nursery, playground, and workshop—theirs and their children's"—their home, in short (94). Throughout the ideal country of Herland, everything is "beauty, order, perfect cleanness, and the pleasantest sense of home over it all" (19). Home, that is, is a civic quality as much, if not more, than a private one.

Believing, as a character in the story "Their House" asserts, that "[s]urely it's a woman's business to make the home!" (209), Gilman extended that "business" to civic spaces. An editorial comment in the 26 January 1895 issue of the *Impress* asserts, in response to a news brief that two women had won a competition for the best design for a San Francisco sanitarium:

> Our domestic architecture, and our public architecture in the nature of the large home a great sanitarium should be, offer a specially inviting field for women workers—one for which the heredity of housekeeping and the heart and conscience development of women has peculiarly fitted them. . . . [O]ne of the most important results of extending the sex's activity outside the home is the making of better and more beautiful homes—not to mention better women and therefore better mothers. After all, perhaps architecture and decoration are not outside the home—anymore than is municipal administration. (2)[6]

Home design, a peculiarly appropriate public activity for women, who can apply "hereditary" advantages to compete equally with men, is here conflated with the design of "homelike" public buildings. Gilman thus effectively blurs the line between difference and equality, private and public, domestic and civic.

One group of stories, which might be identified as a distinct subgenre in Gilman's writings, puts into fictional form a sort of "how-to" guide to creating ideal communities that fulfill Gilman's theories of private/public home design.[7] Three short stories, "Five Girls" (1894), "Bee Wise" (1913), and "Maidstone Comfort" (1912), briefly outline the steps by which idealistic groups of talented young women create a "model tenement" and "sample town" ("Five Girls," 85; "Bee Wise," 229). These exempla include features fundamental to Gilman's ideal living arrangements. Each house or community is designed by educated, talented women, with an eye to both practical and aesthetic concerns. Although the house or community requires a substantial financial investment at the outset, each rapidly becomes self-sustaining at the least, profitable at the best. Unlike in a commune in which each resident or household takes a turn at each task, the work of upkeep is performed by specialists—in cooking, housekeeping, teaching, and so on. Professionalization of the housework improves its quality and leaves the other residents time, space, and energy to pursue activities that match their talents and inclinations—and to contribute them to the community as a whole. Specialization also helps make living spaces simpler, cleaner, more pleasant, and more private.

"Five Girls" contains the typical ingredients of a Gilman house-making story. Each of the five girls who design "one of those splendid compound houses that are so beautiful and convenient" is an artist; one is an architect (84). This balance of the "beautiful and convenient" typifies the literary home-making ideal. The five girls plan their apartment house to be "artistic and hygenic and esthetic and everything else; with central kitchens and all those things; and studios and rooms for ourselves, and a hall to exhibit in and so on" (85). Once the house is built, they rent apartments to families, whose rent, along with that paid for the studios, supports the project. One girl's "redoubtable Aunt Susan"—one of Gilman's super-housekeepers whose domestic skills rise above the requirements of a single home—keeps house, and "declared that she never had had half a chance to show what was in her before"; another girl's widowed mother acts as chaperone (86). Gradually, the girls fulfill the plan articulated by one: "[I]f we do marry we don't mean to give up our work I hope. I mean to marry some time, perhaps—but I don't mean to cook! I mean to decorate always, and make lots of money and hire a housekeeper" (84–85). As the girls marry, they move into the apartments; and "the charming little kindergarten in the south wing grew fuller and fuller" (86). In short, the story illustrates not only the creation of an ideal building but the ability of the structure to facilitate both female success in public-sphere terms ("make lots of money") and an idealized family life.

Like the eponymous "five girls," the young founders of the town of "Bee Wise" possess complementary talents: there are girls nicknamed Mother, Teacher, Nurse, Minister, Doctor, Statesman, Manager, Artist, and Engineer (227). The entire California community is self-sufficient, with a reservoir at either end of town to supply drinking water, irrigation, and power, the "clean, economical electric energy" also supplied by "wind-mills on the heights and tide-mill on the beach" and later a "solar engine" (230)—in short, a clean, renewable power system well ahead of its time (or ours). Using locally available materials, "they built houses of stone and wood and heavy sheathing paper, making their concrete of the dead palm leaves and the loose bark of swift-growing eucalyptus, which was planted everywhere and rose over night almost, like the Beanstalk—houses beautiful, comfortable, sea-shell clean" (231). Once again, Gilman reconciles the beautiful and the clean. She also replaces traditional private domestic arrangements with an efficient, professional domesticity: "There were no servants in the old sense. The dainty houses had no kitchens, only the small electric outfit where those who would might prepare coffee and the like. Food was prepared in clean wide laboratories, attended by a few skilled experts" (233). Central to Gilman's conception is that the town be, as its fictional founder insists, "'planned, built, and managed—' her voice grew solemn, 'by women—for women—and *children!* A place that will be of real help to humanity'" (230).

"Maidstone Comfort" is less a community than a profitable summer resort, a village of cottages—kitchenless, of course. Built by "landscape architects and concrete constructors and sanitary engineers and all sorts of people," whose sex is not specified (229), it nevertheless embodies the feminist principles of Gilman's other ideal housing projects, and was founded by two women. The beautiful town has feminine curving streets, not "gridiron angles" (228), and an "astonishing variety in the houses, both in shape and color," though all are small and each has its own garden, enclosed by walls—providing, Gilman emphasizes, privacy. Inside the cottages, each guest has a separate bathroom, and here Gilman becomes atypically specific:

> A funny little bathroom with a tub solid with wall and floor, though smoothly enamelled inside; and a basin that jutted out from the wall like a shelf in a cave, also smooth and pearly within like a big seashell.
>
> "Must be one of those moulded houses," I thought, and turned the faucet marked "hot" with a forgiving smile. The water steamed.
>
> Amazed and grateful I enjoyed a luxuriously hot bath, the one renovator after a day of travel. (228–29)

Apparently a triumph of the "sanitary engineers," this very up-to-date bathroom avoids such cleaning nightmares as freestanding claw-foot tubs and boasts easy-to-clean surfaces, not to mention genuinely hot water. Doubtless the "drains" conform to approved sanitary standards. The bathroom thus offers maximum comfort for residents while requiring minimal labor for the "skilled employees who come in by the hour" (229). Furthermore, even this bathroom, with its "pearly" seashell-shaped basin, combines the antiseptic and the aesthetic. This perfect resort cottage, like those in all Gilman's pragmatopias about building model communities, illustrates the sanitary, aesthetic, and practical advantages of her ideal, woman-designed, professionally maintained, public/private, kitchenless homes.

In the chapter on "Domestic Art" in *The Home: Its Work and Influence* (1903), Gilman asks, "What is there in home-life, as we know it, which proves inimical to the development of true beauty?" (144). Not surprisingly, her first explanation is the kitchen, because it is ugly in its own right and because its sights, odors, and sounds infiltrate the house. Furthermore, Gilman argues, small houses, by their nature, violate the fundamental aesthetic principles of unity, simplicity, harmony, and restraint. The feudal castle "was beautiful because it had one pre-dominant idea—defence"; the modern home, by contrast, with its kitchen, reception area, and sleeping areas, has "absolutely contradictory themes" (147, 148). A closely related problem is that the person most responsible for decorating, the woman, "continually has to do utterly inharmonious things" in her "patchwork life" and thus is unlikely to develop the appreciation of simplicity and harmony necessary to beauty (151). By the same token, woman's confinement to the home, which has hampered her evolutionary development, contributes to a "magpie taste that hoards all manner of gay baubles," however incongruous (158). Ultimately, however, Gilman posits no complete solution to the problem of the home's lack of true beauty. She simply declares the truly beautiful home "impossible" (156). "Great art," she writes, "is always public, and appears only in periods of high social development" (157). That being so, homes will become more beautiful only when women live more public lives: "A larger womanhood, a civilised womanhood, specialised, broad-minded, working and caring for the public good *as well as the private,* will give us not only better homes, but homes more beautiful" (158; emphasis Gilman's). That is why Herland, which has erased the public/private dichotomy, is so beautiful.

And, by the same token, that is why Gilman's best-known example of interior design, the titular yellow wallpaper, is so horrifying. Gilman's portrayal of this infamous paper is significantly illuminated by attention to her literary housekeeping ideas: her parallel insistence on the importance of maintaining personal privacy and of "working and caring for the public good," her simultaneous emphasis on aesthetic and health concerns.

Whatever else it represents, the paper is surely ugly, "committing every artistic sin." As we have seen, for Gilman, the debased state of home decoration reflects the suppressed condition of human evolution, which in turn results from women's repression. As she writes in her discussion of the arts in *The Man-Made World,* "The house is the physical expression of the limitations of women; and as such it fills the world with a small drab ugliness" (82). This ugliness reflects the narrowness of its inhabitants' lives and their lack of opportunities to develop a "civilized art sense," but also, paradoxically, the fact that "the decorator is the man" while woman is the consumer (73, 72). The narrator of "The Yellow Wall-Paper," unlike the average woman, "know[s] a little of the principle of design," and is therefore capable of being offended that in the room her husband insists she sleep in, the walls are covered with a paper that is "not arranged on any laws of radiation, or alternation, or repetition, or symmetry, or anything else that I ever heard of" (9).

In invoking "the principle of design," Gilman, an admirer of William and May Morris, identifies with "art decoration" of the era, including its denigration of Victorian decorating styles.[8] The rented house containing the paper "has been empty for years," so its decor not surprisingly resembles the style that house beautiful advocate H. J. Jennings calls "the tasteless fashions of the early Victorian era." Characterizing that era, Jennings quotes a description of its wallpapers: "Their very patterns are pernicious, producing—unknown to the victim—irritation of the retina, confusion of the brain, vertigo, and nightmare" (19). Similarly, Rhoda and Agnes Garrett suggest a simple paper for a bedroom, one with "an all-overish pattern that cannot be tortured into geometrical figures by the occupant of the chamber, who, especially in hours of sickness, is well-nigh driven to distraction by counting over and over again the dots and lines and diamonds which dance with endless repetition before his aching eyes. For the same reason it is well to avoid the use of light or bright colours, and especially to study harmony of effect, and to eschew contrast" (69). In deploring a mid- or early-Victorian decor, Gilman thus participates in the rhetoric of art decoration typified by Jennings and the Garretts, but invests in it a broadly feminist social significance.

Another aspect of the paper should not be overlooked: the fixation on wall-paper in late nineteenth-century medical discourse on housing and health—both mental and physical. To be sure, Gilman's primary emphasis—her "purpose," as she explicitly called it—in "The Yellow Wall-Paper" is on the devastating psychological effects of the narrator's isolation and forced inactivity.[9] That said, Gilman participated in discussions of sanitary issues, read Dr. Benjamin Richardson's *Diseases of Modern Life* in 1883,[10] and would have endorsed the often-stated observation by Richardson and others that unhealthy conditions in the home most threatened those family members who spent the most time there: women and children. In "Why I Wrote 'The Yellow Wallpaper'?" Gilman writes, "I wrote *The Yellow Wallpaper,* with its embellishments and additions to carry out the ideal (I never had hallucinations or objections to my mural decorations)" (331–32). In other words, she added the wallpaper to her story as an objective correlative—a particularly evocative one that has practically created its own cottage industry of critical interpretation. On the other hand, in *The Living of Charlotte Perkins Gilman,* she reports that an editor of the *New England Magazine,* in which the story first appeared, wrote to ask if the story were true, because, he told Gilman later, "he had a friend who was in similar trouble, even to hallucinations about her wallpaper, and whose family were treating her as in the tale, that he had not dared to show them my story till he knew that it was true, in part at the least, and that when he did they were so frightened by it, so impressed by the clear implication of what ought to have been done, that they changed her wallpaper and the treatment of the case—and she recovered!" (121). Gilman herself might not have been maddened by her walls, but she was easily persuaded that another, similarly confined woman might be. That the narrator of "The Yellow Wall-Paper" is sickened not only mentally and emotionally by her confinement but physically by the house itself simply reinforces Gilman's "ideal." Presumably Gilman selected this particular "embellishment" because it so effectively combines aesthetic and sanitary issues that impacted the late nineteenth-century domestic environment.

At the turn into the twentieth century, many writers warned homeowners that wallpaper could be toxic. Wallpapers took the blame for ills ranging from nausea to "bodily lassitude" to "violent sickness and headache" (Edis, 359, 340). In a milieu in which dust was feared as a disease carrier, doctors and designers warned that flocked papers act as a "dust trap" that will "contaminate" a room's air (Parkes, 233). Even smooth papers threaten residents' health, especially in bedrooms, where "impure air" that accumulates each night creates "unwholesome smells"—and bad smells were themselves still linked to illness. As one sanitarian explained, "the absorbent nature of paper must necessarily cause it to retain a certain proportion of the deleterious atmosphere," an accumulation that could be removed only by changing the wall covering frequently—at least every two years (Edis, 343). But the sizing and paste used for paper was itself subject to "putrefactive change," even when fresh, while old paste, if not completely removed prior to repapering, was likely to "decompose." Old paper had to be removed before new paper was applied also because "each covering of paper only adds to the absorbent nature of the walls, and helps to increase therefore the unhealthiness and stuffiness of the room" (Edis, 340). In short, wallpaper was counterindicated for the healthy home.

At the most extreme, advice books alerted readers to the horrors of papers containing arsenic: "danger is lurking at the present moment unsuspected in many a home," Dr. Malcolm Morris exhorts his readers in frantic italics, because "*it is no uncommon thing for men and women to die, poisoned by arsenic in wallpaper*" (366). Morris's discussion of this danger, although unusually detailed, resembles in its general purport similar discussions in numerous advice books, including the book by Richardson that Gilman is known to have read. According to Louis C. Parkes, for example, manifestations of the "chronic form of poisoning" caused by inhaling or swallowing "arsenical dust" from wallpaper include "conjunctivitis and lachrymation, cough, nausea, sickness and diarrhœa, colic pains, cramps, dryness of the mouth and throat with much thirst, headache, and debility becoming gradually very marked, with actual paralysis of the extremities, terminating in convulsions and death" (236). Few of these symptoms appear in Gilman's tale, though "lachrymation"—excretion or shedding of tears (*OED*)—matches the narrator's observation, "I cry at nothing, and cry most of the time" (9). Some of the case studies Dr. Morris outlines resemble Gilman's story. Symptoms in these cases included intolerance of light, "malaise," great depression, restlessness, wakefulness, and loss of sleep—all consistent with the narrator's "nervousness," obvious depression, and habit of creeping around the room all night.

Dr. Morris's explanations of the mechanisms of arsenic poisoning from wallpaper also echo Gilman's descriptions: "some of the more potent forms of arsenic are very volatile, and become gaseous at a very low temperature, as evidenced by their odour and yellowish colour; and though the ordinary observer may not detect the vapours, they are carried and diffused by the motion of the air in the moist warm days of summer, and stealthily invade the skin and lungs in quantities that render them very potent for evil" (369). This description bears a remarkable similarity to the narrator's observations. For example, she says, "But there is something else about that paper—the smell! . . . Now we have had a week of fog and rain, and whether the windows are open or not, the smell is here" (14). The odor appears, as Dr. Morris predicts, when the summer weather turns humid. His description of these "vapours" as "stealthy" resembles Gilman's idiosyncratic diction: the narrator says that the smell "creeps all over the house," is "hovering in the dining-room, skulking in the parlor, hiding in the hall, lying in wait for me on the stairs" (14). Furthermore, as Dr. Morris explains, the dye containing trioxide of arsenic, "when dry cracks and peels off with the slightest friction" (369), a detail consistent with Gilman's paper, which "stained everything it touched" with "yellow smooches" (13). Presumably, as the narrator begins to tear off the paper, even more dust is released, accelerating the arsenic's effects.

Ultimately, of course, the crucial point is that had the narrator controlled her own physical environment, neither the wallpaper nor forced inactivity would have overcome her. Whether its influence results from putrefaction or arsenic or crimes against Aestheticism, the paper would have been removed in a far more conventional fashion, or the narrator would have moved herself to the pretty downstairs bedroom—or she would have left altogether for the "visit to Cousin Henry and Julia" that John would not permit (10). Although this story is in many ways atypical of Gilman's writings, its narrator's lack of control over her living space does reflect Gilman's insistence that the home as currently organized creates an environment that is unhealthy—physically, mentally, aesthetically, and politically—not only for women but for men and children.

In contrast to the horror of "The Yellow Wall-Paper," Gilman's fictional portrayals of kitchenless homes and professionalized housework are almost relentlessly upbeat. In her utopian novels *Moving the Mountain* and *Herland,* kitchenless homes and their accompanying improvements represent a fait accompli, to the delight of all except such unredeemable conservatives as

Herland's Terry. Others of her stories portray her heroines (or occasionally heroes) organizing efficient boardinghouses or creating ideal living arrangements, often in the face of skepticism or outright opposition. Invariably, reason and economy—and kitchenless living—triumph in the end. It seems reasonable to inquire, therefore, why the kitchenless home has failed to catch on in modern America. Ruth Schwartz Cowan, in *More Work for Mother,* argues persuasively that the invention and marketing of "labor-saving" devices like washing machines discouraged previous practices of sending laundry to be washed outside the home, while items like vacuum cleaners and improved stoves encouraged the American trend toward a woman's "doing her own work." Such trends, along with advertising that associated status with owning the new products, provided powerful counterforces against the comparatively weak movements toward more collective arrangements. Meanwhile, aggravating as *Herland*'s Terry may be, his rigid insistence that "a man wants a home of his own, with his wife and family in it" (97) suggests other reasons why Gilman's proposals have never come to fruition. The problem with her plans is not so much that they are unreasonable. All her facts and figures, arguments and evidence suggest that that the schemes would save quantifiable time and money. And up to a point, Americans have adopted many of Gilman's ideas, especially regarding food, as eating out and reheating frozen microwave dinners permeate the lives of busy two-income families. But even though Gilman insists that her plans are not communalism, the fact is that, reasonably or not, many people feel their privacy and independence would somehow be violated by having someone else washing their undergarments or cleaning their bathrooms. As in *Herland,* Gilman seems to overlook problems that arise when a conflation of the domestic and the communal threatens the individual's need for the privacy of concealment and withdrawal.

Ruskin and Drains: Ward and the Building of "The House Beautiful"

For Gilman, houses are primarily of interest within a larger feminist theory of community; for Grand, houses and their decor function primarily as symbols; but for Ward, many houses seem simply to exist for their own sake. In addition, they function as aesthetic objects, as problems of sanitary science, and as expressions of the character of their inhabitants. Like Gilman, Ward was fascinated by the politics of building design, but unlike Gilman, Ward enjoyed a series of opportunities throughout her life to see her ideas embodied in actual buildings, including public buildings. Ward's work with the "decoration of houses" may in turn underlie the generally optimistic tenor of her portrayal of relations between homes and the public realm: she suggests not only that private efforts can improve the public sphere but also that it is possible to balance beauty and usefulness in spaces that bring together the private and the public.

Ward's ideas about domestic spaces were deeply influenced by the Arts and Crafts movement. In her autobiography, she describes her first home as the wife of an Oxford tutor: "[W]e all gave dinner-parties and furnished our houses with Morris papers, old chests and cabinets, and blue pots. . . . Most of us were very anxious to be up-to-date and in the fashion, whether in esthetics, in housekeeping, or in education. But our fashion was not that of Belgravia or Mayfair, which, indeed, we scorned! It was the fashion of the movement which sprang from Morris and Burne-Jones" (1:159, 160). Across the street from the young newlyweds lived Walter Pater and his sisters, whose "beautiful little house," "'Paterian' in every line and ornament," with its Morris papers and delicate framed embroidery, "drew me perpetually" (1:165–66). In Oxford, Ward was also influenced by Arts and Crafts and Paterian aesthetics in her first foray into designing a space to simultaneously serve public and private functions: the residential building of one of Oxford's first women's colleges, Somerville Hall—later Somerville College. Ward's engagement diary for 1879 records "the decision to purchase the lease of 'Walton House,' . . . the builder's estimate for alterations ('£540 for raising the roof and making twelve bedrooms'), the letters about drainage, or cretonne, or armchairs and fenders" (Trevelyan, 31). From these early days, Ward attended not only to armchairs and fabrics— the artistic touches—but also to items firmly identified with sanitary science: the roof and drainage. She also donated several blue pots (Sutherland, 65). A balance of science and art, domestic comfort and feminist determination would be necessary, she knew, to the success of Somerville. Indeed, in its promotional materials the Association for the Education of Women pragmatically compared Somerville Hall—the name for both the institution and its residence—to an "English family," thus blurring the line between acceptable domesticity and a groundbreaking foray into the intellectual public sphere.

A change of residences for her own family invariably occasioned attention to decoration in Ward's life, as in her fiction: the decorating choices reflect her attitudes toward aesthetic, political, and sanitary issues. When the Wards removed to London in 1881, following Humphry's appointment to the *Times,* they settled in a "charming old house" in Bloomsbury (Trevelyan, 35). As we have seen, eighteenth-century houses were in vogue, and the feature that appealed to the Wards in the Russell Square House, built in 1745, was one that writers about houses most frequently missed in contemporary houses: an attractive entry "hall." The house had one significant deficiency—inextricably connected to its eighteenth-century charm—its ancient plumbing. The Wards' youngest child, Janet, who lived there from age two to nine, apparently absorbed—with childish distortions—the adult anxieties about the house's sanitary fittings, for she recalled the "lurking horror" that lived on the top landing, "where the taps dripped in a dreadful little box-room, and if the taps dripped you knew that the water-bogy, *who lives in taps,* might at any moment escape and overwhelm you" (36; emphasis Trevelyan's). And indeed, the family was overwhelmed by some kind of plumbing bogy in February of 1886, when, according to John Sutherland, the Wards had to beat a hasty retreat from a "stinking house" when "the never-very reliable Russell Square drains" burst from the strain of a series of freezes and thaws (111). In an era when dampness and "sewer gas" were still blamed for disease, the Wards lived with powerful reminders of the difficulties of balancing health and aesthetic charm in domestic space.

Early in her writing career, in her constant effort to balance the practical and the beautiful, her public writing vocation with her needs for privacy, Mary Ward realized that the "powder-room" at Russell Square could not protect her concentration from the inevitable London distractions, so in 1889 the Wards invested profits from *Robert Elsmere* to buy land near Haslemere, where they built a house of fashionable red brick, designed by Edward Robson, an associate of the famous architect J. J. Stevenson, influential advocate of the Queen Anne style. Ward's daughter recounts that Ward "took the keenest interest in every detail of the new house, planning it out in daily letters to her husband" (Trevelyan, 93). Ultimately, however, she found the house unsatisfying: the neighborhood proved too busy to provide a secluded work environment, but, at least as important, as the house itself "drew near completion she could not help rebelling at its very newness" (93). Soon afterward, the family leased "Stocks," a 120-year-old house in western Hertfordshire.

Imagining a house beautiful was as important in Ward's fiction as it was in her life. In the fiction, characters frequently struggle to reconcile their desire for or pleasure in a beautiful living environment with what they see as a competing impulse for political justice. This internal conflict reflects an ambivalence Ward herself occasionally suffered. Regarding the expense of living at Grovesnor Place, the Wards' London home after 1890, Ward's daughter explains:

> Sometimes she would have searchings of heart over this, or even momentary spasms of economy, but it sprang in reality from two fundamental causes—one her delight in beautiful things . . . ; the other this constant ill-health, which made her incapable of 'roughing it,' and rendered a certain amount of luxury indispensable if she was to get through her daily task. Good pictures and the right kind of furniture gave her a definite joy for their own sakes, while the arrangement of the chairs and tables in the manner best calculated to encourage talk was always a fascinating problem. (Trevelyan, 190)

For Ward, engaged as she was in the settlement movement's efforts to assist the urban poor, living in luxury might well have inspired compunction. To justify her beautiful surroundings as necessary for health, for enabling her to complete the writing that helped finance her projects, and for hosting the "at homes" at which she drummed up support for the projects must have provided some comfort. But the dilemma recurs in her fiction.

In many cases, the house beautiful is implicitly associated in Ward's fiction with English tradition, a seeming conservatism that runs counter to her characters' more radical impulses. Nevertheless, as we have seen, in late-Victorian thinking influenced by Ruskin and Morris (as Ward's was), artistic evocation of tradition styled itself as progressive. In Ward's books, houses frequently symbolize a past that must be recovered or preserved for future generations, as for example Mellor and Maxwell Court in *Marcella,* Bannisdale in *Helbeck of Bannisdale,* or Monk Lawrence in *Delia Blanchflower.* The Elizabethan mansion Monk Lawrence is "steeped in fragrant and famous memories, English history, English poetry, English art, breathing from every room and stone of the house"

(197). To radical suffragist Gertrude Marvell the house represents only conservatism, and destroying it thus protests more than the antisuffrage position
of its cabinet minister owner. Gertrude gazes at the house just after having set
the arson fire: "'It's beautiful,' she was saying to herself—'and precious—and
I've destroyed it.' Then—with a fierce leap in the blood—'*Beauty!* And what
about the beauty that men destroy? Let them *pay!*'" (378). To her, both tradition, symbolized by the house, and the relishing of beauty represent oppression.

This attitude helps explain why Delia, Gertrude's former pupil, worries
that decorating is directly at odds with politics. Like many of Ward's heroines,
Delia finds herself the new owner of family property, and her immediate impulse is to redecorate: to make certain practical and sanitary changes—build
wardrobes and bookcases, and install electricity and a bathroom—as well as a
number of aesthetic ones: "And she fell into a reverie,—eagerly constructive—wherein Maumsey became, at a stroke, a House Beautiful, at once modern and æsthetically right" (58). Delia's fashionable taste might well yield a
practical and pretty house, but her plans are no sooner formulated than rejected with revulsion: Delia sees that money used to redecorate (and "playing
the heiress—patronising the poor people") is money not invested in suffrage
causes. In this novel, Ward all too frequently descends to the antifeminist
cliché that politics and beauty, of whatever sort, are mutually incompatible. Yet
she complicates this dichotomy, for Delia's "patronising the poor people" expresses another political interest. Moreover, all but the book's most militant
suffragists oppose destroying Monk Lawrence, and Delia maintains her suffragist position even while redecorating—and while falling in love, marrying, and
setting up housekeeping.

Another duality frequently associated with home design—that between
health and beauty—appears prominently in Ward's fiction. It is typified by a
passage from *Robert Elsmere*:

> "It seems to me," said Langham musing, "that in my youth people talked
> about Ruskin; now they talk about drains."
>
> "And quite right too. Dirt and drains, Catherine says I have gone mad
> upon them. It's all very well, but they are the foundations of a sound reli-
> gion."

"Dirt, drains, and Darwin," said Langham meditatively, taking up Darwin's *Earthworms,* which lay on the study table beside him, side by side with a volume of Grant Allen's *Sketches.* (170–71)

Ruskin and drains, Langham suggests, are incompatible enthusiasms, a belief shared by the novel's enthusiasts on both sides: by the saintly Catherine, who distrusts art as a distraction from God; by Catherine's sister Rose, who dismisses both nursing and religion as distractions from her music; and by the scholarly Squire Wendover, who delegates responsibility for his tenants to a corrupt agent in order to work on his book undisturbed in his beautifully furnished library. To be sure, the eponymous Robert appreciates both the artistic and the sanitary, but he never successfully reconciles the two. The novel juxtaposes a loving description of carpets, sculptures, valuable pictures, and artfully designed shelving in the library of Squire Wendover's Tudor mansion with, a page or two later, an account of "a miserable group of houses, huddled together as though their bulging walls and rotten roofs could only maintain themselves at all by the help and support which each wretched hovel gave to its neighbor," on the squire's land (202). The little hamlet offers a textbook case of problems identified by sanitarians, and Ward in a sense identifies it as such:

> It belonged to that old and evil type which the efforts of the last twenty years have done so much all over England to sweep away: four mud walls, enclosing an oblong space about eight yards long, divided into two unequal portions by a lath and plaster partition, with no upper storey, a thatched roof, now entirely out of repair, and letting in the rain in several places, and a paved floor little better than the earth itself, so large and cavernous were the gaps between the stones. (203)

The hamlet abuts "a sort of open drain or water-course, stagnant and noisome" (202), and its residents suffer from precisely those diseases doctors in the latter half of the century attributed to insanitary housing: typhoid, tuberculosis, diphtheria, and "fever." Squire Wendover has ignored his tenants' living conditions because he wants no imposition on either his leisure or his scholarly endeavors, and has no patience with "new-fangled ideas of a landowner's duty" (258). When a new epidemic breaks out, Elsmere and a local doctor, in between attending dying patients, repair what they can, summon a sanitary in-spector, haul water from a well on higher ground, and begin plans to "drain and repair and sink for a well ourselves," even if money remains unavailable from the squire (285). When Wendover finally sees the hamlet, he realizes the enor-mity of the problem, as Robert shows him "what the water supply had been till now, . . . the roofs, the pigstyes, the drainage, or rather complete absence of drainage," and the mud floors of the tumble-down cottages (293). Finally, Wendover sees the makeshift hospital, where a child is even then dying, and learns that seven have already died from diphtheria or fever. Having witnessed the reality of the problem—or, as Robert observes, having *"felt"* (295)—Wen-dover accepts that he is answerable for his tenants' living conditions and has their cottages rebuilt in a healthier location—presumably according to the best modern principles of cottage construction.

This incident—one of the first sequences involving building or remodel-ing in Ward's books—marks a turning point in the novel. The events at Mile End awaken in the squire a fresh respect for Robert, to whom he then lends books and encouragement. Ironically, of course, Robert's research ultimately leads to his crisis of faith, thus putting an unintended twist to Robert's asser-tion that drains are "the foundations of a sound religion." Robert continues to work among the poor, but leaves the Church to found the New Brotherhood in London. Furthermore, the Mile End episode may have an even more direct impact, for in addition to contracting in Wendover's library the "infection" of historical knowledge that undermines his faith, Robert may catch the tubercu-losis that kills him from Wendover's tenants at Mile End.[11]

In *Robert Elsmere,* drains and Darwin, representing science, and Ruskin, representing art and beauty, are held to be incompatible; in *Marcella,* Ward at-tempts to reconcile the two worlds. (To be sure, Ruskin himself, with his em-phasis on accurate representation and the political and ethical content of much of his writing, would have thought them fully compatible.) Marcella, a former art student who has read Ruskin (91) and Morris (47), understands from her arrival at Mellor that her family's inheriting the estate entails inheriting prob-lems of housing, which are problems of health: "'The village water-supply is a *disgrace,*' she said with low emphasis. 'I never saw such a crew of unhealthy, wretched-looking children in my life as swarm about those cottages. We take the rent, and we ought to look after them'" (52). Marcella's new socialist awareness of rural poverty is repeatedly linked to housing: she witnesses "girls and boys and young children already blanched and emaciated beyond even the normal Londoner from the effects of insanitary cottages, bad water, and starvation food" (61).

Like Squire Wendover in *Robert Elsmere*, Marcella's father is a landowner who refuses to take responsibility for the water supply serving his tenants. Richard Boyce argues that such civic duty and his own home maintenance are irreconcilable: "What have I got to do with a water-supply for the village? It will be as much as ever I can manage to keep a water-tight roof over our heads during the winter" (52). Marcella herself recognizes that her house, no less than those of the villagers, has been "neglected and unkempt" and lacks such fundamentals as "sound roofs, a modern water-supply" (57). But to her mind that does not lessen the landlord's obligation. Observing the poverty on her father's property intensifies Marcella's socialist convictions, as she explains to Aldous, "[W]hen I see these cottages, and the water, and the children, I ask what right we have to anything we get. . . . Yes, indeed!—it *is* too great a risk to let the individual alone when all these lives depend upon him" (68).

Ward suggests that this response—abolition of private property—is excessive, but so is private abdication of public responsibility by landowners like Boyce and Wendover. Here and elsewhere, Ward advocates compromise between individual and state efforts. This "middle way," of public regulation balanced by individual responsibility, is suggested in small ways, as when Marcella refers to the "local authority" who ought to force Boyce to repair his cottages (52), and when, later in the novel, in her official capacity of district nurse, she summons a sanitary inspector to a squalid tenement. Of the social issues in *Marcella* and its sequel, *Sir George Tressady*, Ward observed, "[T]he difficulty lies between the individualist theory, which makes too little of the right and responsibility of the community, and the collectivist theory, which makes too little of the right and responsibility of the individual" (Westmoreland edition, 7:xiii). One character who attempts to find a balance is the venturist (Fabian socialist) Edward Hallin, who states Ward's philosophy directly: "[T]he big changes may come—the big Collectivist changes. But neither you nor I will see them. . . . Meanwhile—all still hangs upon, comes back to, the individual" (523).

In her own social welfare efforts Ward attempted to put into concrete form this idea of balancing public and private responsibility. Both Ward's memoirs and her introduction to *Marcella* in the 1911 Westmoreland edition of her then complete works mingle accounts of *Marcella*'s composition, reception, and ideas with recollections of her work developing the settlement then called University Hall.[12] The two are connected by more than biographical chronology. Both concern the efforts of a wealthy woman to help England's poor and to challenge existing relations between the classes—and both are tightly bound up with building. *Marcella,* which returns almost obsessively to building design, especially, but not exclusively, the design of houses, was written in 1892 and 1893 while Ward was involved in a continuing series of building and remodeling projects. To understand the portrayal of houses in *Marcella,* it is useful to understand the building project that engrossed Ward during the book's composition.

The settlement movement was inspired by the life of Arnold Toynbee (1852–83). Toynbee, who was also the model for the character Edward Hallin of *Marcella,* was a young historian and economist—the coiner of the term "industrial revolution"—who took up residence in the London slums with the goal of bringing culture, religion, and political and historical knowledge to the poor. The first settlement house, opened in 1884 after Toynbee's early death and named Toynbee Hall, was, like its successors, located in a working-class district, and housed students, academics, and clergy who taught the urban poor and worked to solve social problems, while the settlement building provided a social and cultural center for its working-class neighbors. The goal was to encourage mutual friendship and understanding between groups of people who ordinarily lived in widely separated neighborhoods. Ward's own settlement house, University Hall, was founded in 1890 with the intention of bringing together university and working-class men; the primary goal, at least initially, was to promote religious teaching along the lines proposed in *Robert Elsmere.* Unlike previous settlements, which were in London's notorious East End, Ward located hers in a west-central London square "surrounded on three sides by districts crowded with poor" (qtd. in Trevelyan, 84). In Ward's mind, this location would itself help further cross-class communication: "A spirit of fraternization was in the air, an ardent wish to break down the local and geographical barriers that separated rich from poor, East End from West End" (*A Writer's Recollections,* 2:147). The settlement grew and evolved during the early 1890s, with less preaching and more casual "fraternization," including the games and recreation that sprang up to accommodate neighborhood children. In response to this evolution, Ward sought funding for a building that would better serve the settlement's needs, eventually receiving it from the philanthropist Passmore Edwards. The settlement, called the Passmore Edwards Settlement in his honor, was renamed the Mary Ward Settlement after its founder's death.[13]

Having reimagined her settlement plans, beginning in 1892 as her work on *Marcella* was also commencing, Ward was, by early 1895, consulting with experts—typically, an artist and a social thinker, the prominent architect Norman Shaw and the Fabian socialist Graham Wallas—about the general form of a new settlement building. It would have five stories, electric light, rooms for eighteen residents and for their servants, "hotel-standard kitchens," a dining room/lecture hall, a gymnasium, a concert hall, a library, a smoking room, classrooms, and a workshop (Sutherland, 222–23), in short, a balance of public spaces and private accommodations. Shaw, "the architect of choice to the artistic community" (Gere and Hoskins, 42) and one of the originators of the Queen Anne style, was persuaded to judge a public competition for the settlement's design. The winners, the architects Arnold Dunbar-Smith and Cecil Claude Brewer, were former pupils of Shaw and residents of University Hall—and thus had contributed to the evolution of its mission and activities.

The architects' familiarity with the settlement's mission may help explain the success with which the building embodies that mission and philosophy. Adrian Forty persuasively argues that "both in its purpose and in its architecture—and there is a remarkable congruity between the two—it was meant to make people think about class relations" (30). As might be hoped of a building commissioned by a writer with a social conscience in consultation with an artist and a socialist and designed by socially conscious architects, the Passmore Edwards building, as a private residential facility dedicated to the public purpose of enriching the lives of London's poor, balances the artistic, domestic, practical, and political. Forty argues that the interior "stressed humility and the absence of hierarchies, and protested against artificiality," conveying this message, for example, through the design of doorways. Unusually low outer doors represent "a Voysey-ish device for self-abasement"; the oak planks of the Tavistock Place door (the street entrance to the residential section of the building) resemble those of a "humble cottage"; and relatively low interior doors also resemble cottage doors: "These and other details contradict the customary grandeur of late nineteenth century buildings for middle-class occupation and, moreover, by being repeated in all rooms of whatever size and degree of importance, erase the conventional distinctions between public and private rooms" (Forty, 38).

When Ward said she envisioned a building "devoted . . . not to the private pleasure but to the public end," a building that would be recognized as "the House Beautiful," where people would discover the "nobler pleasures" of culture ("Social Ideals," 5), her phrase echoed not only the "artistic house" movement of the late-Victorian era, but the expression that inspired the term "house beautiful," John Bunyan's "Palace Beautiful," from *Pilgrim's Progress,* a lodging for "the relief and security of pilgrims." That is, the phrase itself conflates the aesthetic with the spiritual and ethical. Certainly the building's Aesthetic credentials are impeccable: when completed in 1897, the building was lauded in the *Studio* as "one of the happiest examples of the influence of the 'Arts and Crafts' movement upon architecture" (G. LL. Morris and Wood, 18).

The settlement's most immediate "domestic" function was as a dwelling for idealistic young men—in one notable gesture toward hominess, no two rooms are alike, despite sharing many architectural details with one another and with the public rooms. Yet the settlement's most innovative and enduring legacy was its children's play center, discussed in the previous chapter. With the play center, Ward fulfilled with red bricks, gardens, rooms full of toys, and concerted political effort the theoretical goals of "child gardens" envisioned by Gilman. Ward's efforts to help children and their mothers in the public/domestic settlement house fulfilled the literary housekeeping function of moving maternal care into the public sphere.

But of course Ward was a writer before she was a reformer. Indeed, the settlement itself realized a plan first articulated in *Robert Elsmere*'s fictional "New Brotherhood"—and to some extent was financed by income from Ward's fiction. It was partly while the author was accompanying her sister-in-law, Gertrude Ward, on her rounds as a district nurse, as research for *Marcella,* that she developed her understanding of the needs of slum families—an understanding that contributed both to her settlement projects and to her portrayals of working-class living conditions. Accordingly, many of the ideas that find physical embodiment in the Passmore Edwards Settlement find literary embodiment in Ward's fiction.

One of the most fundamental internal conflicts suffered by Marcella Boyce is that between her "passionate intensity of pleasure" in her new home (35) and her socialist conviction that "we have no right to it!—it ought to be taken from us; some day it will be taken from us!" (68). By the end of the novel, however, Marcella develops a new politics of the beautiful. She explains that after "going about all day in those streets and houses, among people who live in one room—with not a bit of prettiness anywhere—and no place to be alone in, or to rest in," she no longer wants to take beautiful things away from the wealthy as she did before. Instead, consciousness of the "*ugliness* of being poor" makes her "only want to be sure that the beauty, and the leisure, and the freshness are *some*where—not lost out of the world" (431; emphasis Ward's). This is also the philosophy that underlay Ward's insistence on making her settlement house a beautiful building, in which working people could "sit in a pleasant and quiet room, well-lit and warmed, to read a book or listen to music" (qtd. in Trevelyan, 129).

After inheriting Mellor, Marcella sets about to sell railway shares to raise cash for "cottage-building in the village" and "altering the water-supply" (521). Marcella also completes the refurbishing of the house. Ward focuses on its library, which Marcella has made publicly accessible by a door opening onto the garden:

> The beautiful old place had been decently repaired, though in no sense modernised. The roof had no holes, and its delicate stucco-work, formerly stained and defaced by damp, had been whitened, so that the brown and golden tones of the books in the latticed cases told against it with delightful effect. The floor was covered with a cheap matting, and there were a few simple chairs and tables. A wood fire burnt on the old hearth. Marcella's books and work lay about, and some shallow earthenware pans filled with home-grown hyacinths scented the air. What with the lovely architecture of the room itself, its size, its books and old portraits, and the signs it bore of simple yet refined use, it would have been difficult to find a gentler, mellower place. Aldous looked round him with delight.

> "I hope to make a village drawing-room of it in time," she said casually
> to Frank as she stooped to put a log on the fire. "I think we shall get them
> to come, as it has a separate door, and scraper, and mat all to itself." (519)

Here we have a room restored to ancestral dignity, its very architecture evoking its aristocratic pedigree while promising to welcome rural laborers into a new social order, in which their community "drawing-room" will invade the Lady Bountiful's private library. The garden entrance, designed to avoid intimidating potential users, nevertheless reifies class distinctions. The room's appurtenances challenge the traditional gendered division of the house, in which the more private drawing room, boudoir, and morning room were the women's space and the more public dining room, smoking room, and library were the men's. Here, the traditionally masculine books balance with the library's new owner's "work"—that is, needlework. Marcella's new competence manifests itself in the room's balance of beauty and utility, past and present, masculine and feminine, public and private. Like Ward's work at the Passmore Edwards Settlement, it demonstrates a literary housekeeping philosophy. A woman's individual dreams of social improvement, inspired by her reading and portrayed in a work of fiction, become manifest in beautiful buildings that simultaneously embody domestic and pubic functions, which in turn foster social changes that help regenerate the larger community.

≈

Simply to portray a woman in control of decorating a home is to turn from one significant tradition of Victorian narratives, in which the hereditary house and property come as a sort of package deal with the wealthy, titled husband, or in which finding and furnishing a home are the work of male characters, with little input from the future housekeeper herself. In Dickens's *Bleak House* and *Our Mutual Friend*, Trollope's *Dr. Thorne*, and George Paston's *A Writer of Books*, for example, it is a man who finds and furnishes the home. These traditional homemaking episodes signal a couple's retreat into the private, domestic realm. Gilman, Grand, and Ward's portrayals of women building or finding and decorating domestic space—with their delicate balancing of the private and the public, the personal and the political, the traditional and the modern, the aesthetic and the scientific, the literary and the literal—thus echo homemaking traditions while radically subverting them.

In literary housekeeping, analysis of physical space involves interrogation not only of physical situation but of social and political territories and boundaries. The politics of space speak fundamentally to the shifting boundaries between public and private spheres, not to mention issues of property, class, nation, and empire. This was Virginia Woolf's famous argument in *A Room of One's Own,* and it holds fundamental importance as well to literary housekeeping, in which the need for a private "room of one's own" balances uneasily with women's growing power to redesign living spaces both within and beyond the family dwelling. To design a house of one's own, these narratives tell us, is, paradoxically, a public act, one that requires a distinctive feminine strength and that embodies the power and influence of the literary housekeeper.

"Loaf Givers"

Providing Food for the Human Family

IN "OF QUEENS' GARDENS," John Ruskin explains, "Lady means 'bread-giver' or 'loaf-giver,' and Lord means 'maintainer of laws,' and both titles have reference, not to the law which is maintained in the house, nor to the bread which is given to the household; but to law maintained for the multitude, and to bread broken among the multitude" (138). For all his talk of the queenly power of giving bread to the multitude, Ruskin nevertheless limits the woman's public role to "assist[ing] in the ordering, in the comforting, and in the beautiful adornment of the state," a responsibility consistent with her "wifely subjection" within a "vestal temple . . . watched over by Household Gods" (121, 122). Grand, Ward, and Gilman shared Ruskin's belief that the woman is the loaf giver, but they held that loaf giving entails applying the domestic work of food preparation to the world beyond Ruskin's "shelter of home." The womanly task of feeding people might seem the least controversial of activities, but in literary housekeeping, portrayals of food growing and preparation interrogate traditional demarcations between the domestic and the public spheres. Indeed, discussions of food in literary housekeeping texts inspire some of these works' most radical challenges to conventional social and family roles.

A "Mighty Garden": Agriculture in Literary Housekeeping

Sociologists and anthropologists frequently observe that food, eating, and their related activities express fundamental social values, including national identity, class affiliation, and of course gender ideologies. Sherrie Inness, in her study of "Kitchen Culture," has argued that traditions associated with food are particularly powerful at teaching "correct" gender-linked behaviors. In most cultures, each of the stages of food provision has clear gender associations: production and distribution of food are primarily the responsibilities of men and boys, while cooking and clearing up after meals are the responsibilities of women and girls. In preindustrial cultures, all these processes occur almost exclusively within a family or a small, self-sustaining community; in industrialized societies, production and distribution remain primarily masculine responsibilities and take place in the public sphere, while the preparation, consumption, and clearing up of meals remain women's private-sphere activities. But in literary housekeeping, the male, public-sphere activities of growing and distributing food are realigned as womanly and "domestic," even as they retain their public, civic, and economic significance, while cooking itself, which generally retains its traditional connection with women, is reenvisioned as a public responsibility.[1]

With a few significant exceptions,[2] Gilman, Grand, and Ward tend in most of their writings to accept standard gendered divisions of behavior and labor. Rather than challenging ideas about what men and women can do, they are generally more concerned to redefine the scope and meaning of women's domestic activities. Yet perhaps because cooking and serving food are so clearly associated with women, all three writers seem eager to broaden the woman's role in loaf giving to include the earlier stages of food provision usually associated with men. Literary housekeeping texts frequently portray women successfully engaging in traditionally male activities of farming and, in Grand's case, hunting and fishing. And in most instances, challenging gender boundaries seems part of the point.

In Grand's *Beth Book,* Beth not only violates her mother's class prejudices by learning to cook, but she overturns gender expectations by learning to set snares: when her fatherless family lacks food, she sneaks onto her wealthy uncle's estate and poaches rabbits. Showing remarkable resourcefulness, she "skinned and cleaned [a rabbit] herself, boiled it, carved it carefully so that it might not look like a cat on the dish, covered it with good onion-sauce, and garnished it with little rolls of fried bacon, and sent it to table, where the only other dish was cold beef-bones with very little meat on them" (157). Her mother so clearly enjoys the unaccustomed meal that Beth "determined to go hunting again, and see what she could get for her. Beth would not have touched a penny of Uncle James's, but from that time forward she did not scruple to poach on his estate, and bring home anything she could catch. She had often prayed to the Lord to show her how to do something to help her mother in her dire poverty, and when this idea occurred to her, she accepted it as a direct answer to her prayer" (157). Beth also fishes successfully, and cooks her catch as well, on one occasion producing "a whiting on toast, all hot and brown" (177). In each case, Grand balances the gender-bending masculine behavior with superior cooking, but there is no doubt Grand wants readers to admire Beth's ability to step into the male role of family provider, and even valorizes the theft as divinely approved.

Similarly, in *Adnam's Orchard,* when men show themselves incompetent, a woman steps up. Agricultural reform is a major theme of the novel, and although most of the agriculturists in the book are men, there are a few important exceptions. In the book's titular plot, Adnam Pratt employs scientific techniques of "intensive agriculture" to reclaim a neglected orchard and "old lay field." In so doing, Grand repeatedly explains, he reverses decades during which "agriculture has fallen into a deplorable state of neglect." Owing to misguided decisions by incompetent landowners, "land has gone out of cultivation at a perilous rate. England has fallen far behind the times. The area cultivated having been reduced, the agricultural labourers have been either sent or driven away to swell the ranks of the unemployed in the cities. Here, in this fertile region, this fine climate, one sees field after field given over to what you call 'permanent pasture'—grass three inches high and thistles in profusion, hardly enough to feed one cow on each three acres; yet this land might be producing rich and profitable crops" (409–10). Grand thus emphasizes that conservative agricultural methods damage both local rural economies and England's overall strength. And simply by commenting authoritatively, Grand claims for women expertise on improving English farming methods. She shows Adnam's experiments succeeding and local agriculture beginning to revive as his methods are adopted by a few of his more progressive neighbors, including Ellery Banks, whose initial investment his daughter Ella advances him from her lace-making profits. In this indirect way, Grand suggests, a forward-thinking woman, even a delicate lace maker, can contribute to a nation's agricultural economy.

Two women have more direct impact on food production in *Adnam's Orchard.* Ella's stepmother carries on the traditional, relatively private duties of a farm woman: raising chickens, gathering eggs, and making "the best butter in the county," in addition to performing daily housework to support the male family members who work the fields (89). On the other hand, Godiva Pointz, the daughter of one of the most negligent local landlords, is groomed to inherit the Pointz property when Squire Pointz finally realizes that his corrupt agent has run the property into the ground. Disinheriting his dissolute eldest son Algernon for lacking the "sense of honour to make him respect the rights of the next generation," Squire Pointz elects to leave the property to his daughter, who becomes his "aide-de-camp" as he carries out the advice of Seraph Pratt in his efforts to rebuild his land to a level of productivity comparable to the Pratts' (442, 443).

The collaboration between Seraph Pratt and Godiva Pointz affords Grand opportunities to remark on connections between agricultural and human eugenic progress or decline. Godiva promises to be a superior steward of the land, says Grand, not despite but because of her womanhood. Grand asserts, "The last worth lingering in decadent families is usually found in the women. Godiva had character and ability enough to manage the property herself, all that she needed was the training, and moreover she knew this, and made haste to acquaint Seraph with the fact as soon as he was installed in office" (467). When Seraph remarks that the British landowner seems unable to learn how to develop the land, Godiva confidently insists, "*I* intend to learn. There is nothing occult in a knowledge of agriculture, and I shall want it if I ever have property of my own to manage. I have seen enough of what comes of not minding your own business" (469). Perhaps, that is, the problem has been the concentration of land in male ownership. As for the growing influence of that "weedy specimen" Seraph Pratt, Grand has one observer remark, "Seraph Pratt may be a weed . . . , but he does know his own business. They say there's no better farmer in the county. It's with men as it is with plants, isn't it? Some weeds may be developed by cultivation into fine flowers; while some flowers, because they have been neglected in important particulars, rapidly degenerate into unlovely weeds" (433).

Accordingly, the expected marriage between Godiva and Seraph promises to yield, in the never-written third volume of the trilogy, a cross-pollination that regenerates the combined Pointz and Pratt properties. Even before the marriage, the couple achieves impressive success: "In one short year the changes for the better at Pointz became the marvel of the neighborhood, but the improvements on the property were less remarkable than the improvement in Godiva. Nothing embellishes like love and hope, with plenty of congenial work that is worth the doing, done in close companionship with the one and only" (470). On the other hand, Grand takes pains to show that Godiva's love for the "uncouth" Seraph illustrates the "insidious persuasion" of sex, and hints that after their marriage, Godiva, like other mismatched wives in Grand's novels, will recognize in Seraph "an inheritance of baseness" (469, 470). Thus, although the potential power of the woman landowner is muted in this, the first volume of the trilogy, one might imagine that in the third volume, Godiva would come into her own as her knowledge, combined with her inherent strength, triumphed over Seraph's fundamental weakness. Alternatively, Godiva's superior management might enable her to "cultivate" Seraph into a "fine flower." In Grand's writing, women's eugenic superiority parallels and enhances their potential superiority in agriculture, while farming represents yet another way that women can contribute to human progress in the public sphere.

Gilman, too, links women's agricultural work to her eugenic project. In the utopian worlds of *Moving the Mountain* and *Herland,* as well as in her briefer "pragmatopias," women transform domestic gardening from a means to sustain an individual or family into the foundation of a business or even a community or nation. The initial plans for the woman-designed "Beewise" include "great gardens and vineyards." As its instigator exclaims, "We can make a little Eden!" (229). In "A Council of War," the women plan to start their alternative community with "a series of business undertakings," beginning with "farms, market gardens, greenhouses, small fruits, preserves, confections, bakeries" (238). The women plan "a great spreading league of interconnected businesses," so they can assist one another, and employ women under ethical conditions, with "proper hours, proper wages," and so on, to foster their economic independence and a "steady increase of power" (238, 239). Controlling the chain of production and consumption of food at all stages affords the opportunity to create "a world within a world," specifically, "a woman's world, clean and kind and safe and serviceable" (243).

The "Eden" that Beewise achieves in a small California community, and the "woman's world" that is only imagined in "A Council of War," Herland realizes on a national scale: "a land in a state of perfect cultivation, where even the forests looked as if they were cared for; a land that looked like an enormous park, only it was even more evidently an enormous garden" (11). A "mighty garden," as Gilman also describes it (77), suggests more a woman's space than would "a mighty farm," and Gilman also identifies the landscape's general tidiness with its female originators. Van praises its "perfect roads, as dustless as a swept floor; the shade of endless lines of trees; the ribbon of flowers that unrolled beneath them; and the rich comfortable country that stretched off and away, full of varied charm" (43). The entire country is carefully cultivated, revealing "a people highly skilled, efficient, caring for their country as a florist cares for his costliest orchids" (18). Herland "gardening" methods, devised and implemented exclusively by women, utterly surpass Ourland's agriculture in both beauty and efficiency.

Herland's garden encompasses an entire country the size of Holland (77), its harvest and the country's population carefully correlated: "Having improved their agriculture to the highest point, and carefully estimated the number of persons who could comfortably live on their square miles; having then limited their population to that number, . . . they habitually considered and carried out plans for improvement" (79). Most of Herland's agricultural methods would impress a twenty-first-century environmentalist:

> These careful culturists had worked out a perfect scheme of refeeding the soil with all that came out of it. All the scraps and leavings of their food, plant waste from lumber work or textile industry, all the solid matter from the sewage, properly treated and combined—everything which came from the earth went back to it.
>
> The practical result was like that in any healthy forest; an increasingly valuable soil was being built, instead of the progressive impoverishment so often seen in the rest of the world. (80)

For space and economy's sake, Herland has "eliminated all the grazing cattle. . . . Also, they worked out a system of intensive agriculture surpassing anything I ever heard of, with the very forests all reset with fruit- or nut-bearing trees" (68).

Even more important than their soil-building techniques is the Herlanders' selection and breeding of plants. They have replaced unproductive species with useful ones:

> Now every tree bore fruit—edible fruit, that is. . . . They had early decided
> that trees were the best food plants, requiring far less labor in tilling the
> soil, and bearing a larger amount of food for the same ground space; also
> doing much to preserve and enrich the soil.
>
> Due regard had been paid to seasonable crops, and their fruit and nuts,
> grains and berries, kept on almost the year through. (79)

In their agriculture, as in their own reproduction, Herlanders employ eugenic
principles, not scrupling, for example, to drive to extinction a species of moth
that threatens the obernut tree (100–101) and engineering a particularly
beautiful tree species so it will also produce edible seeds. Indeed, the Herlanders learned human eugenics from observing plants, explaining differences
among themselves by "the law of mutation" which "they had found in their
work with plants, and fully proven in their own case" (77). In an analogy reminiscent of Grand's description of Seraph Pratt as a "weed," Gilman comments
that Herland children "compared with the average in our country as the most
perfectly cultivated, richly developed roses compare with—tumbleweeds. Yet
they did not *seem* 'cultivated' at all—it had all become a natural condition"
(72). The Herland women's parthenogenetic production of eugenically superior offspring thus parallels the women's production of a nutritionally superior
"mighty garden." Agriculture in an Eden populated, planned, and planted by
Eves rather than by Adams offers a redemptive model for Ourland.

Ward, like Grand and Gilman, portrays food provision as a civic responsibility for women. She began early, in 1874, when she wrote a pamphlet on
"Plain Facts about Infant Food" for distribution in the Oxford slums. More
practically, she recognized when she opened the "Invalid Children's School" at
the Passmore Edwards Settlement that the standard three halfpennies that
London schoolchildren brought for "dinner money" would not cover the special nutritional needs of her ailing students, who had previously been ex-
empted from attending school on the grounds of ill health. According to her
daughter, "the arrangements for the children's dinners . . . were a subject of
constant interest and delight to Mrs. Ward" (Trevelyan, 135–36). She supple-
mented the meal that the children's money could buy with eggs, cream, hot
meat, fruit, and fresh vegetables—some of which came from the Wards' own
country property (Sutherland, 227). In the face of opposition from the Char-

ity Organization Society, Ward even provided free meals to those who could not afford the dinner money, setting yet another precedent and defending it strenuously in the *Times;* she pointed out that the children at the center were growing physically healthier and performing better intellectually as a result of their healthy lunches. Ward lobbied successfully for the extension of such schools—complete with kitchens and subsidized lunches—throughout London and then throughout England (Trevelyan, 136–41).

Women's civic role in providing food becomes an issue in Ward's fiction, as well. Like *Herland,* two of Mary Ward's last books, *Elizabeth's Campaign*[3] and the posthumously published *Harvest,* portray women in the ordinarily male, public-sphere activities of large-scale agricultural production. Both novels demonstrate Ward's admiration, also expressed in her nonfiction accounts of the Great War in Europe, for the women on the home front who moved from private life into traditionally public masculine activities.[4] Her other war writings portray women in factories and hospitals; these two novels celebrate women's contributions to agriculture. Although the underlying cause—supporting the war—couldn't be more conservative, Ward portrays its manifestation as creating a fundamental social revolution affecting both gender and class.

In *Elizabeth's Campaign,* Elizabeth Bremerton, an Oxford-educated classicist hired as private secretary to Squire Mannering to organize his collection of Greek antiquities, has "got a bit of an organizing gift—like the women who have been doing such fine things in the war" (104), and quickly organizes not just the artifacts but Mannering himself and the entire estate, especially its twelve thousand acres of land. Mannering opposes the war, not as a pacifist but as "an individualist gone mad" (56), or, more accurately, as another landowning Aesthete like Squire Wendover of *Robert Elsmere.* Mannering is "a most excellent scholar" with "a most delicate and unerring taste" who refuses to contribute in any way toward the war, because he resents the "bungling diplomats and 'swashbuckler' politicians" whose war prevents his "long-cherished scheme of exploration in the Greek islands" and excavations in Asia Minor (57, 71, 70). The other members of the household, though patriotic, are helpless against Mannering, but Elizabeth quickly organizes them—behind Mannering's back—into conserving food and resources. This is a purely domestic success. But she also analyzes the estate's larger problems, from a public perspective:

To her trained, practical mind the whole clan seemed by now criminally careless and happy-go-lucky. The gardens were neglected; so was the house; so was the estate. The gardens ought to have been made self-supporting; there were at least a third too many servants in the house; and as for the estate, instead of being a profit-making and food-producing concern, as it should have been, it was a bye-word for bad management and neglected land. She did not pretend to know much about it yet; but what she did know roused her. England was at grips with a brutal foe. The only weapon that could defeat her was famine—the sloth and waste of her own sons. This woman, able, energetic, a lover of her country, could not conceal her scorn for such a fatal incompetence. (73)

Elizabeth uses all her powers of persuasion, with the result that a corrupt and incompetent land agent is replaced, land is cleared and plowed for crops, and a large stand of valuable timber sold for military use, with the profits funding the rebuilding of tenants' cottages. The new land agent, a discharged soldier who lost an arm in the war, is impressed by Elizabeth:

Astonishing, to see a woman taking this kind of lead!—asking these technical questions—as to land, crops, repairs, food production, and the rest. . . . And all through he was struck with her tone of quiet authority—without a touch of boasting or "side," but also without a touch of any mere feminine deference to the male. She was there in the Squire's place, and she never let it be forgotten. Heavens, women had come on during this war! Through the young man's mind there ran a vague and whirling sense of change. (186)

Elizabeth combines nontraditional scholarship with old-fashioned domestic skill, demonstrating that a womanly "organizing gift" not only can make a household run efficiently but can manage a large estate, feed an army, protect a nation, and lead a great change in society as a whole.

In *Elizabeth's Campaign,* a woman is a manager, but the land is owned and worked by men; in *Harvest,* as in Gilman's *Herland,* men are absent, the women self-sufficient. *Harvest* celebrates the Women's Land Army's achievements in bringing in a record harvest in the months prior to the November 1918 armistice. Rachel Henderson, a graduate of Swanley Horticultural College for Women, leases Great End Farm along with her friend and fellow graduate

Janet Leighton, who takes charge of the housekeeping, dairy, and poultry. The novel emphasizes the femininity of the women and the womanliness of their task of providing food to a hungry world, while showing that their work in the international war effort, and the concomitant changes of sensibility and economics, create an entirely new definition of womanly contributions to the public realm.

The book is replete with imagery that juxtaposes the women's feminine and masculine traits. Some of the work on the farm, Janet's in particular, carries fairly traditional gender associations. Janet cooks, cleans, and mends for the household. Her dairy and poultry work, associated as they are with milk and eggs, also represent tasks traditionally delegated to farm women. Maternal images fill the scene in which Rachel is "caressing two little calves whom Jenny was feeding by hand" (91).[5] Moreover, even farming itself, as the provision of food, is portrayed as a naturally feminine activity. Whether or not Ward knew of theories that women invented agriculture, she certainly exploits the long association of agriculture and fecundity with womanhood, with frequent allusions to Demeter. In contrast to the petite heroines who grace some of Ward's novels (Laura Fountain in *Helbeck of Bannisdale* or Elise Delaunay in *The History of David Grieve,* for example), Rachel's beauty is Greek, eugenic even, in its size and strength. But that makes it no less sexually alluring to Rachel's suitor, George Ellesborough: "Her soft brown head, her smile, showing the glint of her white teeth, her eyes, and all the beauty of her young form, in its semi-male dress—they set his blood on fire" (304–5). Indeed, the land girls are beautiful not despite but because of their androgynous dress, exemplified by an early description of Rachel at the evening meal: "Rachel had merely put on a blue overall above her land-worker's dress. But her beautiful head, with its wealth of brown hair, and her face, with its sensuous fulness of cheek and lip, its rounded lines, and lovely colour—like a slightly overblown rose—were greatly set off by the simple folds of blue linen; and her feet and legs, shapely but not small, in their khaki stockings and shoes, completed the general effect of lissom youth" (31).

At the same time, the women's activities are portrayed in terms that emphasize their successful adoption of masculine roles and activities. Agriculture may bear feminine symbolism, but the literal labor requires muscles and skills not traditionally associated with womanhood, such as "'pitching' the sheaves on to the harvest cart" (85). It also entails working with heavy, sometimes dangerous machines—the plow, harrow, reaper, and thresher that are mentioned in the book—under hot and dirty conditions: "Rachel and the girls . . . were all in the high barn, feeding the greedy maw of the threshing machine; a business which strained muscles and backs, and choked noses and throats with infinitesimal particles of oil and the fine flying chaff" (304). This image of "feeding" a hungry, filthy monster, in order to process grain, radically revises the usual imagery of women working together preparing food.

The feminine and masculine imagery echo in the novel's meditation on the relationships between the private and public worlds. Ward repeatedly suggests a Ruskinian opposition of the safe domestic retreat and the threatening, masculine, public world—and then complicates it. In Great End Farm Rachel has intentionally selected "a lonely situation" with "not another house, not even a cottage, anywhere in sight" (11–12). When she learns that the woods surrounding the farm have been commandeered by the government to be cut, she is disturbed by the news, not on account of the scenery, but, she explains, because "I don't like to have a lot of strange men about the farm, . . . especially when I have girls to look after" (21). This response corresponds to Rachel's "shrinking from the ugly or merely physical facts of life, as of one who had suffered some torment in connection with them" (36). References to Theocritus and Virgil (86)—that is, to the pastoral tradition of withdrawal from a corrupt urban world to an idealized rural *locus amoenus*—reinforce this theme. Although Rachel's opportunity to run a farm largely derives from conditions created by the war, for Rachel the farm itself represents retreat from the war: "Rachel was in the mood to feel a certain childish exultation in the plenty of the farm, amid the general rationing. The possession of her seven milch cows, the daily pleasure of the milk, morning and evening, the sight of the rich separated cream, and of the butter as it came fresh from the churn, the growing weight and sleekness of the calves; all these things gave her a warm sense of protection against the difficulties and restrictions of the war" (81–82). As a self-supporting farm, Great End is exempt from government rationing and in that sense removed from public participation, but of course its raison d'être is to share the farm's "plenty" with the public world in its war efforts.

Despite her ignorance of current affairs, Rachel cannot retreat far from the public sphere; on the contrary, her success is defined in the most public ways. It is honored at the Millsborough harvest festival, sponsored by the County Agricultural Committee in honor of the successful harvest and the contribution of the woman land workers. The festival is a large gathering: "All Millsborough, indeed, was in the streets to look at the procession," and the committee "had summoned the land lasses from far and wide" for "speeches in the market-place, and a final march of land girls, boy scouts, and decorated wagons to the old Parish Church, where a service was to be held" (98). In the procession's second wagon stands Rachel, looking stunning in androgynous "full land-dress—tunic, knee-breeches, and leggings" (100). Among the speakers is "a land girl who had played a rousing part in the recruiting campaign of the early summer," a young woman with the presence to speak up, "clearly heard by the crowd," and thus to participate in public discourse. This young woman, representing the spirit of the Woman's Land Army, boasts of "the biggest harvest that England's ever known!—the harvest that's going to beat the Boche" (103). Women's farming is thus represented not merely as their foray into economic independence—abandoning the private domestic sphere for the public marketplace—but as a "public service," mandated by the public sphere (here, the central government), which at this time saw any "private enterprise" aspect of agriculture as subordinate to the public function of feeding the military. Women's job of providing food has thus expanded to the winning of a world war.

To be sure, Ward never loses track of the conflict in Rachel between this public purpose—which becomes more important to her when her American suitor winds up his work harvesting timber and volunteers for active duty on the front—and her private preoccupations. Indeed, Rachel is "crassly ignorant about many current affairs," "could not have given . . . the simplest historical outline of the great war" and "was quite uncertain whether Lloyd George or Asquith were Prime Minister" (69). Even on November 10, the eve of the armistice, as Janet prays for peace, Rachel remains strangely indifferent: "But her own heart seemed dead and dumb. She could not free it from its load of personal care; she could not feel the patriotic emotion which had suddenly seized on Janet" (238).

In fact, Rachel is not just indifferent to the war: she could be perceived as coldly benefiting from it. Ward has captured the complex and contradictory relationships between public and private gains and losses in time of war, for she shows that by outgrowing the old limits on what they, as women, could contribute to the public food supply, Rachel and her peers not only perform a genuine public function but also potentially challenge the status of the men whose places they are filling so well. Early in the novel, Rachel muses, "*The War!* She felt towards it as to some distant force, which, so far as she personally was concerned, was a force for good. Owing to the war, farming was booming all over England, and she was in the boom, taking advantage of it" (38). Immediately upon having this thought, Rachel is "ashamed." As she remembers her bailiff's wounded son and imagines others like him, the tears come into her eyes. Ward deals with a very real phenomenon, described by Sandra Gilbert and Susan Gubar as a major source of the antagonism toward women felt by male combatants and veterans: "[W]hen their menfolk went off to the trenches to be literally and figuratively shattered, the women on the home front literally and figuratively rose to the occasion and replaced them in farms and factories." Rachel exemplifies this other conflict between public and private, "the exuberance with which these women settled into 'the Amazonian countries created by the war'" (Gilbert and Gubar, 271). In *Harvest,* the women have come into their own and have shown themselves as competent as the men, if not more so, as is the case of the young woman on the Harvest Festival platform: "She's Farmer Green's girl, out Ralstone way. Ee says there ain't nothing she can't do. Ee don't want no men while he's got 'er. They offered him soldiers, and ee wouldn' have 'em" (103–4).

Women's economic displacement of men is paralleled by another public sphere gain for women: the vote. In 1918, shortly before the events portrayed in *Harvest,* Parliament rewarded women's contributions to the war effort by granting national suffrage to women over thirty (a group that includes the thirty-two-year-old Janet but not twenty-seven-year-old Rachel). Although Ward continued her public opposition to women's suffrage through the final battle in the House of Lords, she privately admitted to a fellow leader of the antisuffrage movement that "the war has changed so many things" and that to concede the vote would be far less dangerous in 1918 than it would have been before (qtd. in Harrison, 205). Ward had earlier argued that women should not vote in national elections because women did not participate in the national defense and because Parliamentary decisions require knowledge of matters such as agriculture, heavy industry, and finance, which she considered to belong solely to men's sphere. Ward's war reporting in *England's Effort* and elsewhere, and her several war novels, including *Elizabeth's Campaign* and *Harvest,* with its "harvest that's going to beat the Boche," amply demonstrate her recognition of women's important contributions in all these areas. In *Harvest,* written in 1919, when woman's suffrage was an irrevocable fact, Ward makes the connection between women's new achievements and their enfranchisement, in a dialogue between two elderly laborers, Peter Halsey and Joseph Batts, who provide a sort of Greek chorus at the novel's beginning. As Mr. Halsey remarks, "Well, these be funny times to live in, when the women go ridin' astride an' hay-balin,' an' steam-ploughin,' an' the Lord knows what. . . . An' now they've got the vote" (3). Ward seems, if anything, to celebrate the competence of women to decide independently:

> "Well, onyways the women is all in a flutter about the votin','" said Halsey, lighting his pipe with old hands that shook. "An' there's chaps already coomin' round lookin' out for it."
>
> "You bet there is!" was Batts's amused reply. "But they'll take their toime, will the women. 'Don't you try to hustle-bustle me like you're doin','" says my missus sharp-like to a Labour chap as coom round lasst week, 'cos yo' won't get nothin' by it.' And she worn't no more forthcomin' to the Conservative man when ee called."
>
> "Will she do what *you* tell her, Batts?" asked Halsey, with an evident interest in the question.
>
> "Oh, Lord, no!" said Batts placidly, "Shan't try." (4)

Batts and Halsey's exchange, which subtly disavows the arguments that women would be subject to manipulation by party operatives or by their husbands, prefigures the novel's portrayal of a world in which women not only act independently but, if anything, dominate men.

Batts and Halsey's discussion of the vote immediately precedes their musings on a related issue, one that shows that Ward recognized that the radical changes wrought on gender relations by the war corresponded to changes in class relationships:

> Prices were high, but they would go down some day; and wages would not go down. The old men could not have told exactly why this confidence lay so deep in them; but there it was, and it seemed to give a strange new stability and even dignity to life. Their sons were fighting; and they had the

> normal human affection for their sons. They wished the war to end. But, after all, there was something to be said for the war. They—old Peter Halsey and old Joe Batts—were more considered and more comfortable than they would have been before the war. And it was the consideration more even than the comfort that warmed their hearts. (6)

The women and the aged farm laborers share in common a previous disempowerment, on account of sex in the one case, class in the other. Indeed, Rachel raises wages not merely in response to supply and demand or government mandate (she "raised her wages before the award of the Wages Board" [102]), but as a matter of principle, as she explains when Lady Alicia, a local aristocrat, complains of what she sees as "the awful—the *wicked*—wages" (101). Lady Alicia in turn recounts the conversation in scandalized tones: "It was high time, she said, that the labourer should have enough to live on—*decently;* really thrown the word at you" (102). Lady Alicia dismisses Rachel and Janet as "dreadful Socialists!" but Ward suggests that the partners are simply enthusiastic participants in a larger social upheaval that Ellesborough describes: "We're supposed only to be fighting a war. . . . But all the time there's revolution going on beside it—all over the world! . . . All I know is that the people who work with their hands are going to get a bit of their own back from the people who work with their heads—or their cheque-books" (130–31). And, one might add, from the people like Lady Alicia, who don't work at all. Rachel's private business decisions on her farm thus inevitably participate, whether she intends them to or not, in enormous systemic changes in both class and gender relations, with broad historic implications for the public sphere.

"Six Mortal Hours": Gilman and Cooking

Six hours a day the woman spends on food!
Six mortal hours a day . . .
. . . .
Six mortal hours a day to handle food,—
Prepare it, serve it, clean it all away,—
With allied labors of the stove and tub,
The pan, the dishcloth, and the scrubbing-brush.
Developing forever in her brain

The power to do this work in which she lives;
While the slow finger of Heredity
Writes on the forehead of each living man,
Strive as he may,"His mother was a cook!"

("Six Hours a Day," 1–2, 18–26)

For visions of the relationship between food preparation and widespread systemic challenges to the social order, one need look no further, of course, than the writings of Charlotte Perkins Gilman. Unlike Grand and Ward, Gilman wrote of food preparation from a position of extensive, lifelong, firsthand knowledge and experience. Anyone who reads *The Diaries of Charlotte Perkins Gilman* must necessarily be struck by the proportion of entries devoted to food and food preparation, beginning with the second entry, for 3 January 1879,[6] in which the eighteen-year-old Charlotte Perkins reports, "Enter into a solemn contest with Miss Salisbury & Blanche Vaughn to which of us makes the best bread" (6). We never learn who won this contest, but we do know that Gilman got plenty of practice at bread making, an activity reported in literally dozens of entries throughout the journals, along with the preparation of (among other items) biscuits, griddle cakes, peas, potatoes, soup, cod, chops, roast mutton, steak, chicken, gingerbread, cake, blancmange, and the occasional pie. Many of these meals turn out "delicious," "perfectly delectable," or simply "*Good!*" Not surprisingly, the bulk of the entries about cooking appear in 1884–85, the first year of her doomed marriage to Walter Stetson, and one cannot help noticing that menus stand where the accounts of art projects had been in earlier entries and where lists of writing projects would emerge in journals of later years. (By contrast, for the first six years of her second marriage, to Houghton Gilman, Gilman, her husband, and her daughter enjoyed a "home without a kitchen" in a New York boardinghouse [*Living*, 283].) We know from Helen Campbell's testimony that Gilman could "cook to a turn" ("Famous Persons," 7), and Gilman recounts with humor her systematic experiments as a young bride determined to perfect her cooking.

But while Gilman herself may in fact have been a good cook, cooking, generally speaking, is portrayed negatively in her nonfiction and poetry. The problems that Gilman identifies with private preparation of food form the foundation of a large body of her writings and a set of wide-ranging theories about modern social organization and the ways it should be reformed, beginning in the kitchen. Throughout these writings, Gilman objects to home cooking on several grounds: it is inefficient in terms of both time and resources; it yields low-quality food; the kitchen detracts from the physical comfort and efficiency of the individual home; and private cooking hinders the development of human culture and thus of human evolution. Yet if Gilman's nonfiction focuses on the problems, her fiction, typically, frequently provides exempla for solutions. Here, Gilman provides overtly or implicitly utopian visions of worlds in which professionalized cooking produces social progress and even "perfectly delectable" meals.

One of Gilman's main objections to private cooking is its inefficiency. Cooking, says Gilman, "takes up half the working time of half the population of the world" (*The Home*, 95), or, as she frequently calculated, six hours daily, time better spent on other activities. In the chapter on "Home-Cooking" in *The Home: Its Work and Influence,* Gilman calculates that the cooking for 200 families with one cook per family of five (an estimated 1,000 people) consumed 1,200 working hours a day; but if a block of 200 apartments were served by a single central kitchen, the cooking could be completed by only thirty cooks, for a savings of at least 920 working hours daily—probably more, since the more organized specialists could complete their work in less than six hours (133). Separate kitchens entail tremendous duplication of appliances and cooking utensils, and require more space and fuel. Food is more expensive when purchased in small lots at retail, and more of it goes to waste; furthermore, Gilman argues, its quality is inferior: the individual, untrained housewife is more likely to be sold adulterated or spoiled food than would be a trained, professional chef. Because of the housewives' ignorance, not only are filth diseases and other food-borne illnesses harming the population, but the kitchens in individual homes create dirt that attracts flies and other disease-bearing vermin.

In *Women and Economics,* Gilman acknowledges that the situation is unlikely to change so long as "the sexuo-economic relation" of the sexes makes women economically dependent on men, who demand private cooks. The principle that "the way to a man's heart is through his stomach" insures that women will cook to please rather than to nourish, thus fostering a culture of self-indulgence rather than of social responsibility. Overall human development is thus retarded, because people are ill-nourished and intemperate, and because half the population remains in a primitive condition of unspecialized labor rather than evolving toward increasing specialization: as Gilman says in the poem "Six Hours a Day," "[T]he slow finger of Heredity / Writes on the forehead of each living man, / . . . 'His mother was a cook!'" Gilman calls our continuing irrational and ultimately antisocial and primitive attachment to private cooking "kitchen-mindedness": "Being kitchen-minded we cannot see that health is a public concern; that the feeding of our people is one of the most vital factors in their health, and that the private kitchen with its private cook is not able to keep the public well" ("Kitchen-Mindedness," 10).

Recent feminist discussions of recipe sharing, whether in community cookbooks or more informally, have stressed what Susan Leonardi calls "the social context of recipe sharing—a loose community of women that crosses the social barriers of class, race, and generation" (342). Ann Romines sees an "empowering heritage" of creative authorship in the community cookbook's signed recipes (76). Yet Gilman, despite participating in similar communities of shared recipes,[7] rejects this traditionalist approach to community as insufficiently scientific and progressive. Broadening her point of view from "community" to nation and race, she writes, "A million women are making bread as their mothers made it. How many women are trying to lift the standard of bread-making for their country? How many even know the difference in nutriment and digestibility between one bread and other? They do not think 'bread,' but only 'my bread'" ("Kitchen-Mindedness," 11). Gilman repudiates these approaches, adopting instead the "scientific" approach to cooking advocated by the American home economics movement and its allies in such enterprises as the Boston Cooking School.

In the short story "A Partnership," the exemplary protagonist, Margie Haven, had begun "lifting the standard of bread-making" early in her marriage. Her husband is a flour dealer in "a Middle Western city in a famous wheat district," and "when they were 'changing girls' in her young, less experienced days, she had often heard Gerald complain that such first-class flour should go to make such fourth-class food" (258). So Margie, "[s]purred by her husband's criticisms," had "perfected herself in the not too abstruse art of bread-making, and took great pride in her 'homemade' rolls, her white and graham and whole-wheat loaves" (258). Later, Margie learns that "baker's bread" in Europe is far superior to that in the United States, and so

> there had grown in her mind a determination to do something to lift that standard.

> "The lady is the loaf-giver, they are always telling us. We ought to give better loaves then. If the man can't we must."
>
> That is why Mrs Gerald Haven went into the baking business. (258)

This passage conveys several crucial points. First, Margie has taken literally what Ruskin had meant more metaphorically, and, in doing so, has overthrown his larger premise, that the sexes should not compete and that the home should be a "shelter" from the public world of business. Nevertheless, Gilman does treat "loaf giving" as quintessentially female, for, as Gerald observes, "After all if breadmaking was not a woman's business, what was?" (260). Second, and consistent with Gilman's philosophy of social progress, Margie enters business not solely for the pleasure of the work—though indeed it is a source of "growing joy" for this woman whose children are now grown (259), but for the good of her country. In the spirit of literary housekeeping, woman's domestic expertise thus serves the broader public.

Gilman's account of Margie Haven's growing company (eventually a "partnership" with her husband, when the partner in his flour dealership absconds with its funds) is a recipe for turning a domestic activity into a business. Margie starts the pointedly named New Home Bakery small, selling through a "woman's exchange"—a favorite type of institution for Gilman—and building business through word of mouth, "quite naturally and safely, on the advertisement that follows the pleased customer." As sales increase, she opens a small shop and expands the merchandise to include "her own especial gingerbread, the 'hot water' gingerbread, smooth, sweet, dark, and as porous as a sponge. Also her own sponge cake, real sponge cake that, soaring aloft on unaided eggs" (258–59).[8] Gilman provides vivid melt-in-your-mouth details here to establish Margie as a particularly good cook—lifting the standard. Gilman then implicitly contrasts Margie with the mediocre average and points out the advantage to even the best cooks of access to professionally prepared, high-quality baked goods: "Almost any woman is glad to avoid the baking if she is sure of getting as good and as reliable products outside; and the New Home Bakery furnished better goods than most of its patrons were able to make" (259).

For Gilman it is only a beginning that a few midwestern housewives can buy good bread. The influence of Margie's business reaches well beyond her immediate neighborhood, because she shares her experiences with others: initially she gives a paper at her women's club on "Bread-making, Domestic and Foreign"; then she addresses local cooking classes, which were important tools of the burgeoning turn-of-the-century domestic science movement. As her business grows, Margie is "asked far and wide to give 'Bread Talks' to schools and clubs" (260). One subject of those talks—and one secret of her success— is Mrs. Haven's management approach. She always treats her workers with respect and fairness, and with concern for their welfare. Her business begins with "paying her excellent cook an extra price for extra work," and when she needs to hire a second cook, Margie trains her personally (258). As the business grows into its own building with several employees, "Clean comfortable women worked for reasonable hours, and rested under the trees in their leisure moments" (260). Gilman shows that providing pleasant working conditions not only helps the workers but improves the product and even enhances sales:

> A Social Service lecturer spoke in the town on labor conditions, and disclosed the revolting circumstances in which so much of the baker's bread is made. She was stirred to the depths by this revelation and her ambition took new shape.
>
> With the profits of three years' work and the base of a steadily widening patronage she opened a Model Bakery. She remembered a sign she had seen over a little London dairy: "The Inspection of the Public is Invited," and invited it here. . . .
>
> One girl was detailed to take visitors through the place, and the exquisite shining cleanliness, the glass and marble and nickel fittings, the big gas ovens, only heated for the actual hours of baking, the white-capped, white-uniformed workers, all had their effect on the purchasers. (259, 260)

This description, with its emphasis on cleanliness, shows that a well-appointed bakery can avoid the sanitary problems that were one of Gilman's primary objections to private cooking; indeed, the very public quality insures the food's safety, and that, in turn, further increases sales.

The effects extend further still, as "one of the pleasantest results was an emulous improvement in other bakeries. That kind of competition is indeed 'the life of trade.' Everywhere in the town the standard of bread and of bread-making was raised by this woman's honest work" (260). As the Havens start new branches in neighboring towns and cities, Gilman promises that these same good effects—higher standards of bread and breadmaking—will follow. The Havens' bakery echoes pioneering home economist Ellen Richards's plan for the New England Kitchen, an establishment in which Boston working people could purchase low-cost sanitary and nutritious foods, including soups and breads, prepared in the open where customers could watch. The establishment was designed as an educational enterprise; scientific experiments in cookery would be carried out and the poor would witness and learn "principles of exact cookery" (Shapiro, 140). Like Richards, Gilman believed that efforts by a small number of skilled housekeepers who take their skills and product into the public sphere could bring about widespread social improvement. From a drag on social development, cooking could become a spur to social progress.

This point is made on an even larger scale in the novella *What Diantha Did,* in which one woman's basing a business on her housekeeping skills helps reorganize an entire community. Gilman emphasizes that although the "deadly Average" woman (*The Home,* 141) probably has no gift for housekeeping, Diantha Bell is far from average. The novel begins by portraying her deftness in her mother's kitchen, where she sets the table "with light steps and no clatter of dishes," prepares biscuits almost by instinct and without spilling a speck of flour; then "Diantha put her pan of white puff-balls into the oven, sliced a quantity of smoked beef in thin shavings, and made white sauce for it, talking the while as if those acts were automatic" (25, 26). When Diantha takes her first job at Isabel Porne's, Mr. Porne comes home not to the ill-cooked, much-delayed dinners his wife has been providing, but to food that is "well-cooked and well-served, and the attendance showed an intelligent appreciation of when people want things and how they want them" (82). Such descriptions show Diantha's expertise, in contrast to the fumbling failures of more ordinary women; moreover, by describing improvements Diantha brings these individual households, Gilman invites female readers to wish for similar benefits.

Among these benefits is the money Diantha saves the Pornes, despite the relatively high rate she charges, because she knows how to shop wisely (Gilman lists the costs of foodstuffs). Very soon Isabel marvels,

> "I don't even order the meals now, unless I want something especial. She keeps a calendar of what we've had to eat, and what belongs to the time of year, prices and things. When I used to ask her to suggest (one does, you

know; it is so hard to think up a variety), she'd always be ready with an idea, or remind me that we had had so and so two days before, till I asked her if she'd like to order, and she said she'd be willing to try, and now I just sit down to the table without knowing what's going to be there." (96–97)

Diantha supplies a specialist's expertise on seasons and prices—a regular home economics curriculum's worth—along with the imagination of a knowledge-able chef, with many recipes at her command. Nevertheless, Gilman knows that objections will be raised, so she attributes them to one of the book's less pleasant characters, a conservative woman aptly named Mrs. Dankshire, then allows Isabel to refute her:

> "But I should think that would interfere with your sense of freedom," said Mrs. Ellen A. Dankshire. "A woman should be mistress of her own household."
> "Why I am! I order whenever I specially want anything. But she really does it more—more scientifically. She has made a study of it. And the bills are very much lower."
> "Well, I think you are the luckiest woman alive!" sighed Mrs. Ree. "I wish I had her!" (97)

Mrs. Dankshire's argument is a classic appeal to privacy, in the sense of indi-vidual freedom from interference. Gilman's answer is twofold: first, on partic-ular occasions when the individual needs to be in control, there will be no interference; and second, the "freedom" in question is not as valuable as as-sumed, for a trained—"scientific"—outsider will produce more satisfactory results in both quality and price. But perhaps the strongest answer to Mrs. Dankshire is Mrs. Ree's heartfelt "I wish I had her!"

Gilman's larger point, of course, is that Mrs. Ree *can* have Diantha once Diantha "goes public" with her food delivery service and other housekeeping businesses. Thanks to the backing of the local women's club, investment by the wealthy widow Weatherstone, and agreement by a local grocer to supply food at wholesale, Diantha opens a "Business Men's Lunch" (166), which thrives be-cause it provides inexpensive but excellent food and drink: sandwiches made with "perfect bread, excellent butter" and "flavorsome" fillings (167). Mrs. Weatherstone next invests in a delivery truck and specially designed carriers for delivering food, drink, and utensils, so that cold food is served cold, hot food hot, and all is delicious. Diantha's soup—she provides a different kind each day of the month—inspires dinner guests to "keep silent in supreme contentment while the soup lasted" (196). Everyone says, "I don't see how she does it!" (198), but Gilman lets the reader see that it's simply good business sense. And as in "A Partnership," a successful business will grow ever more successful: Diantha's first efforts spawn a large and flourishing complex of kitchenless homes and apartments, and her growing international fame assures readers that beginning in one efficient kitchen, Diantha has created a worldwide movement. Gilman's theories harness capitalism's economic "private sector" to eliminate the "private kitchen" and thus produce far-reaching public improvements.

The "baby utopia" *Moving the Mountain* describes a future world—1940 America—that has undergone a complete transition to kitchenless homes and "great food furnishing companies," supervised by local Food Boards and a National Food Bureau (71). The change began, we are told, when "most of the women, and some of the men, began to seriously study the food question, both from a hygienic and an economic standpoint" (66). As a result of their study, "they recognized at last that it was their duty to feed the world—and that it was miserably done! So they took hold" (65). In this novel, women in particular take it upon themselves to reform the domestic in the best interests of their families—redefined as "the world." In the new system, the "best scientific knowledge is used to study food values, to improve old materials and develop new ones" (71); "We have learned very definitely what people ought not to eat; and it is not only a punishable but a punished offense, to make or sell improper food stuffs" (66). Because food is "bought and prepared by people who know how" (66)—specialists, that is—it is not only hygienic and nutritious but delicious. "Grub's better, by square miles" remarks an old sailor (48), and the narrator takes three servings of a casserole that "gave forth so savory a steam as fairly to make my mouth water," and praises a "crisp and toothsome bread," a "suave, cool salad," the "most delicate little cakes" and other culinary triumphs (63). The world of kitchenless homes, Gilman assures her readers, not only will bring us inexpensive, "scientifically" prepared, and "savory" food, but will hasten utopia as well. For Gilman, the reorganization of bread baking and of all food production, a reorganization to be spearheaded by women, is an essential step in the social evolution of the entire human race. Although the old "sexuo-

economic relation" of the sexes created the "kitchen-mindedness" that has op-
pressed women, by keeping them in the kitchen, and suppressed human evolution, Gilman shows that women are particularly well qualified to take charge
of the scientific reform of cooking. Women's "business" of bread making is thus
transformed from a drag on human progress to the yeast that helps humanity
to rise.

"A Variety of Good Solid Food": Sarah Grand and the Art of Cooking

Gilman's friend and colleague Helen Campbell described cooking as an art,
but immediately acknowledged,

> At present, to be sure, there is little sign of this art sense among our cooks;
> but what do we expect? We may find philosophers among servants, but we
> do not find artists. The artist is always free. If we had a hired poet or musi-
> cian in every household, or if our poetry and music were practiced only by
> the overworked and uneducated housewife, poetry and music would be to
> us only what cooking is now, an ill-performed duty, a source of low pleas-
> ure and much evil. (*Household Economics,* 180)

Although Gilman suggests a kind of artistry in Diantha's creations, she seems
more interested in the science of cooking—and in the current state of cooking
as "ill-performed duty." As we saw in chapter 1, she was more inclined to reverse the metaphor and portray literature as "world-food." For perspectives on
cooking itself as an art, we need to look instead to Sarah Grand's writings, in
which the preparing, eating, and sharing of food, including bread, are linked to
the public sphere through repeated analogies between food and art.

Just as Grand distrusted the Aesthetic movement's creed of art for art's
sake, so she deprecated taking pleasure in food purely for pleasure's sake rather
than eating for health's sake. Grand's portrayals of eating convey an ambivalent
attitude toward the pleasures of eating. On the one hand, in "The Human
Quest," a lecture whose subtitle concerns "the art of happiness," Grand quite
explicitly commends enjoying food: "The strongest bent of our nature is to
pursue happiness and to avoid pain; and every healthy function of mind and
body helps the endeavour. It is a pleasure to eat when we are hungry, to drink
when we are thirsty" (157). But Grand distinguishes such happiness from

"amusement" or "excitement," which sacrifices permanent peace for a "momentary gratification" that "endangers the two great sources of happiness: health of body and strength of mind" (175).

In fact, the only people whose pure enjoyment of eating Grand seems to condone are children, whose unabashed pleasure in food she treats with affectionate humor. The Tenor in *The Heavenly Twins,* observing the "Boy's" middle-of-the-night pleasure in frying large quantities of eggs and potatoes, reflects on "the wonderful provision of nature which endows the growing animal not only with such strong instincts of self-preservation, but with the power to gratify them, and to take itself off at the same time and be happy in so doing, thus saving those who have outgrown these natural proclivities from some of their less agreeable consequences" (391). This passage emphasizes the wholesomeness of "natural" juvenile appetite, because it contributes to "self-preservation," while clearly indicating that it is a stage to be "outgrown," lest there be "consequences." The passage also explains the clandestine quality of Grand's portrayals of children's eating: Angelica and Diavolo cheerfully stealing food from their grandfather in midnight kitchen raids; Babs Kingconstance demanding food from her neighbor in the middle of the night, and secretly raiding her mother's kitchen and henhouse; Beth Caldwell poaching rabbits.[9] Their pleasure in clandestine eating "saves" adults from the temptation to join them.

But in adults, such clandestine eating—and thus the animal-like pure pleasure in food—suggests arrested development at the very least; at worst, there will be "consequences." Thus in *The Heavenly Twins,* the hungry "Boy" turns out to be the grown woman Angelica, and her unrestrained eating turns out to have helped impoverish the Tenor, thus contributing to his tragic death. Remorse over her thoughtless actions (actions symbolized by her eating) leads her to reassess her behavior and her marriage. The more mature Angelica that we see in the novel's final pages and in *The Beth Book* no longer filches food in midnight raids.

The consequences of seeking food merely for pleasure's sake are at the center of *Babs the Impossible,* in which the upwardly mobile Mr. Jellybond Tinney, having assessed Mrs. Kingconstance's wealth and possessions and having judged marriage to her as the best means to his entering Parliament, sets about to win her by manipulating her immature attitude toward food. Since the way to Mrs. Kingcontance's heart is certainly through her stomach, Jellybond cooks for her.

As a good student of what folklorists call "foodways," he realizes that the effect of a "food event" depends as much on time, place, and participants as on the actual menu. He thus invites Mrs. Kingconstance to an isolated cottage for a clandestine "picnic" of his own preparing. He orchestrates an "adventure" in which the two abandon their carriage and send on the servants, in order to conceal their retreat to a "little house deep in the forest" hidden behind a privet hedge (245). Inside, the atmosphere is dark and richly colored, the light entering through diamond-shaped panes. Before she so much as smells the food, Mrs. Kingconstance begins "to thrill" and becomes "flighty and giggly" (245). Here, legitimate, healthy enjoyment of food is subordinated to childish, clandestine "excitement." Indeed, "[t]hey both knew that the cooking, cordial, cigarettes, and coffee would have quite a different flavor when they could be had without difficulty; and . . . life would again become as insipid as exercise on a wooden horse" (253). This is a perspective on both food and matrimony that Grand, who believed that "marriage is the most perfect state," completely disavowed.

The description of Mr. Jellybond's food preparation emphasizes that this is not merely cooking, but art. He explicitly associates his cooking with art and with France—the country Grand and others associated with the Aesthetic movement as well as with the "scientific" methods of literary naturalism. Jellybond explains, "I have a laboratory in my own house where I pursue the science and art of *la haute cuisine*" (248). For the picnic he has assembled from his aesthetic laboratory "several plated pannikins and a spirit lamp," a sort of miniaturized, aestheticized kitchen. With great ceremony, "Mr. Jellybond peeped into the pannikins, then he lighted the lamp, and then began to stir and beat and watch with the absorbed interest of an artist in his work." The results, Jellybond calls "dainties" (247). Employing what folklorist Amy Shuman has called "the rhetoric of portions," Jellybond composes a series of miniature servings to titillate the palate: "Mrs. Kingconstance took a morsel of each, and loved the morsel as she ate it; and, while waiting for the next course, discussed its merits as a morsel with more intelligence than she was wont to bring to the discussion of any other matter. Yet very little was said. When the senses are satisfied the mind has but scant appeal" (258). As Jellybond describes his ideal of "Paris and *la haute cuisine*," "Each *plat* has its own aesthetic value" (109). The focus is not on nourishment, not on conversation and the mind, but purely on enhancing sensory pleasure.

Grand rejects this exclusive focus on food's aesthetic appeal as unhealthy. Mrs. Kingconstance's corpulence so inhibits her ability to move that when Jellybond first invites her to the forest picnic, he doubts her "little feet" can support her (244). Moreover, Grand's equating the degenerative effects of aestheticizing food with the "degeneracy" of the Aesthetic movement in art is demonstrated by her use of the same language to describe Mrs. Kingconstance's lifestyle that she would later use to describe that of Col Drinden, the Oscar Wilde–like poet who calls himself "Joyday Flowers" in *The Winged Victory*. Mrs. Kingconstance, Grand observes, was responsible for her surroundings, "but the luxury about her was in turn responsible for what Mrs. Kingconstance was becoming. She was already more ample than a woman of thirty-eight need be in active life. Not that she was fat, but fat was threatening. At present she was only just full-blown; but she *lolled* too much on luxurious cushions, she tasted every morsel of her food too scrupulously when it was specially to her liking—which it generally was—and she cultivated content to an extreme that was dangerous" (8; emphasis added). Significantly, "loll" reappears in Grand's description of Col's rooms, whose decoration, we are told, was influenced by the "usages" of "degenerates": "The deep, springy, softly padded easy-chairs were made to recline in; the broad divan piled high with big down cushions covered with soft satin, to *loll* upon" (*Winged*, 313; emphasis added). As I have noted, the word "loll" indicates that lazy Col is no "use in his day," as Dr. Galbraith of *The Beth Book* would say, and the same could be said of Mrs. Kingconstance, obsessed with food to the point of jeopardizing both her own health and the safety of her children, whose welfare she subordinates to her gastronomic pleasures.

Heather Evans, in her examination of eating in Grand's *Babs the Impossible*, makes an excellent case that "Grand associates feminine powerlessness, dependence, and oppression with a woman's inability to satisfy the needs of her body for nourishment and pleasure, while she celebrates women who acknowledge and address their own appetites without compromising their womanly duties" (138). But Mrs. Kingconstance's failing is not simply that she is selfish and obsessed with her appetite, as Evans observes, though these are indeed her faults. Grand's rejection of Mrs. Kingconstance's sensuality—and of the culinary arts that arouse that sensuality—is part of Grand's larger rejection of Aestheticism, pleasure for pleasure's sake.

The analogy between food and art was a favorite with Grand, who emphasized "solidity" in both. In *Adnam's Orchard*, for example, Ursula Pratt observes that "a good deal of heartburning and bitterness might be laid to the score of art," suggesting a type of spiritual indigestion arising from Aestheticism. She continues with an analogy reminiscent of the "dainties" fed to Mrs. Kingconstance in *Babs the Impossible*: "Personally I cannot see any good in art except as a means to an end. To make art the great object of life is like trying to live on the *hors d'oeuvres* handed round as an introduction to dinner. They are delicious, and wholesome, too, I dare say, in their proper proportion and place; but the body must have a mixed diet to live on, or it loses its health, and so does the mind. A variety of good solid food is essential to the well-being of both" (450–51). "Dainties" for dainties' sake are unhealthy for body, mind, and spirit. Similarly, Dr. Galbraith in *The Beth Book* comments, "The mind craves for nourishment; and the extraordinary success of books in which any attempt, however imperfect, is made to provide food for thought, as distinguished from those which merely offer matter to distract the attention, bears witness, it seems to me, to the involuntary effort which is always in progress to procure it" (372). Shortly thereafter, Dr. Galbraith explicitly distinguishes such "nourishing" writing from that of "the stylists" (374), which was Grand's term for the Aesthetes: "But above everything, mind that you are not misled by the cant of art if you have anything special to say. If a writer would be of use in his day, and not merely an amuser of the multitude, he must learn that right thinking, right feeling, and knowledge are more important than art" (375).

Thus it is not surprising that when Beth, the "woman of genius," cooks, she makes "good solid food" that is simultaneously tasty and nourishing. As a child, Beth befriends the family maid-of-all-work, who has a "talent for fiction" and tells "thrilling" stories in exchange for Beth's assistance with her work (134, 122). From Harriet, who was formerly a kitchen servant, Beth learns cooking skills: "from cleaning a fish and trussing a fowl to making barley-broth and puff pastry" (123). Grand thus links Beth's storytelling and cooking from the start. Beth's cooking achievements are all the more notable because of her mother's reluctance to impart housekeeping skills to her daughters: "With regard to Beth's cooking, it is remarkable that, although Mrs. Caldwell herself had suffered all through her married life for want of proper training in household matters, she never attempted to have her own daughters better taught. On the contrary, she had forbidden Beth to do servant's work, and objected most strongly to her cooking, until she found how good it was" (175). In addition to the tasty meals Beth prepares from poached rabbits and from the fish she catches, she also sometimes mixes up a bread pudding from discarded breakfast crusts: she "steeped them in hot milk in a pie-dish, beat them up with an egg, a little butter, sugar, currants, and candied peel, and some nutmeg grated" (196). All these recipes, somewhat ironic from an author who could not cook, emphasize the seemingly autobiographical Beth's kitchen talents.

But the cooking given the most emphasis in *The Beth Book* is Beth's cooking for Arthur Brock when he is ill: true "sickroom cookery," accentuating the point that food is primarily for health. As Arthur recovers from rheumatic fever under his neighbor's care, he proposes to try the "Salisbury" treatment, a regimen devised by Dr. J. H. Salisbury and promoted by Mrs. Elma Stuart, whose book *What Must I Do to Get Well? and How Am I To Keep So?* Arthur apparently owns, as he refers Beth to "a little work on the subject among my books" (505). About a year before the publication of *The Beth Book,* Grand interviewed Mrs. Stuart for *The Humanitarian.* In the interview, Grand lavishes praise on the Salisbury treatment, which she credits with curing a kinsman's asthma, and which, in this interview alone, Mrs. Stuart identifies as a cure for at least eight ailments, including cancer. The Salisbury treatment involved drinking four pints of hot water daily, at precise intervals, punctuated by a diet that at first consisted solely of beef that is "finely minced by sending it through a machine three times," then made into "cakes" and "grilled well through, lightly on both sides" (Stuart, 31–32)—that is, hamburger. The Salisbury recipe operated on principles congenial to turn-of-the-century ideas about nutrition, as it was supposedly highly "digestible." (At that time, both vitamins and the value of fiber had yet to be discovered, so fresh fruits and vegetables were viewed with suspicion.) In contrast to Mrs. Kingconstance's variety of aestheticized "morsels," the Salisbury diet is bland and unvaried, but "solid."

If food is for health, then fasting would seem to be nearly as unacceptable as overeating, but Grand suggests that in some circumstances self-denial can be admirable. In her analysis of food consumption in *Babs the Impossible,* Heather Evans interprets Ally Spice as representing an angelic, self-sacrificing model of womanhood that Grand rejects (Evans, 144). To be sure, poor, foolish Miss Spice hardly represents a role model, but I would argue that her willingness to entertain her wealthy neighbors when she cannot afford bread for herself comments mainly on her neighbors' greed and Ally's inability to distinguish worthy objects of generosity from unworthy ones, for in other books Grand presents similar sacrifices as admirable. For example, Lena Kedlock in *Adnam's Orchard* recounts that the nuns at her convent school withheld food from students as punishment. Lena used to steal food for another girl, less strong than she, but Lena abstained from eating the food herself, as penance for stealing. To be sure, in *The Beth Book,* Grand shows that Beth is merely being exploited when, "in order to indulge" her husband, "and keep the bills down besides, she went without herself; and he never noticed her self-denial" (340). Since the self-indulgent Dan—labeled by Beth's friends a "plausible hog"—married Beth for her money, steals her savings, and provides her an inadequate allowance, he hardly deserves her sacrifice. But when Beth pawns her possessions in order to feed minced beef and buttered toast to the convalescent Arthur Brock, while she "lived principally on the crusts she cut off the toast" (507), it is idealized as the "homiest time" that Arthur has had in England or that Beth has had since her aunt's death, and is explicitly contrasted with Beth's marriage: "Now that she had some one she could respect and care for dependent on her, whose every look and word expressed appreciation of her devotion, the time never hung heavily on her hands, as it used to do in the married days that had been so long in the living" (504). In the one situation, Beth's sacrifice only abets exploitation by Dan, who would be healthier eating less of the rich food on which he gorges himself, and who neither notices nor much cares that Beth does not eat. In the other situation, there is mutual love and affection; moreover, Arthur, who is unaware that his own money is gone, genuinely needs the simple, nourishing food, yet would have refused it had he realized that Beth was sacrificing herself. Indeed, on one occasion, Arthur inquires why she does not eat and is satisfied only when she claims to have dined already.

The economics of this situation also point to the class implications of eating and loaf giving in Grand's books. In *The Beth Book,* loaf giving is actually buttered-toast giving and rabbit poaching, as Beth goes to great lengths to feed hungry loved ones. Her own experiences of physical privation enhance her compassion for even hungrier people, as she angrily watches starving children scraping up the rice thrown at a fashionable wedding, "cursing the greedy rich who wallow in luxury while children starve in the streets" (507). Babs Kingconstance does give literal loaves, in a basket "crammed with good things" stolen from her mother: chicken, tongue, pâté de foie gras, dinner rolls, butter, tea, cakes, and sugar that she gathers for Miss Spice whenever she visits (*Babs,* 364, 370–71). This tradition began, she explains, after an occasion when Babs visited Ally and found "there wasn't bread enough. I hardly like to tell you. It makes me feel ashamed. Don't you know? don't you feel it?—feel that there is something shocking in the fact that there wasn't enough bread—*bread* even!—enough! That's the kind of thing that gives me positive pain when I think of it" (365). Thus, scenes of loaf giving afford Grand the opportunity to contrast the hunger of the poor and the self-indulgence of the wealthy. By implication, art for art's sake resembles wealthy people's greedy or wasteful overeating: it is not only unhealthy but it deprives others of the intellectual and spiritual nourishment necessary for "health of mind." In portraying this analogy, Grand carries out in her own writing the mandate Dr. Galbraith describes in *The Beth Book:* to write a book that both entertains and provides "food for thought."

"The Earth Bread without—The 'Bread of Life' within": The Communal Meal

Theologian Kathryn Allen Rabuzzi and sociologist Stephen Mennell, among others, have identified cooking with sacred rituals, a perspective adopted by several feminist literary critics, most notably Ann Romines. This is a perspective with which Gilman had no patience, however. In the words of a satisfied customer of Diantha Bell's meal delivery service in *What Diantha Did,* "Such talk is nonsense! I don't want *sacred* meals—I want good ones—and I'm getting them at last!" (238). Despite Gilman's scorn, food's association with religious and cultural rituals is fundamental to human society. In the nineteenth century, these ancient connections came under increasing scrutiny by scholars such as James Frazer, whose work Mary Ward apparently knew.[10] Bread, in particular, with its Eucharistic function, stands at the center of Christian theology, and bread has from thence become particularly potent as a symbol of social communion, or commensality, to use the sociological term. Louis Marin has argued that the process of changing raw food into dinner parallels the transformation of lived experience into language. In the Eucharistic meal, the bread becomes flesh through language. In Ward's *Harvest,* the harvesting of grain by the women, the baking of bread by Janet, and the sharing of meals by the "family" of women at Great End suggest both the creation of a community and a sharing of communion, expressed not only in the "family's" shared reading of the Bible but in the words of Ward's novel itself. In Ward's portrayal, women's loaf giving, a secular economic triumph, is also a spiritual victory, in which women radically adopt the traditionally male Christian symbolic roles.

Early in *Harvest,* Ward portrays a representative domestic evening, full of images of feeding and sharing food:

> The two land-girls had finished giving food and water to the cattle and a special mush to new-born calves. Everything was now in order for the night, and Janet, standing on the steps of the farm-house, rang a bell, which meant that supper would be ready in a few minutes. The two partners and their employees were soon gathered round the table in the kitchen, which was also the dining-room. It was a cold meal of bacon, with lettuce, bread and jam, some tea made on a "Tommy's cooker," and potatoes which Janet, who was for the present housekeeper and cook, produced hot and steaming from the hay-box to which she had consigned them after the midday dinner. (41)

In many ways this is a typical evening scene on a farm: the animals must be fed before the people, who then share fairly homely fare, perhaps the more so because the cook herself works the fields. Yet the circumstances differ from the standard domestic scene in subtle and not-so-subtle details, many of which carry significant gender implications. The meal's informality and its relatively unconventional preparation contrast with the kind of domestic rituals Ann Romines has identified with the domestic realm—the world that has been disrupted by war. Significantly, Janet makes the tea not on a standard kitchen stove but on a spirit stove like that issued the troops, drawing a connection between the worlds of farm and front, women and men. To be sure, the scene around the table, lit by a small oil lamp and decorated with a pot of wild flowers, has a familial quality, but Ward emphasizes the differences: "The scene was typical of a new England. Women governing—and women serving—they were all alike making their way through new paths to new ends. It was no household in the ordinary sense. The man was wanting. The two elder women were bound to the two younger by a purely business [public] tie, which might or might not develop into something more personal" (41–42). As in *Herland,* we see a small, self-contained, agrarian world of women. In *Herland* this world was left to women after the men were destroyed by war, but in *Harvest,* although the agrarian world partly represents a retreat, it also functions in support of the war effort.[11]

The images in *Harvest* of ordinary domestic community quickly shift to images of spiritual communion. In Herland, the deity is God the Mother; in *Harvest,* Ward too hints at a woman-centered theology. The novel alludes repeatedly to Demeter, Greek goddess of agriculture, especially in descriptions of Rachel: "[T]he atmosphere of the harvest field, its ripeness and glow, seemed to be still about her. A classically minded man might have thought of some nymph in the train of Demeter, might have fancied a horn of plenty, or a bow, slung from the sunburnt neck" (31). The image combines beauty and power, specifically a spiritual power, linked closely to the "plenty" that the goddess provides. More radically, Ward portrays all facets of the Eucharist being carried out by women. At the close of the typical domestic evening, the farm girls join for evening prayers. Janet's leading family worship places her in a role traditionally held by the paterfamilias, whose role in this circumstance was understood to echo that of a clergyman—or God the Father. On this night prayers begin with a reading from John 6, the account of the Last Supper: "'Verily, verily, I say unto you, he that believeth on Me hath everlasting life. . . . I am the Bread of Life. . . . I am the living Bread which came down from Heaven.'" As Janet says "a few simple things about the Words of Christ, and how the human soul may feed on them," Rachel quietly enters the room, and together the women contemplate "the wide cornfield beyond the open window, where the harvest moon, as yet only a brilliant sickle, was rising. The Earth Bread without—the 'Bread of Life' within" (46). Ward thus conflates the biblical Word made flesh with women's provision of grain, and with their baking, serving, and sharing of bread.

In this early scene, Ward sets the novel's tone of foreboding and hope. For Rachel, farm life represents a way to put her sad past behind her, an approach significantly couched in culinary language: "*Work!* that was the receipt—hard work!" (48). What she had not planned on was the renewal fostered by the commensality of friendship and by love. By the end of the novel, Rachel discovers that "love makes new," a spiritual concept Ward embodies in the botanical metaphor "her life had put out a new flower" (344, 275). Janet sees her friend moments before Rachel goes to meet Ellesborough, to whom, at Janet's urging, she has finally confessed her entire past, and in whose arms she dies when her ex-husband shoots her. To Janet, Rachel seems "transfigured," with "the look of one for whom the Valley of the Shadow is past" (347). Janet, a pastoral figure in a literary and animal husbandry sense, has functioned as a spiritual pastor, facilitating Rachel's confession and absolution of sin, while Rachel figures in the novel both as a sinner who finds comfort in traditional Christian forgiveness and also as a kind of sacrificial figure herself. As the person most credited in the novel with producing "Earth Bread," Rachel is a type of Christ figure whose death paradoxically heralds the birth of a rejuvenated postwar England.

To be sure, one could interpret the novel's tragic ending as retribution for Rachel's sins: the brief extramarital affair after her baby's death due to her drunken husband's neglect, and her subsequently concealing her past from everyone who now knows her.[12] But Ward clearly rejects this view, implicitly by portraying Rachel's murderer as deranged, and explicitly in Rachel's last journal entry: "In the Gospel, it was the bad women who were forgiven because they loved 'much.' Now I understand why. Because love makes new. It is so terribly *strong*. It is either a poison—or life—immortal life" (344). The promise that "love makes new" is a classic statement of redemption and rebirth. Harvest, a time of gathering, is also a time of death. Yet the harvest death offers a promise of rebirth in the spring, and Rachel's final confessions suggest spiritual promise, for, as she had written in the final words of her journal, "I think I do now believe in immortality—in something within you that can't die—when once it has begun to live" (344). Similarly, out of the death and destruction of the great war will come, Ward believes, a new and better England for the survivors, an England improved because the poor have won new respect and because women have harvested new public powers.

~

In the mid-nineteenth century, Ruskin's attribution of queenly loaf giving to the middle-class woman offered, from his perspective, an appropriately feminine form of power. By the end of the century, many women—the literary housekeepers among them—could no longer find satisfaction in Ruskin's purely private brand of domestic power. Literary housekeeping, even Gilman's version, with its kitchenless homes, does not abandon the "lady's" responsibility for loaf giving; rather, literary housekeeping invests loaf giving with wider, more public significance. The literary housekeeper doesn't so much "get out of the kitchen" as bring the kitchen into the marketplace and extend loaf giving to grain growing, grain milling, bread baking, bread marketing, meal serving, and even soul saving. Moreover, for Grand, art offers "food for thought"; for Gilman, art is "world-food"; and for Ward, art is food for the human soul. Thus defined, the literary housekeepers could agree, "After all if breadmaking was not a woman's business, what was?"

Cleaning House

Sanitation and Social Purity

Women—mistresses of households, domestic servants—are the soldiers who are deputed by society to engage in this war against dirt. Let them not make the mistake of regarding the foe against whom they stand as insignificant and not worth an attack. Where dirt reigns, disease, misery, and crime stand erect around his throne; liberty, progress, and enlightenment hide their heads in shame. . . . Where dirt has been driven out, purity and enlightenment have found a congenial home; and it has always been found that to become clean is to take the first step in becoming good, wise, and great.

Phillis Browne, "House-Cleaning"

WHEN SARAH GRAND ASSERTED that the New Woman's mission was "to set the human household in order," she was issuing a rallying cry with international appeal, not least because so many women took it not metaphorically but literally. For example, Helen Campbell, in her popular book *Household Economics,* contended, "To keep the world clean—this is one great task for women. Not in the old sense of scrubbing away at her own steps, back or front, . . . but in the newer one of making the whole world so clean that her own bit of it must perforce be the same" (206). To argue that women should "set the human household in order" or "keep the world clean" is to challenge long-held beliefs about housecleaning: that it is trivial, mindless drudgery for menials, within the purely private realm of the individual residence. By the end of the nineteenth century, the domestic science movement, bolstered by the findings of microbiologists and the exhortations of sanitarians, could argue not only that housecleaning is vitally important to the private home, but that it represents a momentous civic responsibility best assigned to the experts: women. Grand, Gilman, and Ward participated enthusiastically in this discourse of "municipal housekeeping," portraying cleaning and disease prevention both literally and metaphorically as treatments for fundamental cultural maladies.

To be sure, cleaning does not always appear in a positive light in their writings. For Grand and Ward, who did little cleaning themselves, such work is frequently linked to class. Grand is mainly interested in metaphorical dirt, but on one of the few occasions that she portrays literal cleaning, young Montecute Kingconstance complains that a housekeeper's dusting is "tiresome" (*Babs,* 72), because it detains her from feeding him. Although Grand observes in *The Beth Book* that doing a "lazy servant's" dusting and sweeping provides valuable "physical training" for Beth, one result is that her mother (who is unaware of the arrangement) is horrified that Beth's hands are unpleasantly "cracked and begrimed, . . . as if the child had to do dirty work like a servant!" (503, 123). When Beth gets older and becomes concerned with maintaining a ladylike appearance, she wears gloves to dust (231). In Ward's *Sir George Tressady,* Sir George dryly undercuts his wife's insensitive suggestion that the miners who work for him are overpaid, judging from their houses, by observing, "Well, after all, darling—you see, you don't have to live in those houses, nice as they are—and you don't have to do your own scrubbing" (156–57).[1] The comment is double edged: Letty should sympathize more with working-class women's domestic labors—and should be grateful that she need not share them.

Gilman, whose diaries are peppered with references to housework—sweeping, dusting, washing dishes, washing the refrigerator, doing "chamberwork," and scrubbing the outhouse—never glosses over the drudgery of cleaning. In her poem "To the Young Wife," Gilman mocks the idealizing of housework that finds nobility in private domestic labors, rhetorically asking,

> *Are you content with work,—to toil alone,*
> *To clean things dirty and to soil things clean;*
> *To be a kitchen-maid, be called a queen,—*
> *Queen of a cook-stove throne?*

(5–8)

As this stanza illustrates, Gilman, no less than Grand and Ward, finds cleaning demeaning: to clean is to "be a kitchen-maid" or resemble the "old dreary creatures with pails of dirty water, scrubbing out . . . offices" ("What Do Men Think," 15). "To the Young Wife" echoes Gilman's other writings in blaming much of the household dirt on her constant target, home cooking: "Cleaning is continuous," she writes in *The Home*. "Cooking, of course, makes cleaning. The two main elements of dirt in the household being grease and ashes; another, and omnipresent one, dust" (96). In *What Diantha Did*, Gilman's distaste for cleaning is summed up succinctly by Isabel Porne, a skilled architect but inexpert housekeeper: "'I'd rather plan a dozen houses!' she fiercely muttered, as she fussed about. 'Yes—I'd rather build 'em—than to keep one clean!'" (69). Yet Isabel is a minor character in the book; that Isabel's ultracompetent housekeeper is at the book's center indicates how important cleaning was to Gilman's theories about housekeeping. Although cleaning is drudgery, it is not trivial, and Diantha's "plans" for housework represent something "worth while . . . for *everybody*" (56; emphasis Gilman's). In literary housekeeping texts, cleaning, despite its unpleasantness, figures as a centrally important, broadly social, and even, paradoxically, empowering activity for women.

Germs, Dust, and Domestic Science

The late nineteenth-century obsession with sanitation was a byproduct of the era's general enthusiasm about science and scientific approaches to social problems. This veneration of science, augmented by the breakthroughs in microbiology in the 1870s, 1880s, and 1890s, fostered respect for the concept of scientific laws of cause and effect—that, for example, specific diseases have specific, identifiable physical causes rather than representing divine retribution for moral failings. As such, sanitarians could also successfully argue that diseases can be prevented by eliminating their cause: germs.

As germ theory took hold in the late nineteenth century, the most urgent emphasis came to be placed on dust. This emphasis began with Robert Koch's work on anthrax and his discovery that anthrax reproduces by means of spores that can remain dormant in soil seemingly indefinitely, unaffected by cold or drought, until they are inhaled or ingested by living organisms. Then, in the 1880s, one of Koch's students, Georg Cornet, injected bacteria found in the dust in tuberculosis patients' rooms into guinea pigs, which developed the disease and died. Cornet's findings led to the influential "dust theory of disease": the belief that "fomites"—bits of contagious matter from sick people, including skin particles and dried saliva or other body fluids—could adhere to bed linen, upholstery, clothing, or paper and, like anthrax spores, remain infectious for years. Accordingly, the best means to prevent tuberculosis and other diseases was to eliminate dust that contained fomites. Although further research established in the late 1890s that tuberculosis bacteria spread through sputum and that bacteria in house dust have little infectious capacity, the dust theory of disease continued influential well into the twentieth century (Tomes, 97).[2]

As anxiety about germs at the turn of the century approached hysteria, Gilman was not alone in fearing that "[a]gainst the real dangers of modern life"—by which she meant, in part, sanitary dangers—"the home is no safeguard. . . . Sewer gas invades the home; microbes, destructive insects, all diseases invade it also" (*The Home,* 32). The invisibility and omnipresence of bacteria and their ability to multiply by the millions heightened the anxiety. The prolific founder of the home economics movement, Ellen Richards, in *The Chemistry of Cooking and Cleaning,* ominously cautions readers that bacteria "are now quietly resting on this page which you are reading" (77). To help elucidate the newly discovered threat, Richards called on more familiar fears, explaining that although the "germ-community is like any other typical community" in that the "majority of the individuals are law-abiding, respectable citizens," nevertheless, as in human communities, "in some dark corner a thief may hide, or a cutthroat steal in unawares. If this happens, property may be destroyed and life itself endangered" (78–79). Responsible mothers naturally would protect their families from such menaces.

Once it was accepted that insidious bacteria in dust could destroy one's property and kill one's family, absolute cleanliness became imperative, and standards of housekeeping achieved unprecedented heights. Richards, a trained scientist, recommended approaching housekeeping scientifically, advocating sterilization procedures appropriate to a laboratory: "To the bacteriologist, . . . everything is dirty unless the conditions for germ-growth have been removed, and the germs, once present, killed" (*Chemistry,* 78). The cost of achieving such standards was equal, she calculated, to a quarter of what a family spent on rent; indeed, she considered this sum barely "sufficient to keep the family shelter 'just above the diphtheria level'"; to keep a house in "*really sanitary* condition where risk is nearly eliminated" would require fully half the cost of rent, or 12.5 percent of family income (*The Cost of Cleanness,* 7). Such extreme sanitary procedures demanded time-consuming labor: Richards calculated that removing dust and tracked-in dirt from an eight-room house requires eighteen hours a week, with an additional twenty hours of cleaning four times a year if the home has a furnace or open fires. Window washing requires ten hours a month, and washing blinds and porches eight hours a month. Washing walls and painted woodwork entails two 15-hour cleanings each year, while a house with a library adds four 15-hour cleanings annually. These tasks are, of course, on top of the time required for household tasks like mending, child care, or cooking, which was also being changed by new sanitary standards for purchasing, preparing, and storing food; or for other chores associated with sanitation, such as laundry and even making beds, with the systematic airing of bedding another favorite topic for advice from sanitarians.

Naturally, these tasks fell to women. Phillis Browne was one among many commentators who argued that women had a particular responsibility to learn and apply principles of sanitation. The epigraph to this chapter comes from Browne's contribution to Shirley Forster Murphy's encyclopedic tome *Our Homes, and How to Make Them Healthy.* Browne's language ascribes an unprecedented nobility of purpose to cleaning: because dirt represents a "threat" and a "foe," those who fight it are courageous soldiers for a mighty cause. Nor is the enemy merely the microbe, for dirt causes not only disease but crime, and hampers "purity and enlightenment." Browne and the pioneers in the home economics movement, like Ellen Richards and Helen Campbell, sincerely rejected the view of cleaning as mere drudgery. Richards, who called home economics the "science of controllable environment," believed that a scientifically trained woman would recognize that cleaning is "a fine action, a sort of religion, a step in the conquering of evil, for dirt is sin" (*Cost of Living,* 137–38). Campbell argued that showing a child the "honor" and "wisdom" of "perfect cleanliness" will insure that as an adult, he will give no less "care to the public cleaning than he has known under his own roof. It is because, in part at least, such work is held ignoble and degrading—because only inferiors as a rule fulfil its needs—that our public housekeeping makes us the shame of civilized nations" (*Household Economics,* 205–6).

Advice manuals accordingly laid out precise instructions as to how—and how not—to clean. One French doctor warned, "Dry sweeping and dusting are homicidal practices" (qtd. in Forty, *Objects,* 175). Indeed Sarah Grand's exhortation to "raise the dust" reveals her embarrassing lack of practical house-keeping knowledge, for a ruling guide of up-to-date sanitary housekeeping and fomite control was that, as Campbell explained, one should sweep "not with a long stroke which sends clouds of dust over every thing, but with a short quick one, which only experience can give" (*Easiest Way,* 42). Other cleaning tasks also inspired detailed instructions: S. Maria Elliott, for example, laid out a weekly, ten-step procedure for cleaning a cellar and a daily, three-step proce-dure for cleaning toilets: soaking, brush scrubbing, then cloth scouring with disinfectant soap powder (176–78, 192–93). One of the primary purposes of the American home economics movement was to train women in the science of cleaning, to insure that they had the latest information on the ways that bac-teria and fungus grow and spread, and thus the methods for safe cleaning and food handling, to prevent disease.

Municipal Housekeeping and Literary Housekeeping

The fear of microbes translated readily into assertions of governmental respon-sibility for the people's health—and conversely, the responsibility of individu-als for their fellow citizens. As Ellen Richards exhorted in *The Cost of Cleanness,* "The public has a right to demand that it may eat and drink and travel safely without danger from pistols or microbes of its neighbors' carrying" (44–45). Gilman, in an article ironically titled "Is Health Worth Having?" argued that sanitary issues illustrate that "[o]ur life is collective" (206). The constitutions of children are "modified by social conditions," partly their parents' behaviors— a mother's overwork or poor diet, a father's contagious diseases—but even more their physical environment, for "if children are born in crowded, unsan-itary tenements, and grow up in them, and in crowded, unsanitary streets as well; their constitutions are further injured irretrievably. This is not their fault, nor even their parents' faults, nor that of any one social malefactor; it is our fault—the fault of all of us, for letting such conditions exist" (204). By the same token, Gilman argues, "If so many of us die, we are that much poorer; if so many of us are sick, we are that much weaker." In answer to the question, "What are we to do about it?" Gilman looks mainly to women: "It is to be keenly hoped that with the entrance of women upon political action they will make the public health their especial care" (206).

Mary Ward, too, looked to women in political life to solve sanitation problems. Ward advocated women's participation "on public housing and sanitation committees" and in local government decisions about, among other things, "important matters of sanitation and housing, even the water supply" ("Why I Do Not Believe," 15). Ward called for more women to serve on local governing bodies, specifically so they could contribute their sanitary expertise: they could deal with "the provision of decent houses to live in, the decent sanitation of these houses, the endeavor through health visitors and sanitary inspectors to help the people who lived in the houses to live wholesomely and wisely" ("Needs of Local Government," 12).

The call for women to take the lead in cleaning beyond the home sphere was not a new one. Indeed, it got its first great impetus in the work of Florence Nightingale during the Crimean War. Long before the establishment of bacterial causes for disease, Nightingale's work at Scutari had demonstrated the life-saving effectiveness of sanitary practices in hospitals. Nightingale would insist in *Notes on Nursing* that "the greater part of nursing consists in preserving cleanliness" (87). She testified to the British Sanitary Commission in 1858 that "the woman is superior in skill to the man in all points of sanitary domestic economy, and more particularly in cleanliness and tidiness"; for that reason, she advocated that sanitary reformers "look to the woman to carry out practically their hygienic reforms" (qtd. in Hoy, 32).

The link between cleaning and professional nursing clarifies certain aspects of Ward's *Marcella,* a book that, as we have seen, concerns itself a great deal with issues of sanitary housing. When Marcella enters nursing training, she is assigned to "scrub and polish and wash" (353). As a district nurse, much of her work involves cleaning. Changing dressings on an ulcerated foot entails making it "clean and comfortable" (380). The first task in dealing with a case of apparent puerperal fever is to procure "clean bedclothes and night-gear," then for Marcella "to wash her patient and remake the bed" (342, 341). To a degree, Ward's portrayal of the menial side of Marcella's nursing exploits the idea of nursing as a vocation: a "calling" demanding submission and self-sacrifice. Indeed, a significant element of Marcella's training involves being "taught her place & kept under by a sister, a stupid person, whom as she says, she would never have spoken to at Mellor."[3] Marcella understands in retrospect that she had to be taken "down a peg, or she [would] be no use to anybody" (354). Even

Ward's observation that "[a] hospital nurse, if her work *seizes* her, as it had seized Marcella, never thinks of herself" (342) suggests a delicate balance of personal reward and professionalism on the one hand, and self-denial on the other. Marcella, in her newly humble character, tries to minimize her work: "It's the fashion just now to admire nurses; but it's ridiculous. We do our work like other people—sometimes badly, sometimes well" (353). Ultimately, though, Ward wants her readers to recognize the importance of nursing, indicated by "the fashion . . . to admire nurses" and by Marcella's obvious competence and professionalism in the face of sometimes difficult conditions. The scrubbing and washing, which from a twenty-first-century perspective make Marcella's nursing seem demeaning, actually signify, from the perspective of 1894, its scientific and professional stature. Marcella's nursing skill contrasts with her bumbling efforts to bandage Wharton's burned hand prior to her training, just as her well-planned rebuilding of tenants' housing at the end of the book contrasts with her prior impotence in these matters; Marcella's increasing sanitary competence thus correlates with her moral, intellectual, spiritual, and political growth.

In America especially, professionalization of women's sanitary skills extended well beyond the sickroom or tenants' cottages. Gilman generalized from women's responsibility for domestic housekeeping to suggest that women could take the lead in cleaning urban and natural environments because "a city could and should be dustless. To enter a well-kept city should be like entering a well-kept house. . . . [A]nd the streets, smooth paved from wall to wall, should be as clean as floors" ("Why Make Dust?" 61). In *Moving the Mountain,* we learn that after women "wakened . . . to their own natural duty as mothers," they spearheaded a spurt of social evolution that ensured a "proper . . . environment" in which to raise children (112). The results are dramatic. The narrator marvels at "New York Harbor *clean!*" and celebrates "the beautiful Hudson. Its blue cleanness was a joy. I could see fish—real fish—in the clear water when we were still" (59, 101). In *Herland,* the roads are "as dustless as a swept floor" (43). In *With Her in Ourland,* Herland's Ellador observes the "real" women who are beginning to emerge, and marvels, "[W]hat a glorious time they will have—cleaning up the world!" (188). Gilman undoubtedly had in mind the successful "municipal housekeeping" efforts by actual women, such as the Ladies' Health Protective Association of New York City, the Women's Municipal League of Boston, and the work in Chicago under the leadership of Ada Sweet and

Gilman's friend Jane Addams of Hull House. Women in these and similar organizations spearheaded sanitary efforts to clean streets, improve garbage removal, purify water, ease air pollution, and improve food inspection, as well as to provide information about sanitation to individual households. Like Gilman, the organizers of these efforts aimed, in the famous words of WTCU founder Frances Willard, "to make the whole world homelike." Social progress thus entails erasing distinctions between public and private, turning the world into a "well-kept house."

Yet even as the world is to become more homelike under the care of municipal housekeepers, the house itself, in Gilman's view, should become less a place for domestic work. In the improved world Gilman advocated, young wives would be freed from their "cook-stove thrones" as their work was professionalized: "The home, quiet, sweet and kitchenless, will be visited by swift skilled cleaners to keep it up to the highest sanitary standards; the dishes will come in filled with fresh, hot food, and go out in the same receptacle, for proper cleansing; the whole labor of 'housekeeping' will be removed from the home, and the woman will begin to enjoy it as a man does. The man also will enjoy it more. It will be cleaner, quieter, more sanitary, more beautiful and comfortable, and far less expensive" ("Genius, Domestic and Maternal II," 6). As a professional housekeeper, Diantha Bell provides her first employers with "a clean house—cleaner," says Isabel Porne, "than I ever saw one before" (91–92). Later, Diantha establishes a House Workers' Union, "thirty girls, picked and trained," who "go out by the day" to clean houses for regular wages (169). These well-trained day workers "do more work in an hour than the average slavey can do in three" (179). Gilman acknowledges that women who want "someone to do their will at any moment from early morning till late evening" dislike Diantha's system, but it pleases women who simply want their houses clean and their food well cooked because "the speed, the accuracy, the economy; the pleasant, quiet, assured manner of these skilled employees was a very different thing from the old slipshod methods of the ordinary general servant" (179, 180). Moreover, Gilman emphasizes how much safer, pleasanter, and more remunerative the system is for the workers themselves. In the early *Women and Economics,* Gilman cheerfully predicted that when cleaning becomes "socialized," the professional cleaner (like the soap maker) will be a man; by the time she wrote *What Diantha Did,* Gilman apparently saw in housework commercial prospects for women like Diantha with domestic talent—though Diantha herself, after her period studying paid housework, becomes a manager, while the cleaners themselves are mostly immigrant women. Gilman's solution to the problem that cleaning turns a wife into a mere kitchen maid is unfortunately to hire more kitchen maids, albeit trained, unionized, and better paid.

Pure Milk

Another direct effect of bacteriology and the domestic science movement was the "pure milk movement," a campaign that Grand, Ward, and Gilman all refer to at least in passing, and that deployed appeals to private motherhood for a public cause. For Grand, milk inspires the comment in *Adnam's Orchard* that Seraph Pratt's mother grew up in the bad old days when "municipal ignorance, mismanagement, and neglect of interest in the health of the community generally was enough to make the microbes in the milk carts stand up on their tails and cheer" (21). Grand implicitly blames Seraph's degenerate character on milk his "anaemic" mother drank when she herself was a child, thus supplementing the overt blame of the municipality for neglecting the community's health with a tacit appeal to mothers to protect their own children from similar microbial danger.

Like other sanitary campaigns, women's activism in the pure milk movement represented to Ward a public service alternative to parliamentary suffrage. At an October 1909 meeting of the Kensington Local Government Association, Ward, who was already the most prominent spokesperson for the anti-suffrage movement, spoke in support of women's candidacy for municipal councils, contrasting this "moderate" political activity with the "illegitimate and violent" demands of suffragists, and emphasizing the "advantage of the expertise and advice of women." Women, said Ward, could "see that the Midwives Act was administered, that the sanitary laws were carried out without fear or favour, that the milk sold was pure, that the school managers appointed were of the right sort, and that unemployed women were helped no less than unemployed men." In these activities having to do primarily with health and sanitation, women were "indispensable" ("Women on Borough Councils," 4e). Pure milk is served up again in *Harvest,* written after women's suffrage was a fait accompli. Here, Ward applauds concern with pure milk in the larger context of women's efforts to supply food to win the Great War. Ward refers to a Miss Hall who frightens village mothers with her pictures of "the terrifying creatures that had their dwelling in milk, and what a fly looks like when it is hideously . . . magnified." Although the mothers are skeptical of a woman with no children of her own, "[n]one the less the village ways were yielding, insensibly little by little; and the Miss Halls were after all building better than they knew" (266). With or without the vote, women in the pure milk movement build something valuable for their nation.

For Gilman, by contrast, pure milk was unequivocally "Something to Vote For," as she titled a play in the *Forerunner*'s June 1911 issue. In the course of a rather contrived plot in which the owner of Billings Milk Trust is caught attempting to bribe a milk inspector, Gilman shows a transformation in attitudes of the members of a women's club. Although antisuffrage and resistant even to the word "politics" when the story begins, the club women change their minds in response to a full meeting program: a presentation of statistics about deaths from diseases blamed on bacteria in milk; a tearful account by poor Mrs. O'Shane of her baby's death after drinking Billings milk; a test of a sample bottle of Billings Company milk from Mrs. O'Shane's neighborhood that shows it to be dirty and adulterated with starch; and the inspector's proof that Mr. Billings attempted to bribe him to falsify the test. By the end of the play the club women are proclaiming, "Rich or poor, we are all helpless together unless we wake up to the danger and protect ourselves. That's what the ballot is for, ladies—to protect our homes! To protect our children! To protect the children of the poor! I'm willing to vote now! I've got something to vote for! Friends, sisters, all who are in favor of woman suffrage and pure milk say Aye!" (153).

To Gilman, the goal of pure milk is "a question of practical politics" but also a question that "appeals to the mother-heart and housekeeping sense of every woman"(146). This combination is, of course, the point. In the 1913 story "A Personal Motive," the personal and the public mix in the plot by wealthy Mrs. Geoffrey Miles to "ruin every milkman in New York!" after her only child dies from tubercular milk (114). Mrs. Miles blames an entire system—the man who doesn't wash the bottles, the milker who doesn't wash his hands, the inspector "who was careless—or bribed," the farmer who "knew his cow was tuberculous—or didn't know"—and most of all, "the men of the Milk Trust—who didn't care" (113). Financed by their wealth, Mr. and Mrs. Miles construct a "wide-spread paradise for cows," a model dairy farm to create superior "Meadowsweet" dairy products, then cleverly market the product so it gains upscale prestige while Mrs. Miles philanthropically sells it inexpensively in poor districts (114). By providing good milk and "the taste and texture of real fresh cream and butter," by publicly displaying the "white cleanness" of their dairies and "shining white [delivery] motor-wagons," and by distributing "literature and illustration of the right processes in dairying," Mr. and Mrs. Miles educate the public to demand a superior product. As a result, they "broke the back of every company furnishing less perfect service—which meant all of them" (115). Then, to make sure milk trusts never regain the power to kill babies, Mr. and Mrs. Miles organize a national campaign for municipal milk supply, largely by recruiting "pure milk voters": mothers, because, as Mrs. Miles exclaims, "Mothers appreciate good milk!" Mrs. Miles has chosen not to adopt children because "I'd rather work to save and help continuing millions of babies than to bring up just a few" (117). Her private sorrow has translated into a feeling of public responsibility to "raise the standard for America—for the world" (114) in the name of mothers and babies everywhere. In literary housekeeping, that is, each individual mother's private domestic task of serving wholesome milk to her children is transformed to a wide social problem, in which bacteriology, economics, practical politics, and ultimately public policy are subject to the power of public motherhood.

"Dirt Killers": Soap, Salesmanship, and Purity

One of the more curious episodes of Gilman's career was the period during the early 1880s when she and her cousin Robert Brown designed small collectible trade cards advertising soap for the Kendall Manufacturing Company.[4] It might be tempting to dismiss the cards as irrelevant to Gilman's career as a whole or to literary housekeeping. To be sure, the cards represented a much-needed "source of income," as Gilman would later call it (*Living,* 47); moreover, she attributes the cards' conceptions to Brown: "Robert had a fertile imagination, he devised the pictures he wanted and I drew and colored them"; in other words, there is no way to know exactly which aspects of the cards represent Gilman's ideas. Moreover, Gilman eventually discontinued the enterprise, which she describes in her autobiography just before she discusses her flower painting, abandoned because it was "not conducive to my object—the improvement of the human race" (47). These facts all suggest that Gilman's hawking of Soapine soap merely reflected necessity and employed her drafts-manship for business purposes rather than expressing conviction.

But thirty years later, in early issues of the *Forerunner,* Gilman once again endorsed cleaning products, Fels-Naptha and Soapine. In her ad for Soapine, a general purpose product with which to "wash dishes, wash floors, wash clothes, wash anything," Gilman nostalgically describes her youthful trade card making and remarks, "I could do it with a clear conscience, for my mother always used Soapine and I used it after her." In a comment about the *Forerunner*'s advertising in the following issue, Gilman informs her readers that the endorsed products are "personally known and used by the editor"; she avers that she has written "absolutely true descriptions and recommendations of them" ("Confidential Remarks," 32). Three decades after creating the soap trade cards, Gilman's mo-tives are again economic—to support her publication—but as we have seen in Gilman's repeated portrayals of women's empowerment through capitalism, she considered a market economy fully consistent with, even conducive to, a woman-inspired ethical reordering of society. Thus, it seems reasonable enough to study Gilman's soap cards as an early manifestation of a "literary house-keeping" philosophy.[5] In fact, many of the cards share with Gilman's writings about housekeeping the sometimes awkward balancing of private with public, disdain for domestic drudgery with celebration of domestic power.

Some of the women portrayed in the cards seem immersed in or even overwhelmed by housekeeping tasks, reflecting Gilman's complaint in "An Ex-tinct Angel" that the work of "angels in the house" involves "dealing with dirt" in "every form of menial service . . . which the human creature loathed and scorned" (50). In a card advertising Kendall's French Laundry Soap (fig. 1), a

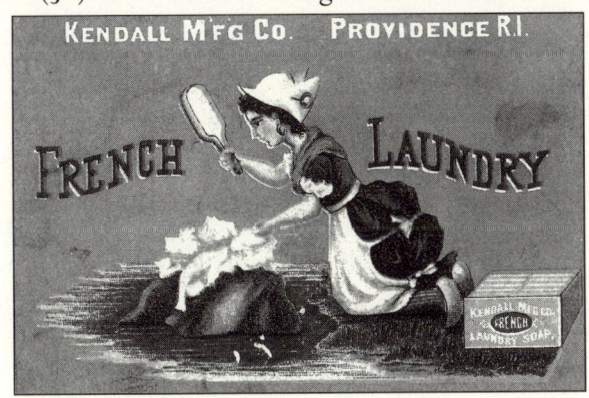

Figure 1

French maid kneels awkwardly to wash clothes on rocks—hardly the latest in domestic technology and an illustration of the "unscientific" methods in home-making that Gilman repeatedly criticized. Although the maid's clothing looks crisp and bright, the apron tied back around her buttocks and ankles is not only protected from wetting but also suggests a form of bondage to domestic obligations. It also anticipates Gilman's complaints about clothing in *The Dress of Women:* "No one who has ever observed a washwoman with an additional layer of wet cotton apron on her wet cotton skirt, getting wetter and wetter with warm water, and then going directly out with soaked clothing and parboiled fingers to hang up the stiffening clothes in a Winter wind, can hold that women's clothes are suitably modified to their economic activities" (6:47). The card's illustration thus undermines any more exotic view of washing that the Kendall Soap Company might have preferred the French maid to inspire.

Similarly, the woman in the "Lady with Clothesline" card (fig. 2)—who seems absurdly overdressed for her labors—bends painfully over her basket, the reason, of course, being primarily to reveal the hanging clothes that spell out "S.O.A.P.I.N.E." on the line behind her. The design, though humorous, is also somewhat threatening, particularly the striped hosiery forming the "P," which seems prepared to kick the stooping woman, and the union suit that forms the "E," which seems to have acquired a life of its own and writhes violently in an apparent escape attempt.

In the conceptually similar "Monster Letters" card (fig. 3), the word spelled is not "Soapine" but merely "soap," and in this card the housekeeper seems understandably terrified by the letters. The "S," a fanged snake poised to strike, faces down the open-mouthed woman, who has dropped her broom. The "O" and the "P" are likewise pointy-teethed monsters: the "P" is formed from the curved back of a grinning crocodile, which threatens to bite the housewife from behind if the snake doesn't get her first; meanwhile, in the background, a fanciful, vaguely feline monster consists almost entirely of its enormous "O"-shaped mouth lined with sharp teeth. Only the "A" is relatively benign, an empty easel, but behind it stands a hideously grinning elf. Behind each of the other three monsters stands a child, in each case in ambiguous relation to the monster: is the child under attack or in alliance with its respective creature? To the extent that the monsters threaten the children, the card plays on children's supposed aversion to soap and inclination to make messes, yet the children appear cheerful, finding entertaining playfellows in the monsters. Perhaps the

Figure 2

Figure 3

children and soap monsters are menacing the dropped broom, as if to suggest that Home Soap will clean more effectively than sweeping or eliminate so much dirt as to decrease the need to sweep. But the card's composition seems more likely to imply a conspiracy against an overworked mother. Perhaps, indeed, the mother is the artist whose easel remains empty because her time is now monopolized by brooms, children, and their soap monster allies. Although clever and memorable, the card seems rather muddled as advertising, representing its product as hideously dangerous. As a comment on housekeeping, on the other hand, the card neatly illustrates the disgust with which Gilman describes women's cleaning duties in *Women and Economics:* "All that is basest and foulest she in the last instance must handle and remove. Grease, ashes, dust, foul linen, and sooty ironware,—among these her days must pass" (246–47). The card reinforces Gilman's argument that so long as women remain relegated to primitive, unspecialized work within the house, they are hampered from producing genuine art or other socially useful products.

Figure 4

Yet there is another group of women in the Kendall Soap cards who maintain firm control over their circumstances. These include the women in "Ironing Day," "Lady Archer," and "Columbia and Universal Family." In the humorous card identified by Dave Cheadle and Bill Lee as "Ironing Day, Kids in French Crate" (fig. 4), the sour-faced woman at the ironing board faces her task squarely, iron raised aggressively. Her work remains uninterrupted—and her children safe from accidental burns—on account of her having cleverly rigged a raised play box for them in a Soapine crate. Here, in contrast to the French washerwoman in the knotted apron, a resourceful woman has taken charge of tying knots that free her from distractions. And although the disproportionately large children could, like the children in "Monster Letters," potentially threaten the mother's equanimity, they seem cheerful, satisfied by the arrangement, perhaps because the alternative is punishment with the strap that lies next to the stove. Naturally, the card's priority is the laundry, since the product marketed is the soap that presumably produced the brilliantly white article of clothing on the ironing board, and whose sturdy box holds three chubby children. Nevertheless, the scene anticipates Gilman's later critique of domestic arrangements wherein cleaning and mothering tasks compete for a woman's attention and children are forced to play in homes that are neither safe nor child friendly.

One of the more remarkable of Gilman's cards, "Lady Archer Hits Dirt" (fig. 5), features a statuesque lady archer in a form-fitting dress with small polonaise bustle and train. The author of the 1915 *Dress of Women* would surely have disapproved of this dress for its constricting, corsetlike cuirass bodice and tight skirt, which would discourage movement. One would imagine a woman so dressed incapable of athletic feats—but not, apparently, archery. She has

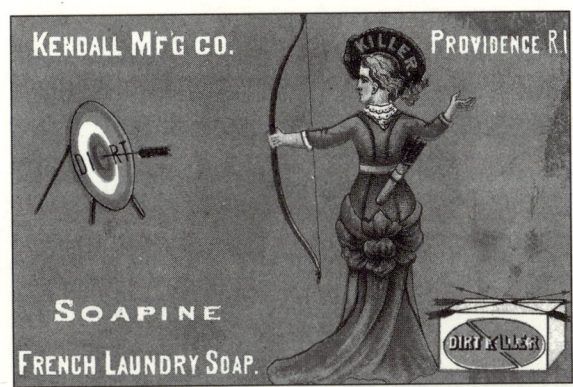

Figure 5

Figure 6

just hit a bull's-eye on a target labeled "dirt." The archer herself wears a large hat with the word "killer" spread across its brim; behind her, on a red, white, and blue soap box labeled "dirt killer," rest more arrows. The archery symbolism evokes images of the virgin goddess Diana hunting prey, combining the athletic and warlike with the refined and feminine, embodied in the woman's fashionable gown and hat. The all-American lady archer suggests the civilized power of the advertised product. Moreover, she anticipates the rhetoric of the municipal housekeeping movement: "Women . . . are the soldiers who are deputed by society to engage in this war against dirt" (Browne, 869).

Less martial but equally poised, the woman in "Watering Plants in Soap Boxes" (fig. 6) has put dirt in its place—as a planting medium for lush flowers in Kendall French Laundry Soap and Soapine crates. Gilman's choice of sunflowers probably alludes to the Aestheticism of Oscar Wilde, whose dubbing sunflowers, along with lilies, as the "most perfect models of design, the most naturally adapted for decorative art" had received wide publicity during his 1882 tour of America (47). The aesthetic sunflower, which had become a favorite image in advertising trade cards, here contributes to a message that Kendall soaps foster a beautiful home and the leisure to cultivate more beauty.[6] The card thus anticipates the ideals of literary housekeeping by attempting to balance the beautiful with the clean and practical.

The "Universal Family" card (fig. 7) broadens the woman's power against dirt, in an American version of the notorious Pears and Monkey Brand Soap advertisements that celebrated British imperialism. Here, a central figure, "Columbia," identifiable by the stars-and-stripes shield at her waist and the white star on her blue cap, tends a large soapy wash tub, labeled "Kendall Mfg. Co." and propped on Kendall soap boxes.[7] She is attended by male figures whose stereotyped features, clothing, and props indicate that they are meant to represent the world's major nations and races. On Columbia's right (the viewer's left), bearing the soap and laundry, are the Europeans, probably representing Switzerland, Scotland, and France from left to right. To Columbia's left, carrying a washboard, are non-European races, including a Native American whose arrows are safely in their quiver (in contrast to those of the Lady archer); and at the bottom is a fallen Irishman, apparently drunk. Presumably, England and Germany, the nations Gilman considered "Aryan," are not separately represented because they supply the superior racial origins of the regal Columbia, who stands above her attendants. As historian Anne McClintock has said of the Pears soap promotions, soap here represents "a technology of social purification, inextricably entwined with the semiotics of imperial racism and class denigration" (212). Cleanliness, associated with Anglo-Saxon virtues, justifies the eugenic supremacy of white America, symbolized by Columbia. On the card's back (fig. 8), beneath the elaborately rendered brand name, "Kendall Mfg. Co. Soaps and Soapine," the caption cautions, "To protect yourself from the evil effects of using soap made of impure materials, see that it bears the name of some reliable manufacturer." Although the "evil" identified is "soap made of impure materials," the card's imagery suggests that Soapine will somehow protect white women from violation, either by purifying the "lower" races or by cleansing society of their contaminating effects. Like the Pears soap advertising, this card subtly confounds distinctions between public and private, identifying the private, domestic activity of washing day with colonial conquest, thus "domesticating" the "inferior" races. As with "maternal power" in other Gilman works, this image of woman's "universal" improving influence is marred by its eugenic subtext.

Figure 7

Figure 8

Finally, the "Dusting Bric-a-Brac" card (fig. 9) brings together several issues we have seen in Gilman's soap cards. Unlike the other women encountering soap letters (and more like the men in two of Gilman's other cards),[8] this woman seems less overwhelmed by than worshipful of the items on her mantle that spell "S.O.A.P.I.N.E." The letters are represented by small pieces of statuary: works of art. Unlike the "Lady with Clothesline," this housekeeper has paused in her cleaning, having tucked her feather duster under her arm as she adjusts the bric-a-brac. To be sure, the duster itself is a daunting item nearly three times the size of the woman's head, and either dates Gilman's knowledge about dust or represents her collaborator's contribution, for by the 1880s both feather dusting and bric-a-brac itself had come under suspicion as threats to domestic hygiene. Indeed, one wonders why the housewife isn't using a cloth dampened with Soapine suds. Nevertheless, in contrast to the "Monster Letters" card, here domesticity and art seem reconciled. The serpentine "S" is now harmless statuary, and although the "A" easel remains empty, the housekeeper may be reaching for it, preparatory to painting; for the picture behind the bric-a-brac might be one of her own compositions, as might the needlework on the

Figure 9

decorative cloth beneath the bric-a-brac. Interestingly, both portraits on either side of the mantle seem to portray women, as does the "P" figure holding the clock; only the sportsman figurine representing the "E" is male. In this woman-dominated domestic space, art and soap become one, and artist and cleaner merge, anticipating the aesthetic that would become literary housekeeping in Gilman's later work.

Whether Gilman originally conceived her card making as consistent with "the improvement of the human race," a case could be made that her later plan to include advertisements for soaps in the *Forerunner* represented more than a pragmatic estimate of the kinds of products marketable to a predominantly female subscription base. For Gilman, as for Grand and Ward, cleaning transcended the domestic drudgery that it inarguably entailed. It was worthy to stand alongside or even to be identified with art, because it represented one part of a larger "object"—"the improvement of the human race"—whether as an imperialist/eugenic project, as a means to eliminating social "corruption," or simply as a scientific endeavor to save lives by exterminating lethal germs.

Social Purity and the Artist:
"Aren't morals closely connected with sanitation?"

Let us return once again to Sarah Grand's paradigmatic literary housekeeping statement: "Let there be light. We suffer in the first shock of it. We shriek in horror at what we discover when it is turned on that which was hidden away in dark corners; but the first principle of good housekeeping is to have no dark corners, and as we recover ourselves we go to work with a will to sweep them out."

Grand's godlike invocation of light duplicates one standard sanitarian prescription; Benjamin Richardson, among others, recommended, "As much sunlight as can be obtained should be allowed to enter into every room of the dwelling at all hours of the day," because "[s]unlight purifies, and is a potent agent for destroying the action of the organic poisons which float in the air" (*Field,* 664). But while Grand does occasionally portray her characters engaged in literal dusting and tidying, she became known as the primary exemplar of the "purity school" of New Women writers because her writings shine metaphorical light onto social poisons. Both Grand and Gilman dedicate significant attention to illuminating and eliminating social pollution, most explicitly men's "biological sin" of infecting their wives and children with venereal diseases, but also the "poisonous exhalations" of literature that promotes "dirt and disease."

In the influential 1966 study *Purity and Danger,* anthropologist Mary Douglas minimizes the more literal justifications for cleaning, such as disease prevention. Defining dirt as "matter out of place," Douglas argues, "There is no such thing as absolute dirt: it exists in the eye of the beholder. If we shun dirt, it is not because of craven fear, still less dread or holy terror. Nor do our ideas about disease account for the range of our behaviour in cleaning or avoiding dirt. Dirt offends against order" (2). Douglas's perspective came out of an era in which communicable diseases seemed on the verge of disappearing altogether; in retrospect, then, Douglas and those she influenced, including many feminist historians of housework, took too little into account the genuine and legitimate fears aroused by germ theory at the end of the nineteenth and beginning of the twentieth centuries, when infectious diseases were the leading causes of death, public health services were limited and unreliable, and rigorous hygiene represented the only known means to prevent most contagions. That said, it is also true that Douglas's theories usefully illuminate the emphasis on "social purity" in literary housekeeping texts and other writings of the era. There can be no doubt, for example, that Grand's and Gilman's cautionary tales about innocent women contracting venereal disease from degenerate men functioned not only as genuine warnings about a previously underreported and very real health threat but also as "analogies for expressing a general view of the social order" (Douglas, *Purity,* 3).

Late-Victorian domestic science informed housewives that dust carries bacteria, but ordinary women rarely had opportunities to visit a laboratory and view dust through a microscope. Hence, fear of bacteria in dust remained as much a matter of faith as had fear of "sewer gas"—or fear of disease as divine retribution for sin. Thus to associate dirt, disease, and evildoing was an easy step. Furthermore, dust's long association with physical decay—"Ashes to ashes, dust to dust"—only reinforced analogies between bacterial infection and social corruption or moral and evolutionary "degeneracy." By the same token, if dust was linked to decay and degeneracy, "raising the dust" was clearly "progressive."

Both Grand and Gilman employ analogies between social corruption, dirt, and disease, especially venereal disease. As we have seen in the context of Grand's ideas about eugenics and the inheritance of vice, she frequently mixes metaphors of inheritance, contagion, and social corruption, as when, in *The Heavenly Twins,* Evadne asserts that to consummate her marriage with Colonel Colquhoun would be "countenancing vice, and . . . *helping to spread it*" (79). In the tradition of Josephine Butler and the campaign against the Contagious Diseases Acts, Grand rejects the social position that blamed prostitutes for spreading syphilis. In Grand's housekeeping analogies for sexual purity, women are clean and men dirty. To be sure, she occasionally vilifies those she calls the "scum of our sex" ("New Aspect," 270), but she far more often endorses the view, articulated by a nurse for a woman who contracted syphilis from her seducer, that "it's the dirty men makes the misery" (*Twins,* 292). In *The Beth Book,* when Beth learns that her husband runs a lock hospital that confines prostitutes under the aegis of the Contagious Diseases Acts, she confronts Dan about the double standard that punishes prostitutes without curing them while ignoring the men who spread the disease to both prostitutes and wives. Dan argues, "[T]hat is not my business. Doctors can't be expected to preach morals. Sanitation is our business." Beth responds, "But aren't morals closely connected with sanitation?" (400). This was also Grand's view in *The Heavenly Twins,* in which the wise Sir Shadwell Rock speculates, "I suppose eventually morality will be taught by medical men, and when it is much misery will be saved to the suffering sex" (639). When Beth finally leaves Dan, "She was like one who has been bathed and perfumed after the defilements of a long dusty journey" (*Beth,* 418). Grand thus conflates physical dirt and disease with "morals," both Dan's particular marital infidelity and the more widespread public issues that inspired the Contagious Diseases Acts and the lock hospital that employs Dan. In his study of "mess" in nineteenth-century art and fiction, David Trotter has rightly observed, "The campaigns against the Contagious Diseases Acts and against vivisection give a public dimension to Beth's private suffering" (275). To leave her husband, that is, represents not merely leaving a bad marriage but joining a social movement. More fundamentally, the episode reinforces Grand's view that personal health and hygiene and private ethical choices are inextricably related to issues of public sanitation, public health, social purity, and public policy.

Charlotte Perkins Gilman, who enthusiastically reviewed *The Heavenly Twins* for the *Impress* in December 1893, echoed Grand's analogy between disease, dirt, and social pollution throughout her career. In *The Crux,* to be free of venereal disease and to have lived the kind of life that would ensure that condition are both to be "clean."[9] Gilman has Dr. Bellair clinically explain that to be certain whether Morton Elder has gonorrhea would require "long microscopic analysis" to identify the suspect bacteria (222), but because she has evidence of his infection with syphilis (based on information from a former prostitute who knows that Morton was "with" several of her friends who had "the sickness" [171–72]), Dr. Bellair can warn Vivian not even to kiss Morton lest she "catch it" (227). Dr. Bellair also uses moral language to explain the sources of a clinical condition: "A man don't have to be so very wicked, either, understand. Just one mis-step may be enough for infection" (226). And ultimately, she uses religious language, explaining that knowingly to marry a syphilitic would be to commit the unforgivable sin: "Beware of a biological sin, my dear; for it there is no forgiveness" (227). Although the scientific is here conflated with the ethical and spiritual, to Gilman, the clinical trumps the ethical. Although Vivian Lane is touched by Dr. Bellair's emotional arguments—and by "true woman" Adela St. Cloud's counterargument that "a good woman's influence" can "make a new man" of a man who has had "temptations" (181–82)—Vivian's ultimate decision not to marry Morton comes only after "she thought and thought." Her "unreasoning horror" of confronting the facts is "met by her clear perception" that she is "old enough to know these things." The chapter ends with the observation "Shy, sensitive, delicate in feeling as the girl was, she had a fair and reasoning mind" (228). Vivian decides, "Wickedness could be forgiven; and she had forgiven him, royally. But wickedness was one thing, disease was another. Forgiveness was no cure" (242). In her review of *The Heavenly Twins,* Gilman had praised "the startling novelty" of "a thinking heroine who acts from judgment instead of emotion" (3). In *The Crux,* she shows that women's trained capacity for reason and scientific knowledge will help them to understand disease and keep them "clean."

Perhaps more fundamentally, Gilman portrays extramarital sexuality, exemplified by Morton Elder in *The Crux* and many other (male) figures in her writings,[10] as a threat to the social order in the sense that Mary Douglas explores. In deprecating extramarital sexuality, Gilman certainly establishes boundaries and behavioral norms. In *The Crux* Dr. Bellair insists, "Marriage is for motherhood," a position Gilman repeats throughout her career. In an article on "The American Social Hygiene Association," Gilman argues that venereal diseases should be reported to the Health Department "precisely as in cases of small-pox or scarlet fever" (257). By the end of the article, however, Gilman has moved from the clinical to the moral and social, arguing, "It is not polygamy which has coarsened and corrupted the human race; it is the continuous and excessive indulgence of the sex-impulse with no regard to parentage. . . . We need continence indeed, in marriage as well as out. But that is a long way off, calling for the breeding and education of a new race of men, clean in mind and body, vigorous and manly, and not tormented by the excessive desires transmitted to them from long generations of intemperate indulgence" (259). In *Herland* and *With Her in Ourland,* Gilman portrays this utopian ideal in the transformation of Van into just such a "clean" and continent man, who learns to forego any sex with his wife until the time comes to conceive a child.

Grand's "social purity" work largely involved lighting the dark corners to publicize the problem of syphilis and the sexual double standard. Many of her comments conflating dirt, disease, and vice concern this crucial task of diagnosing or revealing the problem. In *The Heavenly Twins,* for example, Grand's feminist spokesman Mr. Price, in discussing "inherited vice," observes that "there are sores which must be exposed to view if they are to be prescribed for at all or treated with any chance of success," a metaphor that compares public uncovering of immorality to medical examination of venereal chancres. Pursuing this line of thought, Mr. Price remarks, "The Augean stable of our modern civilization must be cleansed." Hercules' original task, says Mr. Price, was "a very good sanitary measure," though it might not be appreciated "in our day" (187–88). Mr. Price thus equates the not-yet-accepted approach of publicly exposing men who are infected with syphilis to cleaning stables of their disease-fostering excrement, an accepted staple of urban sanitary campaigns, comple-mented by the allusion to Hercules, a traditional symbol of mythic heroism. Nor is it irrelevant that excrement was sometimes euphemistically referred to as "dust," the matter on which Grand's New Woman shines her metaphoric light.

For Grand, literature represents an important "sanitary" tool in the Her-culean task of cleansing modern society, and she delights in metaphors that convey that idea. In her 1923 introduction to *The Heavenly Twins,* she harks back to Mr. Price's reference to "sores which must be exposed to view if they are to be prescribed for at all or treated" by describing the novel in which Mr. Price appears as a "dose" for the "moral health" of the general reader—pointedly gendered male. "My plan was to compound an allopathic pill for him and gild it so that it would be mistaken for a bonbon and swallowed without a suspicion of its medicinal properties. Once swallowed, it would act" (xii). Grand's rhet-oric here challenges Victorian ideologies that linked novel reading with ill health. For Grand, whose books are largely concerned with young women's reading, books like hers might even be considered antidotes to the "exhalations from the literary sewer which streams from France" (*Twins,* 186). Many Euro-pean male writers—especially the French—identified syphilitic madness with poetic genius, celebrating "the privileged decadence of the *poète maudit*" (Showal-ter, "Syphilis," 91), a trope calculated to inspire Grand's fury. Both through her portrayals of "resisting readers" like Evadne and through her own unflinching administration of "doses" of medical information in her books, Grand works through literature to bring her country back to "moral health."

Looking back to the 1893 publication of *The Heavenly Twins* from the retro-spect of 1923, Grand could claim that her prescription was largely successful: "The gilding answered its purpose. Swallowing it for a sweet did not inhibit its medicinal effect" (xiv–xv). In *The Winged Victory,* Grand also speaks opti-mistically of social improvements implicitly linked to her literary housekeep-ing aesthetic. The Duke of Castlefield Saye claims to have observed "a new fastidiousness" in men of the present. By contrast, "Water wouldn't wash the young men of my day clean of their habits, some of them. Then it was thought manly to wallow. Now, manliness is cleanliness" (240). Later in the novel, Mr. Strangworth links the change explicitly both to religion and to literary trends:

> "The Christ Spirit is coming into its own. Col's conversion is symptomatic,
> the extreme of what promises to be a common occurrence. Society has

dipped down to the lowest. It has been mired that it might be made to realise the foulness of corruption. But look about you. See the signs of reaction. It has already set in. Take your modern hero of your modern novel.
Not so very long ago, the hero was the dirtiest of young men——"

"Decadents would have him so still," said the Duke.

"Decadents don't appeal to the normal man and woman. They're a discredited crew, and only speak for themselves. What do you find the hero of
the normal sort? Clean! The women began it, and were plentifully bespat-
tered with mud for daring, but they stuck to it. They exposed the inside of
the cup and the platter, the dirt and disease. They ridiculed the accepted
impossibility. 'There's no reforming a rotten constitution,' they said. 'Let
the mentally and physically tainted be set apart, and give us clean men.'
And now it's the men themselves who are writing each other up clean."
(338–39)

In this passage, Strangworth, speaking for Grand, conflates moral "corruption," "dirt," disease, and literary decadence, and links all of these conditions to
men. But descent into the foul "mire" provoked a "reaction," led by women—
specifically, by implication, women writers, for Strangworth identifies the
change with the "modern hero of the modern novel." In other words, Grand's
character credits writers like Grand herself with "exposing" the "dirt and disease" and ridiculing the "accepted impossibility," that is, the canard that a bad
man can be reformed. Women's writing is thus explicitly credited with cleaning away the dirt and curing the disease of a corrupt culture.

≈

Housecleaning is at the heart of most understandings of "housekeeping." The
reality of the era was that women found cleaning an unpleasant, dirty task, increasingly onerous and time consuming thanks to greater social pressure to
meet standards of cleanliness, and decreasing support from other people in
their households. In literary housekeeping texts, however, Grand, Ward, and
Gilman join their contemporaries in the sanitation and home economics
movements in the daunting effort to find in cleaning nobility, power, and public purpose. Their writings echo the domestic science movement in identifying
cleaning as a task at which women have developed particular expertise, an ex-

pertise that justifies their entering the public sphere to keep the milk pure and to engage in municipal housekeeping. For both Ward and Gilman, municipal housekeeping and pure milk explicitly justify women's political participation, and, as genuinely lifesaving activities, impart an inherent dignity and importance to women's domestic contribution to the public sphere. Gilman, of course, considers the problem of dangerous microbes yet another justification for kitchenless homes and the systemic social reorganization that she associates with professionalizing all domestic tasks, from child care and cooking to sanitation. But the most far-reaching implication of sanitary science for literary housekeeping is its metaphorical deployment in the service of social purity. For Sarah Grand, especially, the threat of disease-bearing dust that terrified her contemporaries extended well beyond the literal dangers of tuberculosis to include social contagions. In turn, the "allopathic pill" of literature would restore society to "moral health."

The Needleworker Reworked

Life has lost a great deal that was beautiful both in character and appearance since women began to neglect their own wonderful little implement, the needle. For one thing, we have lost the source of strength that comes of a tranquil occupation.

Sarah Grand, The Winged Victory

FEMINIST AMBIVALENCE ABOUT HOUSEWORK may reach its highest pitch on the subject of sewing. The feminist critique of sewing begins at the beginning of feminism, with Mary Wollstonecraft's complaint that needlework "contracts" women's faculties by "confining their thoughts to their persons" (172) and Mary Lamb's complaint that "[n]eedle-work and intellectual improvement are naturally in a state of warfare" (50). Strong heroines from Maggie Tulliver to Aurora Leigh, from Jo March to Laura Ingalls, have expressed dislike for sewing. And the plight of the overworked, underpaid seamstress, which became a cause célèbre in England's "hungry forties," was taken up by Lamb, Elizabeth Gaskell, Dickens, Thomas Hood, and countless others.[1] Yet needlework has always had its feminist defenders. British campaigners for women's suffrage consciously deployed the traditional symbolism of pictorial embroidery in order to both invoke and undermine traditional definitions of femininity, in the service of the Cause. The rebirth of feminism in the 1970s saw Judy Chicago's use of needlework in "The Dinner Party" (1974–79) and "The Birth Project" (1980–85) and the journal *Heresies's* special issue on "Women's Traditional Arts." Alice Walker portrayed Celie's liberation through sewing pants and piecing quilts in *The Color Purple* and celebrated, in "In Search of Our Mothers' Gardens," an anonymous black woman from Alabama whose priceless quilt at the Smithsonian Institution reveals "an artist who left her mark in the only materials she could afford, and in the only medium her position in society allowed her to use" (239).

The most interesting recent studies of needlework are those that document the mixed responses of women who recognize the prickly issues that gather around needlework. Susan Gilbert and Susan Gubar, for example, in *The Madwoman in the Attic* document the profound ambivalence toward sewing in such writers as Emily Dickinson and George Eliot, who invoke the power of Ariadne as a muse for the weaving of webs of words and yet also echo the fairy tales in which "sewing signals woman's domestic confinement and diminishment" (520). Rozsika Parker's important history of embroidery, *The Subversive Stitch,* traces shifts and tensions in the cultural status of needlework over some seven centuries. The tensions in feminists' responses to sewing are, of course, reminiscent of those we have seen in portrayals of motherhood, cooking, and cleaning. All reflect feminism's impulses to identify with the masculine world and its values yet also to draw strength from arts and skills developed in the domestic realm; moreover, the shifting responses to sewing reflect the changing social conditions in which needlework has been produced—and in which women of different classes have found themselves.

In the work of Gilman, Ward, and Grand, needlework functions much as other housekeeping tasks function, appearing simultaneously as a womanly private pastime and as an activity with broader public meaning, particularly economic or artistic significance. Needlework stands out, however, as offering particularly strong commentary on the aesthetic value of domestic labor. These writers' portrayal of women's sewing mainly concerns decorative crafts—embroidery, lace making, and weaving—that would seem among the least practical types.[2] Yet sewing has long been referred to casually as a middle-class woman's "work," her sewing supplies lodged in her "work basket." In literary housekeeping texts, the writers frequently play with the ambiguity of the word "work" to evoke tensions among three issues: the assumption that needlework is a leisured, and ultimately useless, hobby; the Aesthetic concept of needle-work as a "work of art"; and the fact that for poor women sewing represented an essential task: provision and maintenance of clothes for one's family—or a source of meager income.

Ward and Needlework

Needlework plays a much smaller role in Ward's writings than in those of Grand and Gilman. Perhaps, having spent the bulk of her childhood at school and away from her own domestic circle, the young Mary Arnold received less instruction in needlework than did Grand and Gilman, and it therefore played a smaller role in her own adult domestic experiences—and thus in her vision of literary housekeeping. Her evenings at home as a bride were, by her own ac-count, spent not sewing but reading and writing: "I see, in memory, the small Oxford room, as it was on a winter evening, between nine and midnight, my husband in one corner preparing his college lectures, or writing a 'Saturday' 'middle'; my books and I in another; the reading-lamp, always to me a symbol of peace and 'recollection'" (*A Writer's Recollections,* 1:220).

Needlework does appear intermittently in Ward's writings. As we saw in chapter 1, Ward frequently used the metaphors of spinning and weaving to de-scribe narrative. Within the fictions themselves, sewing is often simply a prop to be mentioned in passing, but occasionally it is invested with meaning—not always positive meaning. In *Helbeck of Bannisdale,* we learn of one of Helbeck's ancestors, the wife of an abusive husband, who used to sit on a rock seat by the river, "doing needlework, or reading the Little Office of the Virgin, at the hours when her daughters in their French convent would be saying their office in chapel. She died before her husband, a very meek, broken creature" (146).[3] Here, needlework is linked to submissive domesticity and religious self-sacrifice. The rock seat is the very location from which Laura Fountain takes her suicidal plunge to avoid similar domestic submission.

In *Marcella,* on the other hand, needlework facilitates a kind of control. Mrs. Boyce uses embroidery to maintain command of a difficult social situa-tion. In the awkward period after Aldous and his grandfather have refused to sign the clemency petition in Hurd's support and before Hurd's execution, Al-dous attempts to visit Marcella, and is told she will not see him; on the chair in the drawing room he notices that a "needle with some black silk hanging from it had been thrust into the stuffed arm of the chair, the cushion at the back still bore the imprint of the sitter. She had been there, not three minutes ago, and had fled before him" (297). Marcella's sewing, significantly mourning clothes for the Hurd family rather than wedding apparel for herself, stands as mute testimony to her alienation from her fiancé. Beside the chair is correspondence from Harry Wharton, Aldous's political and sexual rival. When Aldous asks Marcella's mother about the correspondence, Mrs. Boyce "knew well that the moment was critical," so she responds with care, the needlework assisting. As a matter of tactics, she reverts to her sewing as she carefully chooses her words: "She took up her embroidery again before she answered him. In her opinion the needle is to the woman what the cigarette is to the diplomatist" (297–98). This line reflects Ward's repeated portrayal of women's participation in private power struggles as both analogous to and ultimately contributing to larger public power. Mrs. Boyce controls the conversation's pace and direction while seemingly maintaining an appropriate feminine passivity. For both mother and daughter, needlework thus is a subtle but powerful form of communication, a function needlework serves even more prominently in the work of Gilman and Grand.

The Art and Business of Needlework in Gilman's Literary Housekeeping

Gilman made her own clothes, and reports, "Textile construction always delighted me" (*Living*, 65). Hence, although she believed that sewing, like other domestic activities, would benefit from professionalization, it inspires little of the ire that we see in her discussions of cooking. In Gilman's stories, needlework of various types provides talented needlewomen with opportunities as artists, tailors, and other professionals; in many cases, the portrayal of needlework allows Gilman occasion to redefine "domestic" work as a means to reenvisioning society more generally.

In "The Cottagette," Gilman explicitly contrasts embroidery, identified as both work and art, with unproductive kitchen labor. Malda, the story's narrator, is a resident of an art colony: "I did embroidery and made designs. . . . I like to draw from flowers and leaves and things about me; conventionalize them sometimes, and sometimes paint them just as they are,—in soft silk stitches"

(132). This is clearly feminine stitchery, but the terms "designs," "draw," "conventionalize," and "paint" all confirm Malda's qualification to reside in what is portrayed as an exclusive art colony. That hers is not merely domestic sewing is emphasized by the repeated point that Malda's "work" is hampered by her attempts at housekeeping: "[I]t did interfere with my work a good deal"; "I never could work much—at my work—baking days" (135). The conflict is an issue both of time and of the physical incompatibility of the two types of tasks: Malda mourns that "one's hands are not so nice when one cooks and washes dishes,—I need nice hands for my needlework" (134). When Ford Mathews proposes and insists that the condition of their marriage be that Malda not cook, his argument is based on the paramount importance of Malda's art: "But you haven't done half as much of your lovely work since you started this kitchen business, and—you'll forgive me, dear—it hasn't been as good. Your work is quite too good to lose; it is a beautiful and distinctive art, and I don't want you to let it go. . . . Because you are so truly an artist in your special way, seeing beauty and giving it to others" (137, 138). Malda, who was brought up in a manner that encouraged her "domestic instincts" (137), has developed one private domestic skill—embroidery—into a public art form that brings beauty "to others" and thus surpasses the rest in importance. The story illustrates once again that domestic labor can represent an oppressive deterrent to a woman's performing valuable work—or an opportunity for a gifted woman to contribute beyond the private home in uniquely valuable ways.

More often, sewing in Gilman's writing is ascribed economic power, direct or indirect. In her murder mystery *Unpunished,* sewing indirectly restores Jack, Hal, and Iris to their rightful inheritance. It seems that shortly after Jack's father's death, her scheming brother-in-law, who had forced the father to disinherit his daughters, also forced Jack to fire a loyal pair of servants, Jane and Peter O'Connell. The only severance compensation Jack could give was her father's old clothes. A frugal and careful seamstress, Jane managed to mend an old overcoat to keep it wearable for nearly two decades, "with a patch and a darn here and there." But, she explains, "just now, when I was trying to hold the lining together I came upon this—" (183). "This" turns out to be a handwritten will that Mr. Smith had composed only hours before his death, to override the cruel one that had been forced on him. Had Jane not been so skilled and dedicated with her needle, her once and future employers might never have regained their property.

Generally, though, needlework's economic function is more direct. Gilman's ubiquitous "good villain," Benigna Machiavelli, at first sees sewing as an activity inferior to boys' work, but learns its practical "advantages" and eventually discovers how needlework may be employed to obtain economic independence and personal dignity. Learning the "science" of sewing at school and practicing at home, Benigna perfects her sewing as part of her campaign to get "strong" by acquiring as many skills as possible. By taking lessons with a dressmaker, Benigna learns how not to be cheated, and she saves money by making her family's clothing. When as a young woman Benigna embarks on a "wander year," among the many jobs she takes to yield "practical inside knowledge of nine trades" are necktie maker and skirt worker (163). Acquiring these skills and learning the business side of textiles presumably prepares her to move things her way in one of the many stories in which she appears as Mrs. Mac-Avelly, "According to Solomon": Gilman's clever schemer helps a woman attain economic and personal independence by subversively employing the womanly art of weaving to generate income.

Textile work finds its way into Gilman's utopian societies designed by women. The first evidence that Herland is a "considerable civilization" comes through the discovery of a piece of "well-woven fabric, with a pattern, and of a clear scarlet that the water had not faded" (5, 4). The story "A Council of War" portrays a group of women planning an alternative society. Because economic independence is the "foundation stone of all other progress" (239), they plan a group of interconnected businesses, including boardinghouses, laundries, bakeries, gardens, dressmakers, and milliners. Miss Waltress, who has thought out the proposal, uses as her extended example the creation of neckties—a clever choice that symbolizes, subtly though never explicitly, capitalist male power, co-opted to create a metaphorical noose by which to execute the "man-made world." Miss Waltress points out that neckties are easy to make and that women have frequently made them. She adds, "Silk itself was first made use of by a woman, and the whole silk industry might be largely in their hands. Designing, spinning, weaving, dyeing, we might do it all" (240). So acceptable is this behavior that it provides perfect cover for a covert revolution:

> "there is absolutely nothing to prevent our stretching out a slow soft hand, and gathering in the business. We might begin in the usual spectacular 'feminine' way. A dainty shop in a good street. . . .

"Anyhow we establish a trade in neckties, fine neckties, good taste, excellent materials, reliable workmanship. When it is sufficiently prosperous,
it branches—both in town and in the provinces—little by little we could
build up such a reputation that 'Widow Shop Neckties' would have a
definite market value the world over. Meanwhile we could have our own
workrooms, regular show places—patrons could see the neckties made,
short hours, good wages, low prices." (240–41)

Thus the enterprise, built on women's skills with fabrics and thread, exploits
masculine economic power and learns from male business models to create an
alternative model of labor and business.

In the most thoroughgoing portrayal of the transformation of domestic
into public work, "Bee Wise," the community's "supporting industries" include
several related to women's traditional arts of spinning, weaving, and sewing
(230). Citizens raise Angora goats, then at their mill produce yarn, from which
they manufacture "fluffy blankets, flannels and knitted garments." From the
"magnificent cotton" grown there, and "silk of the best," Beewise supplies its
own "[s]mall mills, pretty and healthful, with bright-clad women singing at
their looms for the short working hours. From these materials the designers
and craftswomen . . . made garments, beautiful, comfortable, easy and lasting,
and from year to year the demand for 'Beewise' gowns and coats increased"
(231). As fits an ideal society, the textile work of Beewise not only involves
creating a self-supporting and profitable business out of domestic activities,
but also manages to do so while providing ideal working conditions. As we
have seen again and again in Gilman's work, the most domestic and ostensibly
trivial feminine activities can, if transformed into public work, create the
means for a complete reorganization of society on feminist terms.

Grand and the Economics of Lace Making

In *Adnam's Orchard* and *The Winged Victory*, needlework's economic and social
manifestations take on an even more overt role, for the title character of *The
Winged Victory*, Ella Banks, makes lace professionally. Ella's personal and business success with the lace cooperative she establishes in order to provide a
market and fair prices for the work of working-class lace makers promises for
a time to allow her to bridge class differences and to reconcile the conflicts

between public and private, but by the end of the second book, her efforts have led mainly to disaster, and the delicate fabric of lace proves too flimsy a material to shield her from the hazards of commodifying herself.

Although only one type of handmade lace is made with a needle, the craft qualifies for discussion in this chapter because it is almost exclusively undertaken by women and because, like other forms of "needlework," it involves textiles and thread. Indeed lace is nothing but thread—an ornamental network of fine threads that is attached to the fabric of clothing or other items, such as table or bed linens. According to an 1875 *History of Lace,* by Mrs. Bury Palliser (apparently one of Grand's own sources of information),[4] there are two types of handmade lace: *point,* "made by the needle on a parchment pattern" (26) and *pillow-lace,* which is the kind most frequently described by Grand and which Mrs. Palliser explains as follows:

> The "pillow" is a round or oval board, stuffed so as to form a cushion, and placed upon the knees of the workwoman. On this pillow a stiff piece of parchment is fixed, with small holes pricked through to mark the pattern. Through these holes pins are stuck into the cushion. The threads with which the lace is formed are wound upon "bobbins," small round pieces of wood, about the size of a pencil, . . . on which the thread is wound, a separate bobbin being used for each thread. By twisting and crossing of these threads the ground of the lace is formed. The pattern or figure . . . is made by interweaving a thread much thicker than that forming the groundwork, according the design pricked out on the parchment. (27)

Creating this intricate material requires huge amounts of time—indeed, Ella describes one small piece as the work of "half a century" (*Winged,* 534)—giving fine lace a rarity that enhances its monetary value. Handmade lace is thus a material embodiment of class-based conflicts, for when its quality is highest, it is affordable only by the wealthiest consumers. To wear a large piece of lace is to announce one's wealth, one's taste, and, if the lace is old, the length of one's pedigree. Yet while lace making is an art that Grand repeatedly describes as ladylike, fully appropriate to a princess and a duchess, in England it had long been primarily the inadequately recompensed labor of the rural poor. In Ella, Grand creates a character who hales from both worlds, emphasizing the fundamental ambiguity of both product and producer.

In addition, lace, like many other forms of needlework, embodies tensions between public and private realms, variously defined. Lace is a product with strong feminine associations, traditionally produced by women; and it appears both on clothing displayed prominently on public occasions such as presentation in court, and on lingerie and on linens in the private boudoir. As a family heirloom, produced in family drawing rooms, lace functions purely as a private possession, but when it figures in wills, as Grand says it has, it attains a degree of public notice. A fine art, as Grand repeatedly emphasizes, lace making was one of many crafts idealized by the Arts and Crafts movement, which tried—unsuccessfully—to revive its economic viability. When produced by working-class laborers, often under appalling "sweated" conditions in their private homes, it is always and only a product for public sale—though those who sweat these laborers resist "public sector" interference in the working conditions. This public/private ambiguity thereby embodies class tensions as well.

Ella's situation embodies the tensions among classes, among the varying conditions in which lace is produced, and between the private and public realms. Unbeknownst to herself, Ella Banks is the product of two different economic, social, and genetic communities: the poor laboring class of her servant mother and lace maker grandmother, who raised her and taught her her profession; and the nobility, through her father, the duke. As Ella's case exemplifies, lace making is not only a profession but also an identity, one with ambiguous class markers. Ella comes from a long line of lace makers: "There had been lace-makers in her family on the mother's side for generations" (*Adnam,* 281); moreover, Ella's paternal great-grandmother, the grandmother of the Duke of Castlefield Saye, also produced "exquisite" lace (*Winged,* 535). As a result, Ella's "cleverness with her fingers was hereditary" (*Adnam,* 281).

In addition, the lace itself is bound up in the lace maker's identity: Ella's identification with her lace is apparent from her response to making her first big sale, of a piece of lace on which she had worked for two years: "It was like parting with something of herself, so intimate was her relation to it, so worked up into it were the crowding thoughts, the swift emotions of the long days during which she had been engaged upon it. There was a reminder for her of something felt, planned, suffered, hoped, in every part of the pattern" (*Adnam,* 85). In one remarkable passage, a piece of lace becomes the "text" of a woman's life, which only a skilled reader like Ella knows how to "read." Ella examines "a rare and beautiful specimen of *point à l'aiguille,*—Early Venetian," which portrays "a curious medley of figures, bearing, apparently, little or no relation to each other." Ella, however, identifies it as a "life in cipher . . . a woman's life, an autobiography." The figures begin with an infant, move through a childhood image in which sewing and studying are juxtaposed—"here the young girl with a book, learning; with a pen, writing; with a piece of work in her hand, sewing"—through marriage, widowhood, and finally, in "a different hand," her death and burial (*Winged,* 305). The phrase "different hand" conflates the language of handwriting with the "language" of lace, making both distinctive expressions of self.

Lace made by women of the aristocracy derives its value partly from the identity—and pedigree—of the lace maker. Looking at some lace in her showroom—an item donated purely for aesthetic display, not sale—Ella muses,

> "If I were the daughter of a great house, I should like to leave my descendants a legacy of beautiful work, to keep myself in touch with them. In many of our great families such work—done centuries ago, some of it—is piously preserved, a lovely link in the chain of their descent. Let me show you a piece of lace begun by the grandmother of the present Duke of Castlefield Saye." . . .
>
> She unfolded the work. "See!" she said. "Isn't it exquisite? I can't do better myself, who am a lacemaker by trade. And it is the kind I love best to make, partly bobbin and partly needlepoint. Do you know the feeling it gives me when I look at it? A feeling of continuity, of a past behind and a future in front, which makes it worth while to do things, and to do them well." (535)

The duchess's lace is instantly recognizable, and in Ella's exhibition it is displayed *as* her work: unlike the makers of other lace, the maker of this lace is clearly identified. As readers we know that Grand considers it no coincidence that Ella and the late duchess have produced lace of similar type and quality or that Ella should have a "feeling of continuity" with her unknown great-grandmother, who so resembled Ella that the duke has covered her portrait to protect his secret. Lace here is a publicly displayed manifestation of a private familial link.

Lace making is ladylike not only because aristocratic women produce it in their leisure time: even when the worker is not literally a lady, the task requires ladylike hands, for roughened hands would catch on the delicate threads and hinder, if not spoil, the work. Before Ella makes her first, lucrative sale, her stepmother resents her refusal to help with ordinary household tasks like washing dishes and scrubbing the floor: "'I'll 'ave no fine ladies 'ere,' her stepmother screamed, 'settin' in the parlour makin' lace, and not a dish washed yet. . . . It's jest an excuse to set in the parlour, and act the fine lady . . . an' me slavin' in the kitchen'" (55). Mrs. Banks's resentment seems understandable under the circumstances, and Ella's behavior seems contrary to "housekeeping" in its simplest sense. Yet Ella explains her refusal to do heavy labor: "I can't make lace if I spoil my hands" (55). Here, professionalism and domesticity seem opposed, suggesting that the noblewoman's creation of lace is a fundamentally useless activity, at least from the perspective of an industrious country housewife. But Mrs. Banks changes her mind when Ella brings home three hundred pounds earned from her lace.

Despite the need to maintain ladylike hands, there is nothing aristocratic about the circumstances in which the professional lace maker must labor. Grand, echoing Palliser's information and language, has Ella inform a woman, "The lacemaker, working twelve hours a day, can scarcely produce one-third of an inch a week, and for this labour her daily earnings do not amount to a living wage. . . . Valenciennes like this used to be made in underground cellars by young girls, as a rule, working from four in the morning till eight at night. . . . Many were almost blind before they were thirty. Very seldom was a piece finished by one worker; when it was, the value was enormously increased" (109–10). Grand reminds her readers repeatedly that the very delicacy of fine lace is testament to the intensity and strain of the labor that goes into its production. Observing Ella, Adnam notices, "The white delicacy of her smooth transparent skin was unbroken by the slightest tinge of colour. Her deep blue eyes glittered feverishly. She had worked to the limit of her strength, and her nerves were racked with the irritation of extreme fatigue" (*Adnam*, 41). However "ladylike" an occupation lace making might be, it constitutes not leisure but painful—frequently blinding—and protracted work.

Although Ella manages to sell her lace for a good price, Grand takes pains to emphasize that her good fortune represents an exception, and that conditions for most lace makers remain as wretched as they have been for centuries.

> "This lace of mine is old, old; but the conditions under which such a piece
> could be produced in these enlightened times in the majority of cases

would be as bad as ever to this extent—the worker would still be in want, starving, unable to procure a living wage—to our shame; to the lasting shame of every woman who wears lace, knowing the truth, and troubling herself not at all to relieve the necessity, to come to the rescue of the workers, to save them from their living death." (*Winged,* 295)

Ella's stepmother notes that while Ella's grandmother helped make the lace for Queen Victoria's wedding gown, "she died in a hovel," evidence, even to Mrs. Banks's nonpolitical mind, that "[t]he pounds don't go into the worker's pockets" (55). Ella herself admits publicly, "My earliest recollection is of hunger and fatigue. Hunger—sometimes without even a crust to ease the craving; fatigue—without a hope of rest" (294). Ella risks this public statement of her private suffering in hopes of raising the awareness of the visitors to her showroom. Unfortunately, the London society Grand portrays is hardened and indifferent. Only the duke—his sympathy augmented by his private tie to Ella—develops any compassion. Still, Grand shows that one eloquent woman, moving one powerful man, may influence public policy. The duke decides to take action. Grand describes the duke's past practice sarcastically, significantly employing the polysemic word "domestic" to describe the relevant issues: "He had acquiesced in, by not differing from, the Tory attitude on the subject of domestic legislation, and had at one time agreed that public discussions on the conditions of the working-classes which show that they do not always have within their reach everything that they ought to have to make life bearable, only tend to provoke futile discontent, and were therefore demoralising." After learning of Ella's experiences, however, "he could no longer be relied upon as a party man in domestic affairs" (234). Rather, in the House of Lords, he "insisted on calling it mismanagement, seeing that still, in this wealthiest of nations, seventy-five per cent. of the population were insufficiently housed, clothed, and fed" (234–35). This, of course, is the change in attitude Grand advocates. Ideally, the work and words of a single needleworker can lead to changes in economic conditions and public policy for the benefit of all workers.

Where Ella differs most profoundly from all the lace makers she otherwise resembles is in her business acumen. Nuns produce church lace out of devotion, and wealthy ladies make lace to keep themselves occupied and to produce family heirlooms that, though valuable, are, by definition, not for sale; but the working-class lace maker, laboring under economic compulsion, suffers from dreadful working conditions and starvation wages. Ella refuses to submit to a similar fate. Instead, she becomes an astute businesswoman. One of the first scenes in which Ella appears shows her successfully bargaining with the Duchess of Castlefield Saye (who does not know her identity). The duchess initially offers only ten pounds for two years of Ella's work, but thanks to Ella's skillful negotiations ultimately pays three hundred pounds. Subsequently, the duke, having discovered Ella's identity and wishing to help her, bankrolls her opening a London showroom for lace. But Ella's goals are not merely to market her own wares, which, after all, require so much time to produce that she could not possibly produce enough single-handedly to fill a showroom. Instead, her aims are, first, to educate the public about the lace, its beauty, its history, its meaning; second, to create a market for lace by turning it into a fashionable commodity; and, third, and most important, to provide an outlet for a lace-makers' cooperative. When the duke asks her, "If you were offered one wish, Ella, now, I wonder, what would be the wish of your heart?" Ella promptly responds, "A liberal living wage for every worker" (221). Although incapable of assisting "every worker," she can dedicate herself to lace makers, even at the sacrifice of her own best interests: "Knowing, as I do, what misery is, and what my fellow-workers have to endure, I ask myself, Have I any right to be happy? And I answer myself, No! Not while there is one worker still to be rescued from the cruelties of men, from the callousness of women—from the lot which is death-in-life, a lingering death" (294).

Ella sees her own beauty as a means to selling her product. Recognizing that hers is a commodity for which conventional advertising would be inappropriate, she sets about to create demand by creating a fashion. She explains, "To me life is a big business which I intend to bring to a successful issue. My dress must further my object" (35). She accordingly exploits "the power that lay in her beauty to mould the minds of mankind to her will" (45), and devises a remarkable costume to wear to her showroom's opening: "Her dress—adapted eighteenth century, designed to show how lace should be worn—was an old-world, soft, satiny brocade, tinted with rose of the faintest shade on which lace could show itself, and draped to her figure so that it seemed a part of herself, the making of her as petals are the making of a flower" (282). One part of her shrinks from this display, whose eighteenth-century trappings identify it with Aestheticism, but her dedication to helping lace makers takes precedence over modesty: "The question of dress for her next at home day was serious. Her womanly readiness to sacrifice herself for the benefit of her workers, and her equally womanly horror of attracting undesirable attention, made the choice difficult. She had a consignment of new lace to advertise, and a difference of hundreds and hundreds of pounds more or less for her poor girls depended on how the lace looked when worn, and that meant on how she looked in it. There was no help for it. She must look her best" (590).

Grand portrays Ella's exploitation of her personal beauty for economic advantage as a particularly dangerous blurring of the private and the public, the beautiful and the practical, despite her noble motives. Its danger as a form of prostituting lies in its origins: a lesson she learned from the grandmother who taught her lace making. This grandmother (who at that time was the only person holding the secret of Ella's origins) taught her to view her beauty cynically, as an "inheritance" to "invest":

> "You can live decently on your inheritance, you can squander it, or you can make profit of it, great profit. . . . Set a price for yourself, and you will get it; you will be worth anything you ask. Every woman has her price, they say. . . . All the world over the price a decent woman asks for herself is safety and respect, love and marriage. But look high for love, my girl, you can't look too high. It's in the highest you'll inspire it most. The higher born your gentleman the better he knows the worth of beauty; and beauty he will have, bought or stolen. He'll try to buy or steal it from the poor; that's his way with the poor. But make him pay your price. He will pay it when there's no other way. Stand firm—Marriage! Make marriage your price, and you'll get it." (54)

Ella intends to use her beauty to win the hand of the duke's son. But she recognizes that it is an ideal marketing tool for the lace as well. When she is selling her lace to the duchess and Lord Melton asks, "What is your price?" Ella's reply, "My price is the highest to be had" (*Adnam*, 81), has a double meaning. By describing her demands for her lace using her grandmother's language of setting a high "price" for herself, Ella emphasizes the identification between the lace and its maker, between the marketing of lace and the marketing of her selfhood. Grand thus emphasizes the danger of Ella's situation, that she runs the risk of prostituting herself, or, at the very least, being perceived as a type of prostitute—the very problem she encounters late in *The Winged Victory*. And of course by taking her grandmother's advice that "you can't look too high," Ella looks beyond the match Grand wants readers to see as appropriate to her— that with Adnam Pratt, who like Ella is a natural aristocrat and specimen of eu- genic fitness—and she looks instead to Lord Melton, who, though aristocratic, is eugenically inferior and her own half brother to boot. Ella's superior busi- ness skills are portrayed as one of her admirable traits, but her decision to use her womanly beauty as an economic weapon proves advantageous only when the product is lace; when she attempts to market herself, the plan backfires.

The fact that marriage is her "price," while marriage is intended as a way to avoid prostitution or fallenness (like her mother's), only shows the inherent similarities between prostitution and marriage. Ella's attempts to justify her opinions underline what Gilman calls the "sexuo-economic" relation between the sexes: "[W]omen," says Ella, "are expected—are trained—to trade upon their beauty. Their lives are so arranged that there is no possibility for many of them of trading upon anything else. Half the marriages made are trade unions" (*Adnam*, 341). A poor woman, Ella believes, has an equal right to use her "asset": "Is it putting it to a baser use than my father and mother would have put it to had I been born well enough to be entitled to high preferment in the mar- riage market? It is customary to exploit the beauty of women in one way or an- other. Can it be wrong for a penniless girl to regard this valuable asset as her own bird-in-the-hand?" (340).

Ella's rationalizations serve more to indict marriage as akin to prostitution than they do to justify any, even metaphorical, attempts to commodify herself. Grand shows that, under this way of thinking, marriage, especially with mone- tary or class advancement as a goal, is morally bankrupt, and that becomes even more clear as we realize that Ella has set her sights on Lord Melton. To be sure, she believes that she loves him (and neither is aware of their kinship), but she is also quite consciously calculating in her pursuit of him, cognizant all along of her grandmother's advice. Marriage to Melton would, she believes, secure for her once and for all the economic and social wherewithal not only to free herself from precarious economic circumstance but to make perma- nent the lace-making cooperative that ensures the survival of other working- class lace makers. As the eventual Duchess of Castlefield Saye, she would attain the apparent ideal combination of circumstances: she would be able to make lace at leisure rather than under economic compulsion, in a condition of economic and social power that would allow her to effect social improvement on a broad scale well beyond the private sphere. It would seem a perfect way of reconciling divergent goals: personal, domestic fulfillment and public service, power as a woman in the apparently masculine economic world. In short, Ella's marriage to Melton would seem to provide the perfect platform for literary housekeeping.

But of course it does not. Shortly after the secret marriage, the couple learn Ella's identity; Melton commits suicide; and the duke brings Ella into his family. Ella must confront the ways that she has allowed herself to be controlled by her heredity. Ella is grief stricken but asserts, "If I have to live, I shall live bravely" (*Winged,* 647). As determined as she has been to help her lace makers, she seems unlikely to abandon them now. Yet Grand herself abandoned Ella, Adnam, and the promise of a redeemed world in which the highest development of agriculture and needlework would somehow mend relations between the sexes and among the classes.

The Needleworker Reworked in The Beth Book

Parker, in *The Subversive Stitch,* cites Sarah Grand's *The Beth Book* as an example of a misguided "tendency in nineteenth-century feminism which, by positing women's essential spiritual superiority, inadvertently confirmed the oppressive Victorian stereotype of 'The Angel in the House'" (8). To Parker, Grand's "attempt to validate women's work ultimately reinforces the rigid sexual categorisation and justifies the separate spheres" (7). But I argue that Grand portrayed needlework as a branch of literary housekeeping, as a means to reconcile women's distinctive domestic arts with their public gifts and aspirations.

To be sure, for much of *The Beth Book,* needlework in its many forms epitomizes everything that would seem to discourage the development of the "woman of genius" that Elizabeth Caldwell Maclure is destined to become. For one thing, the bulk of the sewing in the novel is not the ornamental sewing of the leisured middle-class woman but is what Grand calls "the everlasting making and mending" (140): a reflection of the poverty into which Beth is born and whose disadvantages she must struggle to overcome. Grand establishes this connection on the first page of the book, as we see Mrs. Caldwell, nine months pregnant with Beth, her seventh child, "looking up at noon from the stocking she was mending," and feeling a "depression of the spirits." The poor woman "would like to have felt it right to put away the mending," but she "lived in the days when no one thought of the waste of women['s lives]" (1). For Mrs. Caldwell, "it was hard to drag the darning-needle through that worn stocking, and, oh dear! the holes were so many and so big that week, and there were such quantities of other things to be done, clothes mended and made for the children, besides household matters to be seen to generally" (2). Sewing thus becomes a symbol of poverty, an emblem of maternal suffering, and an index of the backwardness of a culture that forces women with no talent for homemaking into an uncongenial activity, because self-sacrifice is their "duty."

Furthermore, Mrs. Caldwell's sewing precipitates an exchange through which Grand illustrates the oppressiveness of mid-Victorian marriage, for Mr. Caldwell, rather than being sympathetic to his wife's condition, merely looks at his pregnant, sewing wife with "critical disapprobation" and complains, "I wonder why it is when a woman marries she takes no more pains with herself. . . . When I married you, . . . [y]ou had more accomplishments than most of them, and now all you do, it seems to me, is the mending" (4). The functional "plain sewing" Mrs. Caldwell must do, far from being an attractively feminine accomplishment, only reinforces her husband's tendency to flirt with other women. Though necessary to her family, Mrs. Caldwell's mending alienates her husband, a quagmire that renders domesticity—and sewing—singularly unappealing.

We might therefore expect the book to follow the pattern that Elaine Hedges and other feminist critics have documented in much nineteenth-century and turn-of-the-century women's writing, in which "[a]n expressed distaste for, or an explicit rejection of, sewing became a hallmark in writing by or about the 'new woman.' Not to want to sew was a sign of intellectual seriousness, of literary or professional ambition" ("Needle," 345). And yet that prototypical New Woman Beth Caldwell actively seeks out sewing. One of the first representations of Beth's creative aspirations and her family's tendency to stifle them is a childhood scene in which Beth, accompanying her mother on her calls, is fascinated to discover the hostess "busy doing black monkeys on a grey ground in woolwork. She was astonished to find that it was possible to do such wonderful work, and she wanted to be taught immediately; but her mother made her ashamed of herself for supposing that *she* could do it, silly little body" (26).

Grand faults Mrs. Caldwell not only for suppressing Beth's impulse to do decorative needlework but also for failing to instruct her sooner in sewing's more practical branches. Mrs. Caldwell dislikes sewing and does it badly because she did not get proper instruction as a child, yet she perpetuates the failing in her own children: "She made and mended as badly as might be expected of a woman whose proud boast it was that when she was married she could not hem a pocket handkerchief; and she did it all herself. She had no notion of utilising the motive-power at hand in the children. As her own energy had been wasted in her childhood, so she wasted theirs, letting it expend itself to no purpose instead of teaching them to apply it" (118). One of the more interesting criticisms of Mrs. Caldwell's insufficiencies as a teacher of domestic skills comes in conjunction with the portrayal of one of her few maternal successes: her practice of reading aloud to her family each evening. In conventional scenes of this sort, the paterfamilias reads surrounded by the ladies of the family— with their work baskets. Here, the family is literally fatherless and figuratively motherless, as Mrs. Caldwell neglects to introduce her daughters to womanly work: "It was a pity she did not try to improve Beth and Bernadine by finding some sewing for their idle hands to do" (130). Instead, of course, Satan finds some mischief, in the form of nightly battles between the sisters—a far cry from the idealized picture of Victorian feminine placidity. Passages like this would seem to confirm Parker's criticism that Grand "reinforces the rigid sexual categorisation and justifies the separate spheres."

I argue, however, that in *The Beth Book,* needlework has a much more complex function—a "literary housekeeping" function. First, simply to look directly at sewing, to interrogate its domestic role rather than to take it for granted, is to take it seriously. The attention paid needlework indicates its intrinsic importance. Moreover, *The Beth Book* portrays Beth's embroidery as genuinely valuable. Beth carefully conceives "a piece of work, something more original and effective than the things usually sold in fancy-work shops, which did not often please her" (355), and when she sends it to a London depot, it is accepted "on spec." in violation of the usual policies, according to which Beth would have to pay a subscription—which she cannot afford—before putting her work up for sale. The secretary agrees to take the subscription out of Beth's first sale because "the committee thought that such an artistically beautiful design as hers was sure to be snapped up directly" (358). Sure enough, "[h]er beautiful embroidery . . . sold for six guineas," and Beth receives "an order from the depot for another piece of work at the same price" (359). Grand thus emphasizes that Beth's work is original and beautiful, a legitimate outlet of aesthetic expression. Its value is further proven by the public-sphere measure of money.

Furthermore, this needlework functions as a challenge to conventional marriage, which rigidly separates the private from the public. Beth originally undertakes the embroidery project in order to pay back the loan her husband wheedled out of her impoverished mother on false pretenses and with no intention of repayment; but then, when Mrs. Caldwell dies before Beth can erase the debt, Beth uses the money to free herself from her husband's control. Although Beth's initial investment in threads and other materials comes from gifts and loans—a reflection of her husband's control over money that ought to be her own—she nevertheless accumulates enough capital to leave her husband and become independent.

In *The Beth Book,* the "literary housekeeping" idea problematizes the standard trope of feminist criticism opposing "the needle and the pen." To be sure, while Beth concentrates on her needlework project, she stops both her writing and her studying, because, Grand explains, "she conceived them to be for her own mere personal benefit, while the task which she had set herself [the embroidery] was for a better purpose" (357). Later, of course, Grand questions that valuation, because Beth's writing serves humanity. But in the meantime, Grand also insists that, paradoxically, Beth's decision to sacrifice personal benefit actually produces even greater benefit—and sewing itself deserves the credit: Grand says of Beth's money-making project, "The exertion alone was inspiriting, and re-aroused the faculty which had been dormant in her of late" (354). Even more important is the way Beth uses her mind while her fingers are active with her needle:

> [A]lthough she did not study as had been her wont, while she sewed she occupied her mind in a way that was much more beneficial to it. . . . Beside her was always an open book, it might be a passage of Scripture, a scene from Shakespeare, a poem or paragraph rich in the wisdom and beauty of some great mind; and as she sewed she dwelt upon it, repeating it to herself until she was word-perfect in it, then making it even more her own by

earnest contemplation. . . . In meditating upon them she taught herself to meditate; and in following up the clues they gave her in the endeavour to discriminate and to judge fairly, by slow degrees she acquired the precious habit of clear thought. . . . Her mind, wonderfully fertilised, teemed again. . . . Purposeful thought was where the mere froth of sensuous seeing had been; and it was thought that now clamoured for expression. (357)

Thus, while it is true that "it was only when [Beth] could no longer ply her needle that she allowed herself to take up her pen" (359), Grand insists that not only the delay, but the fact that the delay is occasioned by needlework, actually strengthens Beth's mind, and thus the needle assists the pen. Instead of "contracting" her thoughts, as Wollstonecraft or Lamb might have predicted, Beth's sewing seems to focus her thinking, to make her reading more deliberate. The private, domestic activity of sewing has enabled Beth's public act of writing.

Grand calls Beth's writing "the delicate fancy work of her brain, a matter of enormous consequence" (358). This expression, "fancy work," generally applied to "frivolous" embroidery and here used to characterize Beth's highly serious writing project, plays as well with the multiple meanings of "fancy." Fancy, in its adjectival sense, implies something decorative, ornamental, even extravagant or impractical, but also suggests technical skill. At the same time, "fancy" in its noun form suggests imaginative creativity. The expression "delicate fancy work of her brain" thus erases the distinction between the work of Beth's needle and the work of her mind and pen. Indeed, in her 1923 introduction to *The Heavenly Twins,* Grand asserts that "there is no better stimulant for the brain of a woman" than sewing (ix).

One of the most puzzling evocations of needlework in *The Beth Book* is Grand's choice to quote a stanza from Tennyson's "The Lady of Shalott" several times in the novel's later chapters:

> *A bow-shot from her bower-eaves*
> *He rode between the barley sheaves,*
> *The sun came dazzling through the leaves,*
> *And flamed upon the brazen greaves*
>   *Of bold Sir Launcelot.*

The romantic ending of the novel, in which Beth's "knight" rides through the barley on the final page, has been criticized by, among others, Terri Doughty for undermining Grand's feminist message. The novel, Doughty says, "vividly and daringly portrays the protagonist's rebellion against the traditional female marriage plot, yet its romantic ending fails to sustain resistance" (185). And that this ending is rendered through allusion to a weaver of tapestry only seems to reinforce Parker's argument that Grand's "attempt to validate women's work ultimately reinforces . . . rigid sexual categorisation." I contend, however, that Grand's allusion unravels conventions and categories to create an alternative feminist literary housekeeping version of the Lady of Shalott's story.

In Tennyson's poem, the lady, like Plato's poet, produces an art at two removes from reality, for the lady's curse apparently prevents her from seeing more than "shadows of the world" in her mirror: "But in her web she still delights / To weave the mirror's magic sights" (64–65). The mirror is an important metaphor for Grand as well—but to very different purpose. The mirror image returns us one last time to "The New Aspect of the Woman Question": "Mirrors may be either a distorting or a flattering medium, but women do not care to see life any longer in a glass darkly. Let there be light. We suffer in the first shock of it. We shriek in horror at what we discover when it is turned on that which was hidden away in dark corners; but the first principle of good housekeeping is to have no dark corners" (276).

As we have seen, in Grand's literary housekeeping, literature is itself a form of housekeeping that sheds light—uncovers the truth about the world, especially about social problems about which women have particular insight. Writing, which supplies the mirror in which to see reality, acts as the "broom" raising the dust and offers "domestic" solutions to the messes it identifies and sets out to clean up—or to mend. In direct answer to the traditional image of the seamstress bent over her work to the exclusion of all else—and to the Platonic/Tennysonian image of the artist who sees only "shadows"—Grand creates a seamstress whose room affords an unusually wide capacity to observe—both physically to oversee and intellectually and spiritually to understand, through her mystical "further faculty."

Tennyson's lady, we recall,

> *weaves by night and day*
> *A magic web with colours gay.*
> *She has heard a whisper say,*

> *A curse is on her if she stay*
> *To look down to Camelot.*

> (37–41)

But whereas Tennyson's weaver was punished with death when "she left the web, she left the loom," Beth's capacity for vision enables her to leave her secluded tower and realize her genius as a speaker for women's rights. Yet at the end of the novel, she once again sits at a window, this time of a small domestic cottage, remembering lines from Tennyson's poem: "A bowshot from her bower-eaves, / He rode between the barley-sheaves" (qtd. in *The Beth Book*, 527). The man Beth, Grand's "new lady," sees riding toward her on horseback is not a sexually adventurous Lancelot but an Arthur, New Man Arthur Brock, who is "fit to help [her] make a home" in the "human household."[5] His arrival as Beth stands at her window casement allows her to complement public success with domestic bliss. She leaves her castle, not in spite but because of her needlework, which has facilitated her book about "the great problems of life" (376). Her singing of her song does not lead to death; as Beth finds her voice, "recognise[s] her vocation," and becomes a great orator, she weaves "words [that] should come with comfort to thousands of those that suffer, who, when they heard, would raise their heads once more in hope" (527).

In *The Beth Book*, Grand portrays sewing as primarily a means to achieve a feminist end, a private, feminine, domestic method for escaping a stultifying domesticity and entering the world of public equality. By creating Beth as an orator, Grand insists on an overtly political function for her feminist "woman of genius," much more political than sewing could possibly be. As we have seen, in the later *Adnam's Orchard* and *The Winged Victory*, Grand would show needlework, as an economic activity, becoming a political force in its own right; but in *The Beth Book*, once Beth has employed sewing to free herself from her husband, it no longer functions as a means for balancing the public and private. Beth's oratory allows her to do for others what her sewing did for her: break the bonds of old ideas.

If *The Beth Book* is partly a conscious response to Tennyson's "Lady of Shalott," it is also, in part, a meditation on Thomas Carlyle's ideas, especially his discussions of duty and his "clothes philosophy" in *Sartor Resartus*. Beth reads Carlyle in her period of self-education after her marriage, during which she is particularly interested in authors' biographies and autobiographies. Much of

The Beth Book is a commentary on one of *Sartor Resartus*'s most famous concerns—duty—though in most cases, Grand rejects traditional obligations that are *mis*named duties. In some instances, such as Mrs. Caldwell's mending at the beginning of the novel, needlework constitutes such a misnamed duty. Most egregiously, Beth conceives her embroidery to be a "duty," in contrast to her writing: "But her very delight in her new pursuit [writing] made her think it right to limit her indulgence in it. Duty she conceived to be a painful effort necessarily, but writing was a pleasure; she therefore attended first conscientiously to her embroidery, and any other task she thought it right to perform, although her eager impatience to get back to her desk made each in turn a toil to her" (358).

Beth's assessments of her duty are portrayed as severely mistaken in this case, but that is not to say that the book altogether rejects the concept of duty. The last quarter of the book devotes a remarkable amount of attention to differentiating true duties from false. In one of her conversations with Arthur Brock, Beth remarks, "The life for a woman to long for—and a man too, I think—is a life of simple duties and simple pleasures, a normal life; but I only call that life normal which is suited to the requirements of the woman's individual temperament" (504). Throughout the book, Grand insists on the importance of Beth's fostering the "requirements" of her "individual temperament" and expresses this mandate in the language of duty. In the final pages of the book, Beth recognizes her "natural gift" for oratory. Having heard "the call," Beth has a duty to produce "art for man's sake," by means of "the mesmeric power which is part of the endowment of an orator" (525), not only because it is her "vocation," but because it is "the way in which she could best live for others" (524). Beth's voyage of self-discovery in this female bildungsroman illustrates Carlyle's idea of "the folly of that impossible Precept, *Know thyself;* till it be translated into this partially possible one, *Know what thou canst work-at*" (163).

Thus, while Grand rejects false "duties," she ultimately endorses a sense of duty that is consistent with Carlyle's, largely because it echoes the "clothes philosophy" of *Sartor Resartus.* Carlyle compares all human institutions to clothes, which simultaneously conceal and reveal the reality beneath. Thus "Church-Clothes" are "the Forms, the *Vestures,* under which men have at various periods embodied and represented for themselves the Religious Principle" (214). Of course clothes, whether literal or symbolic, inevitably become worn out and tattered, and these worn-out institutions need to be discarded—and replaced. Who will replace—retailor—these institutions? Significantly, Carlyle looks, in part, to writers: "What too are all Poets and moral Teachers, but a species of Metaphorical Tailors?" he asks (290). Because "symbols, like all terrestrial Garments, wax old" (224), Carlyle says we must look to "the Poet and inspired Maker; who, Prometheus-like, can shape new Symbols" (225). Beth, formerly a poet, now an inspired orator or "moral Teacher," is just such a metaphorical tailor—or rather a needleworker, reworking worn-out patriarchal institutions. That the "maker" is a woman and the metaphor is not tailoring but dressmaking reflects Grand's insistence that women, led by geniuses like Beth Maclure who possess skill with both the needle and the pen, are, if anything, more qualified than men in the 1890s to remake a worn-out culture.

Oscar Wilde famously asserted, "All art is quite useless." But Grand, like Gilman and Ward, developed her aesthetic of "literary housekeeping" in conscious opposition to art for art's sake, and embraced the useful effects of art that the Aesthetes denied. Like Carlyle, Grand, Gilman, and Ward look to writers to retailor worn-out institutions. They insist that writing is housekeeping and therefore is women's work, and they make sure that their readers know that the "delicate fancy work" of a woman's brain is a matter "of enormous consequence."

EPILOGUE

Literary Dust-ups

Cleaning Out the Housekeepers

THE PHRASE "LITERARY HOUSEKEEPING" can carry an entirely different connotation from that I have been exploring in this book: it can indicate
a kind of canonical spring-cleaning to clear away the rubbish. Without a doubt,
many reviewers took it upon themselves to thus dispose of Ward, Grand, and
Gilman. Contemporary reviewers discerned the three writers' interest in
housekeeping—and held it against them. An *Athenaeum* reviewer of Ward's
History of David Grieve called Ward's writing not realism, but "commonplace,"
the distinction apparently referring to domesticity, for in the "commonplace,"
the author is "like some housewife, insisting upon narrating the utterly unin-
teresting past history of a cook or a housemaid" (142). Ambrose Bierce, who
used his "Prattle" column in the *San Francisco Examiner* to carry out something
of a vendetta against Gilman and the Pacific Coast Women's Press Association,
for which she edited the *Impress,* sniped that "the leading members of the
Pacific Coast Women's Press Association . . . assuredly do not know the difference between poetry and pottery." Attacks on Grand took the opposite tack,
accusing her of purveying filth. A reviewer of *The Beth Book* accused Grand of
making "an unjustifiable show of uncleanness with scarcely a suggestion of
remedy" and recommended, "let us keep our social sewers covered as closely
as possible until such time as we see our way to make them clean" (487, 489).

Gilman, Grand, and Ward knew, of course, that their approach to writing
was artistically unfashionable. Throughout their works we see what I have called

the "judicial" stance in Ward's criticism: an impulse to defend (or perhaps be defensive about) what they saw as women's ways of writing against alternative theories by writers whose prestige seems to have been obvious. These prestigious writers included the naturalists, the decadents (labeled "French fiction"), the Aesthetes or "Stylists," and the "objective" or "self-expressive" modernists. Early in their careers, Gilman, Grand, and Ward could argue that the public, which embraced their books, knew better than the critics who complained about "the novel with a purpose." As the twentieth century progressed, however, all three saw precipitous drops in popularity, as literary and political fashions changed around them. Ward's sales plummeted in the last ten years of her life, and most of her books were out of print within a few years of her death, in 1920. Grand published her last collection of stories in 1922, and by the time she died in 1943, her work was virtually unknown, even by the citizens of Bath, who knew her well as their mayoress. Gilman published no new fiction and fewer than a dozen poems after the *Forerunner* ceased publication, in 1916; and after 1920, her production of nonfiction slowed to the relative trickle of about three pieces a year until her final illness and death in 1935. Every few years throughout the mid-twentieth century, an anthology of horror stories would include "The Yellow Wall-Paper"; and *Robert Elsmere* slipped in and out of print for varying stretches of time. But for the most part, all three writers were forgotten.

Undoubtedly it is the rare author whose popularity long outlives her without the assent of the era's most powerful critical voices. As the twentieth century progressed, those voices belonged to the academic literary critics, and the midcentury academic critics' criteria of literary merit and ways of reading were profoundly shaped by the very modernists against whom Ward, Grand, and Gilman had contrasted their own approaches. As we have seen, literary housekeeping represents an attempt to reconcile private domesticity with public service and literary beauty with practical political "purpose." But the New Criticism, with its formalist emphasis on irony, paradox, and ambiguity, rejected what Poe had called the "heresy of the didactic" and shied away from "a dangerous turn to some special 'use of poetry'" (Brooks, 209), so the literary housekeepers' unapologetic embrace of writing with a purpose made their work, by definition, "heretical." Furthermore, the modernist aesthetic is notably "intent on distancing itself and its products from the trivialities and banalities of everyday life" (Huyssen 47), of which housekeeping is a preeminent example. For the modernists, portrayal of everyday or domestic subjects characterizes "middle-brow," that is, second-rate, art. Moreover, modernism, along with the literary critical culture it influenced, "conceives its formal vocation to be the resistance to commodity form" (Jameson, 134). The very popularity of the literary housekeepers was thus further reason to question their literary value. By midcentury, "Mrs. Humphry Ward" had become a byword for terrible writing; Gilman was remembered, if at all, for one ambiguous little "horror story"; and Grand was utterly unknown. "Literary housekeeping" was not a paradox but simply a contradiction in terms.

To be sure, women modernists—including Woolf, Mansfield, Richardson, Cather, Wharton, Stein, and many others—often portray domestic scenes, and Woolf in *A Room of One's Own* explicitly challenges the critical devaluation of women's experiences in literature. But if the domestic realm can be both the subject of and the inspiration for women modernists' art, as it is in *To the Lighthouse,* for example, neither the art nor the domesticity has the type of practical, public-spirited, forward-looking implications characterizing "literary housekeeping."

For if literary housekeeping was alien to definitions of literature for much of the twentieth century, its effort to reconcile the political and the domestic likewise ran counter to women's cultures of most of the century. Generally speaking, domesticity and public politics were understood as mutually exclusive. Although feminism by no means disappeared after the suffrage victories of 1918, the movement lost much of its cohesion. After the vote was won in Britain, the National Union of Women's Suffrage Societies (NUWSS) became the National Union of Societies for Equal Citizenship (NUSEC), and, led by Eleanor Rathbone, lobbied for family allowances paid to women, protective factory legislation, maternity benefits, easy access to birth control, and other reforms designed to cater to women's distinctive needs at home and at work. This policy of "New Feminism" led to a serious split in the NUSEC when NUWSS founder Millicent Garrett Fawcett, along with many of her allies with a similar equal-rights emphasis, resigned in 1926. Feminism in both Britain and America tended to be identified with Fawcett's allies rather than Rathbone's.

Changes in the American home economics movement reinforced and perpetuated this perception. By the postwar era, such pioneers of the movement as Ellen Richards and Helen Campbell were dead, and the newer generation tended not to share their political and social welfare goals. Many of the civic housekeepers' social welfare concerns were institutionalized in governmental programs under male control, limiting public service opportunities for women. Home economics classes in America and domestic science classes in Britain increasingly focused on training schoolgirls to be housewives rather than to pursue careers in social service, while professional home economists took jobs with appliance or food manufacturers, helping to develop and market products for "Mrs. Consumer" and promoting scientific housework only in order to sell the latest cleanser or kitchen gadget. This, of course, is the home economics that Betty Friedan justly accused of creating the ideology of the happy housewife heroine against which early "second stage" feminists rebelled. To be a "liberated woman" in the 1960s and early 1970s meant, by definition, to reject domesticity. It wasn't until the late 1970s and early 1980s—around the time that Gilman's *Herland* was first reprinted—that feminists began to rediscover the political implications of domestic values, and cultural studies scholars began to look beyond the modernist-defined literary canon.

For nearly fifty years, Gilman, Grand, and Ward were virtually unknown, written out of literary history. But as we have learned in the past thirty years or so, there was more going on in the final years of the nineteenth century and first years of the twentieth century than the "rise of modernism." To reexamine "literature as housekeeping" is, as Grand would say, to illuminate a previously dark corner of literary history: good housekeeping indeed.

NOTES

Introduction

1. In both countries, the numbers of households with servants varied dramatically among regions and between urban and rural areas. For more detailed information on servants, on explanations for their decreasing numbers, and on the difficulties in obtaining reliable statistics, see Horn and Katzman.

2. See, for example, Cathy Davidson, Gavison, Hansen, Reverby and Helly, Kerber, Pateman, and Romero.

3. In the United States, home economics was taught at Wellesley and Smith but not at the other members of the Seven Sisters. For accounts of the history of home economics, see Handlin, Stage and Vincenti, and the far less sympathetic accounts by Ogle and Shapiro. Accounts of domestic arts education in England are more scattered. Among the useful studies are Burstall, Dyhouse, Kamm, and McDermid. Apparently on account of Britain's class and education systems, domestic science education failed to thrive in England as an organized movement or field of advanced education as it did in the United States. Women academics in England—whose access to higher education was more recent and hard-won—scornfully rejected domestic science courses as retreats from academic parity. English promoters of domestic arts classes tended to be relatively conservative educators, who targeted working-class girls—future servants—for classes in practical skills, as an alternative to academic curricula. Domestic science thus tended to reach England's middle-class homemakers through domestic advice manuals and public health campaigns rather than through classroom training.

4. The best sources of biographical information on Ward are her autobiography, *A Writer's Recollections* (1918); *The Life of Mrs. Humphry Ward* (1923) by her daughter, Janet Penrose Trevelyan; and John Sutherland's *Mrs. Humphry Ward: Eminent Victorian, Pre-Eminent Edwardian* (1990). On Gilman, see her autobiography, *The Living of Charlotte Perkins Gilman* (1935); and the biographies *Charlotte Perkins Gilman: The Making of a Radical Feminist, 1860–1896* (1980), by Mary A. Hill; and *To "Herland" and Beyond: The Life and Works of Charlotte Perkins Gilman* (1990), by Ann J. Lane. On Grand, the only biography is *Darling Madame: Sarah Grand and Devoted Friend* (1983), by Gillian Kersley.

Although based on study of documentary material, the material comes primarily from the diaries of Grand's "devoted friend" Gladys Singers-Bigger, who met Grand in 1925; moreover, lacking other information, Kersley is quick to assume autobiographical content in Grand's fiction. For correctives to Kersley, see Teresa Mangum's important study *Married, Middlebrow, and Militant: Sarah Grand and the New Woman Novel;* Carol Senf's introduction to *The Heavenly Twins;* and the documents gathered by Ann Heilmann and Stephanie Forward in *Sex, Social Purity, and Sarah Grand.*

Chapter 1

1. Further references to Ward's prefaces to *The Life and Work of the Sisters Brontë* will use the abbreviation *LW,* followed by the volume and page number.

2. Grand's connection to the New Woman movement is indisputable; Ward's and Gilman's less established. Among contemporaries who linked Gilman to the New Woman is Campbell, "Famous Persons"; on Ward and the New Woman see Barry, Oliphant, Pearse, and "Fiction New and Old."

3. The participants were Walter Besant, Thomas Hardy, and Eliza Lynn Linton.

4. The distinction and terminology were introduced by Hugh Stutfield in 1897 and have shaped many subsequent discussions of the genre.

5. Howells published works by both Gilman and Ward and wrote admiringly of both. Grand praises Eliot repeatedly: especially noteworthy are "Does Marriage Hinder," 119; and "A Page of Confessions," in which she identifies Eliot as her favorite novelist. Gilman wrote "Thurston Gower," one of her early "Who Wrote It?" stories for the *Impress,* in imitation of Eliot, and in the subsequent "Story Study" both praises Eliot's "breadth of vision" and "deep insight" and criticizes her "somewhat heavy style" (5). Ward, whose own narrative approach owes the most to Eliot of the three writers considered in this book, was also the most ambivalent of the three, praising Eliot publicly in her memoirs (*A Writer's Recollections,* 1:144–48) and in her preface to Charlotte Brontë's *Villette* (*LW,* 3:xxv–xxvi), but privately confiding, "[H]ere I am, terribly bored—tell it not!—by *Adam Bede* and obliged to give up on an article I had half promised Mr. Dudley Warner on George Eliot because I cannot be wholly or even mostly on my knees, and it is not seemly for me to be anything else. What a prig is Adam, & what a Sunday school tone most of it has" (Mary Ward to George Smith, 22 October 1896, Department of Special Collections at the Honnold/Mudd Library, Claremont, California, 2:11).

6. See Williams on efforts by Elizabeth Stuart Phelps to manage a similar balancing act at a slightly earlier period and without the literary housekeepers' emphasis on reconciling the private and public spheres.

7. See Black, 282; and Grand's letter of 20 May 1896 to Mrs. Burnett Smith (Annie S. Swan): "A great deal of modern fiction is certainly not true of life at large . . . ; yet all is interesting as an indication of the possibilities of human nature. . . . But I am no authority whatever on fiction. I seldom read novels, and only write of that I know from observation and long study of human nature" (Mildred Robertson Nicoll, ed., *The Letters of Annie S. Swan,* [London: Hodder and Stoughton, 1945], 26. Qtd. in Heilmann and Forward, 2:47 n. 1).

8. All quotations are from the British edition of *Our Manifold Nature,* completed some months after publication of the American edition and featuring substantial revisions, including a reordering of the stories, and significant additions to the preface and to nearly all the stories.

9. All quotations from *The Beth Book* are taken from the Dial Press edition.

10. A nearly identical observation appears in *The Beth Book,* 372.

11. Among the critical discussions that quote this set of statements are Knight, *Charlotte Perkins Gilman: A Study of the Short Fiction,* and Tuttle.

12. "Stetson Reception," *Topeka State Journal,* 15 June 1896, 6. Qtd. in Scharnhorst, *Charlotte Perkins Gilman,* 40.

13. On this parallel between the early short story and the late novel, see Golden and Knight's afterword to *Unpunished,* 226–27.

14. See Knight, *Charlotte Perkins Gilman: A Study of the Short Fiction.*

15. These stories are "According to Solomon" (1909), "Martha's Mother" (1910), "A Coincidence" (1910), "Mrs. Potter and the Clay Club" (1911), "Mrs. Elder's Idea" (1912), "An Innocent Girl" (1912), "Maidstone Comfort" (1912), and *Won Over* (1913). The 1914 *Benigna Machiavelli* is Gilman's prequel to the earlier stories, describing how the character developed her remarkable capacity to "make things move [her] way" (12).

16. "The Study of Poetry" first appeared as the introduction to Humphry Ward's multivolume anthology *The English Poets* (1880), to which Mary Ward contributed introductions to the work of several individual poets.

17. All quotations from *Robert Elsmere* are taken from the University of Nebraska Press edition (1967).

18. Other uses of this metaphor appear in the 1892 preface to *The History of David Grieve* (reprinted in the 1911 Westmoreland edition, *The Writings of Mrs. Humphry Ward,* 3.x), in the 1911 preface to *The Marriage of William Ashe* (12:xvi), and in a letter, written during the war, in which Ward remarked, "I never felt more inclined to spin tales" (Trevelyan, 269). In the introduction to Charlotte Brontë's *Villette,* Ward describes George Eliot and George Sand as "observers of the many-coloured web" (*LW,* 3:xxv–xxvi).

19. All quotations from *The History of David Grieve* are taken from the first American edition (Macmillan, 1892).

20. Thomas Arnold to Mrs. Arnold, 16 June 1870, in *The Letters of Thomas Arnold the Younger,* ed. James Bertram (Auckland, New Zealand: Auckland University Press, 1980), 167.

21. All quotations from *A Great Success* are taken from the American edition (Hearst, 1916).

22. All quotations from *Delia Blanchflower* are taken from the American edition (Hearst, 1914).

23. Mary Ward to George Smith, 6 October 1896, Department of Special Collections at the Honnold/Mudd Library, Claremont University, 2:11. Reprinted in the Broadview edition of *Marcella,* 558.

Chapter 2

1. *The Testing of Diana Mallory* was simultaneously published in England as *Diana Mallory.* Page citations in this study refer to the American edition (Harper, 1908).

2. All quotations from *Marcella* are taken from the Broadview edition (2002).

3. In her several articles that address Grand and eugenics, Richardson explicitly argues against interpretations by Sally Ledger, Elaine Showalter, and Teresa Mangum.

4. See Bland's discussion of the impact of Lamarckianism on turn-of-the-century feminists. Bland points out that in *The Descent of Man,* Darwin resorted to Lamarckian explanations of some phenomena. Lamarckian theories were not discredited by scientists until the 1930s, and the ideas still hold sway in the popular imagination.

5. For discussions of the imperialist implications of the "domestic" in American literature (apart from eugenics), see Kaplan and Romero.

6. The bacterium responsible for gonorrhea was isolated in 1879, but the syphilis spirochete—which would have been of greater interest to Grand—was not identified until 1905.

7. If nothing else, the war rendered highly suspect the overt pro-German sentiments of the first two novels. The 1926 fire at her residence destroyed, Grand told Gladys Singers-Bigger, her poetry and at least one of her lectures. See letters of 25 December 1928 and 15 May 1930 (Heilmann and Forward, 2:119 and 2:138). In her "Personal Sketch of Matilda Barbara Betham-Edwards" (1919), Grand recalls that Miss Betham-Edwards

> had been kindly interested in a book of mine which was designed to have a sequel, and one day on the asphalt path, by way of spurring me on to work, she

gave me what she supposed would be my plot. There was no resemblance. It was like listening to some one who had been misinformed about the doings of friends with whom I had kept in close touch. I knew she was mistaken, yet her circumstantial account implanted a doubt in my mind as to which of us were really the better informed. In effect, it disturbed my certainty without convincing me of error, and the sequel was never written. (xxxiii)

8. Speech to Liverpool Settlement, 1899/1900. Mary Ward Centre Archives, box 25. Qtd. in Lewis, 218.

9. Gilman's identifying powerful women as "aunts" may reflect her attitudes toward her great-aunts, the renowned experts on homemaking, who must have seemed far more commanding figures than her own ineffectual mother.

Chapter 3

1. Clarence Cook, "Beds and Tables, Stools and Candlesticks" (*Scribner's Monthly* 10 [1875]: 354. Qtd. in Handlin, 430).

2. Chase reports one hundred women architects registered in America in 1900 (133). See also the discussions in Walker and Hayden.

3. An important exception is Gilman's role-reversal story, "Her Housekeeper."

4. I am grateful to Kathleen K. Anspaugh for calling this pattern to my attention.

5. See Mouton's excellent study of Grand's use of "The Lady of Shalott" in *The Heavenly Twins*.

6. Attribution by Scharnhorst in *Charlotte Perkins Gilman: A Bibliography*.

7. In addition, several of Gilman's stories and novellas include significant episodes about hotels, boardinghouses, and artists' colonies. These include "Martha's Mother" (1910), "Her Housekeeper" (1910), "The Jumping Off Place" (1911), "Dr. Clair's Place," "The Cottagette," and the novellas *The Crux* and *Benigna Machiavelli*.

8. Heather Kirk Thomas argues that the paper represents a Morris print, but this interpretation overlooks the house's age, and surely misapplies to Morris the paper's violation of all principles of design—for it is unreasonable to fault Morris's papers on this score. Moreover, Gilman was a great admirer of Morris, recording reading his works in several of her diary entries. In her memoirs, Gilman recalled fondly her opportunity to meet Morris when she was in England in 1896: "But I did meet William Morris, both at the Congress and in his home in Hammersmith. Gray and glorious he was, and most kind" (*Living,* 209). Later in the memoirs she recalls, "October 3rd has a heavy black line. 'William Morris died to-day.' That was a great loss to the progress of England, of the world. Fortunately he left large work, large years of glorious giving" (212).

9. Gilman recollected, "But the real purpose of the story was to reach Dr. S. Weir Mitchell, and convince him of the error of his ways. I sent him a copy as soon as it came out, but got no response. However, many years later, I met some one who knew close friends of Dr. Mitchell's who said he had told them that he had changed his treatment of nervous prostration since reading 'The Yellow Wallpaper.' If that is a fact, I have not lived in vain" (*Living*, 121).

10. In her diary entry for 19 April 1883, she writes, "Stop at Tibbitts & Shaw's and buy 10 ct. book 'Diseases of Modern Life,' Richardson" (*Diaries*, 186). On 26 September 1883, she notes, "Go & read 'Diseases of Modern Life' while Eddie [the boy for whom she was governess] fishes" (*Diaries*, 222).

11. In one of the odder moments in the history of marketing, a copy of a pirated edition of *Robert Elsmere* was offered as a free premium with purchase of a cake of Maine Balsam Fir Soap. Perhaps the sanitary subtext illustrated by the Mile End episode helps explain the Maine Balsam Fir Company's sales strategy.

12. See Sutherland, especially chapter 18, on challenges to Ward's vision for the original University Hall, culminating in the residents' move to Marchmont Hall, and Ward's ensuing work to develop the Passmore Edwards Settlement. Sutherland's account is usefully balanced by Trevelyan, 86–91.

13. Today's Mary Ward Centre, a nonresidential adult education institute, is located in another building in Queen's Square. The building designed by Brewer and Smith to be the Passmore Edwards Settlement currently houses the National Institute for Social Work.

Chapter 4

1. Although meals themselves represent significant narrative moments in writings by Gilman, Grand, and Ward—as is the case in much fiction—for the purposes of this study I will discuss only meals whose provision and preparation somehow play a role in the literature.

2. Most notable among these exceptions are, in Grand, a variety of gender-bending behaviors in early episodes of *The Heavenly Twins,* as well as cross-dressing incidents in both *The Heavenly Twins* and *The Beth Book;* in Gilman, Herland's achievement of most modern technological and engineering feats without men, and the portrayal of women in a variety of traditionally male professions—but in little male blue-collar work; in Ward, as well, women's success in professions previously considered male, such as secretary (*Elizabeth's Campaign*) and ambulance driver (*Helena*).

3. The book was published in England as *The War and Elizabeth*. Page citations in this study refer to the American edition.

4. In early 1916, Ward received a letter from Theodore Roosevelt, whom she had met at the White House during her 1908 tour of the United States. The former president, who hoped to influence Americans' sentiment in favor of entering the war in Europe, suggested that Ward, "in a series of articles, put vividly before our people what the English people are doing" (Theodore Roosevelt to Mary Ward, 27 December 1915. Qtd. in Sutherland, 350). In response, Ward obtained permission from the British government to visit the fleet, munitions factories, and even the trenches, access unprecedented for a woman; she assembled her notes into six remarkable "Letters to an American Friend" for syndication in American newspapers, subsequently gathered in book form as *England's Effort,* and followed by two more books of war propaganda, *Towards the Goal* (1917) and *Fields of Victory* (1919). Ward's extensive observation of war work underlies her four wartime novels, *Missing* (1917), *The War and Elizabeth, Cousin Philip* (1919), and *Harvest*.

5. All quotations from *Harvest* are taken from the American edition (Dodd, Mead, 1920).

6. Denise D. Knight's definitive edition begins with selections from the early diaries, beginning 1 January 1879, rather than with Charlotte Perkins's earliest diaries, begun in 1876, when she was fifteen. Unabridged selections begin with the 25 December 1880 entry.

7. For example, during one period when Mrs. Perkins was ill and her daughter had taken over the housekeeping, Charlotte reports, "Aunt C[aroline]. and I are so anxious to have some of '*mother's* sponge-cake' for tea, that we make it ourselves! Inside of ten minutes too" (18 June 1882; *Diaries,* 127). On a later occasion, a few months into her marriage, Charlotte records, "[W]e all revel in chicken soup. *Good!* As good as mother's, Aunt C. said so!" (23 September 1884; 304). On 23 February 1885, "Mrs. Springer comes & makes 'anise brodt' to show me how" (319).

8. Gilman's emphasis on "unaided eggs" is glossed by a remark in *The Joy of Cooking* that "true-blue sponge cake enthusiasts scorn baking powder" (Rombauer and Becker, 669).

9. John Kucich has observed that in both *The Heavenly Twins* and *The Beth Book* Grand links creativity with lying, and associates both with childish high spirits to be outgrown. I would add that Grand's associating creativity with stealing food, as amusing in children but suspect in adults, underlines her ambivalence.

10. See my "The Slayer and the Slain" on Ward's use of the myth of the priests of Diana at Nemi, a central topic of Frazer's study.

11. The echo between the names Ellesborough and "Herland" is probably only co-incidence, but a notable one all the same.

12. Helen Small asks "[h]ow far the taint of adultery made Rachel an unsalvage-able heroine" and notes the "high-Victorian moralism in the novel's presentation of her death" (41). It is certainly the case that women do not divorce with impunity in Ward's books. However, unlike divorcees in Ward's previous novels, Rachel left her husband not on account of thoughtless pique (*Daphne*) or passion for another man (*Eltham House*) but because her brutal husband allowed their baby to die when he chose to get drunk rather than fetch a doctor; the now-ex-husband, Roger Delane, who ultimately murders Rachel, is no saintly wronged husband like those in Ward's earlier novels of divorce, but a horrifyingly well-drawn example of what we would today call a "stalker" determined to control his ex-wife, even if the only way to do so is to kill her.

Chapter 5

1. All quotations from *Sir George Tressady* are taken from the first British edition (Smith, Elder, 1896).

2. Adrian Forty speculates that the peak of the home hygiene movement in the 1920s and 1930s coincided with the adulthood of those whose school years in the first two decades of the century had featured the most intense propaganda about hygiene (*Objects*, 116). One might also observe that the decline in the movement Forty observes after the 1930s coincides with the increasing availability of effective antibiotics in the 1940s.

3. Mary Ward to Mandell Creighton, 20 December 1893, MS letter, Pusey House, Oxford; *Marcella*, Broadview edition, appendix C.2.

4. Knight, "An 'Amusing Source of Income,'" and MacDonnell identify the cards Gilman created and provide evidence for the attributions; the articles are usefully read alongside the illustrations in Cheadle and Lee. For briefer accounts of Gilman's work on the soap cards, see *Living*, 47; Hill, 56; and numerous diary entries from 28 October 1880 to 2 March 1884.

5. In thus studying the cards, I follow Denise D. Knight, whose "An 'Amusing Source of Income'" argues that the cards "reflect [Gilman's] innovative artistic imagi-nation" and "illuminate her social and racial theories" (8).

6. On Wilde's impact on trade card design, see Navarre.

7. The square box end marked with a large "K" for Kendall is a repeated image on Gilman's cards, so the stacks of three "K"s probably do not allude to the Ku Klux Klan and represent only unpleasant coincidence.

8. See, for example, the swallows and stars spelling "S.O.A.P.I.N.E." in "Soapine Telegraph" and "Wizard, Stars and Moon," respectively (Cheadle and Lee, 18, 15).

9. Compare, for example, pages 187, 244, and 245.

10. Compare, for example, Roger Moore in "The Vintage," Mr. Marimor in "Turned," the bigamist Mr. Cunningham/Henderson in "Being Reasonable," and Dr. Armstrong in *Mag—Marjorie*.

Chapter Six

1. See Alexander's excellent study of Victorian representations of needlewomen.

2. I have opted in this chapter to concentrate on the task of sewing itself rather than on clothing as an end product, a topic that could expand into a book in its own right, since all three writers were interested in fashion, and Gilman and Grand wrote extensively about dress reform. See especially Grand's *Two Dear Little Feet* and Gilman's *The Dress of Women*.

3. All quotations from *Helbeck of Bannisdale* are taken from the Penguin edition.

4. For example, in *The Winged Victory* Ella's explanation of the history of the lily as a symbol of the Annunciation in the lace called *potten Kant* (pot lace) uses the very words of Palliser's explanation: "As Romanism declined, the angel disappeared and the lily pot became a vase of flowers" (Grand, 534; Palliser, 106 n. 53); language in other parts of Grand's passage echoes Palliser's closely.

5. As Mangum has noted, the implications of the union are muddied somewhat by the fact that Beth's husband has denied her a divorce.

BIBLIOGRAPHY

Abrams, M. H. *The Mirror and the Lamp: Romantic Theory and the Critical Tradition*. London: Oxford University Press, 1953.

Adam, Juliette. "The Tree of Knowledge." *New Review* 10 (1894): 675–90.

Adams, Annmarie. *Architecture in the Family Way: Doctors, Houses, and Women, 1870–1900*. Montreal: McGill-Queen's University Press, 1996.

Alexander, Lynn M. *Women, Work, and Representation: Needlewomen in Victorian Art and Literature*. Athens: Ohio University Press, 2003.

Allen, Polly Wynn. *Building Domestic Liberty: Charlotte Perkins Gilman's Architectural Feminism*. Amherst: University of Massachusetts Press, 1988.

"Anti-Suffrage Campaign." *Times* (London), 15 November 1909, 14, col. 3.

"The Anti-Suffrage Demonstration." *Times* (London), 14 July 1910, 9, col. 6.

Ardis, Ann L. *New Women, New Novels: Feminism and Early Modernism*. New Brunswick, NJ: Rutgers University Press, 1990.

Armstrong, Nancy. *Desire and Domestic Fiction: A Political History of the Novel*. New York: Oxford University Press, 1987.

Arnold, Matthew. "The Function of Criticism at the Present Time." In *Essays in Criticism*, 1–41. 1865. Reprint, London: Macmillan, 1907.

———. Matthew Arnold to Mrs. Forster, 14 April 1853. In *The Letters of Matthew Arnold, 1848–1888,* edited by George W. E. Russell, 1:34. New York: Macmillan, 1895.

———. "The Study of Poetry." In *Complete Prose Works,* edited by R. H. Super. Vol. 9. Ann Arbor: University of Michigan Press, 1973.

Bakhtin, Mikhail M. "Discourse in the Novel." In *The Dialogic Imagination: Four Essays,* translated by Caryl Emerson and Michael Holquist, edited by Michael Holquist, 259–422. Austin: University of Texas Press, 1981.

———. *Problems of Dostoevsy's Poetics*. Translated by Caryl Emerson. In *Theory and History of Literature,* vol. 8. Minneapolis: University of Minnesota Press, 1984.

Baldwin, Kenneth Huntress. No title. In Knight, *Charlotte Perkins Gilman,* 175–84. New York: Twayne, 1997.

[Barry, W. F.] "The Strike of a Sex." *Quarterly Review* 179 (1894): 289–318.

Barthes, Roland. "Toward a Psychology of Contemporary Food Consumption." In Counihan and Von Esterik, *Food and Culture*, 20–27.

Bauer, Dale M., and Susan Jaret McKinstry, ed. *Feminism, Bakhtin, and the Dialogic*. Albany: SUNY Press, 1991.

Beecher, Catherine E., and Harriet Beecher Stowe. *The American Woman's Home; or, Principles of Domestic Science, Being a Guide to the Formation and Maintenance of Economical, Healthful, Beautiful, and Christian Homes*. 1869. Reprint, Hartford, CT: Stowe Center, 1975.

Bell, Michael Davitt. *The Problem of American Realism: Studies in the Cultural History of a Literary Idea*. Chicago: University of Chicago Press, 1993.

Bierce, Ambrose. "Prattle." *San Francisco Examiner*, 15 November 1891, 6.

Bindslev, Anne M. *Mrs. Humphry Ward: A Study in Late-Victorian Feminine Consciousness and Creative Expression*. Stockholm: Almqvist and Wiksell, 1985.

Black, Helen C. From *Pencil, Baton and Mask: Biographical Sketches*. In Heilmann and Forward, *Sex*, 1:280–84. First published London: Spottiwoode, 1896.

Bland, Lucy. *Banishing the Beast: Sexuality and the Early Feminists*. New York: New Press, 1995.

Bodenheimer, Rosemarie. *The Politics of Story in Victorian Social Fiction*. Ithaca, NY: Cornell University Press, 1988.

Boone, Joseph Allen. *Tradition Counter Tradition: Love and the Form of Fiction*. Chicago: University of Chicago Press, 1987.

Booth, Wayne. *The Company We Keep: An Ethics of Fiction*. Berkeley: University of California Press, 1988.

Brittain, Vera. *The Women at Oxford: A Fragment of History*. New York: Macmillan, 1960.

Brooks, Cleanth. *The Well-Wrought Urn: Studies in the Structure of Poetry*. 1947. Reprint, New York: Harvest Books, 1975.

Browne, Phillis. "House-Cleaning." In S. Murphy, *Our Homes*, 869–94.

Burnett, John. *A Social History of Housing, 1815–1985*. 2nd ed. New York: Methuen, 1986.

Burstall, Sara A. *English High Schools for Girls: Their Aims, Organisation, and Management*. London: Longmans, Green, 1907.

Burstyn, Joan N. *Victorian Education and the Ideal of Womanhood*. London: Croom Helm, 1980.

Callen, Anthea. *Angel in the Studio: Women in the Arts and Crafts Movement, 1870–1914*. London: Astragal, 1979.

Campbell, Helen. *The Easiest Way in Housekeeping and Cooking, Adapted to Domestic Use, or Study in Classes*. New York: Fords, 1881.

———. "Famous Persons at Home. LX. Charlotte Perkins Stetson." *Time and the Hour* 16 (April 1898): 7–8.

———. *Household Economics: A Course of Lectures in the School of Economics of the University of Wisconsin.* Rev. ed. New York: Putnam, 1896, 1907.

Cane, Aleta Feinsod. "The Heroine of Her Own Story: Subversion of Traditional Periodical Marriage Tropes in the Short Fiction of Charlotte Perkins Gilman's *Forerunner.*" In *"The Only Efficient Instrument": American Women Writers and the Periodical, 1837–1916,* edited by Aleta Feinsod Cane and Susan Alves, 95–112. Iowa City: University of Iowa Press, 2001.

Carlyle, Thomas. *Sartor Resartus.* Edited by Charles Frederick Harrold. New York: Odyssey, 1937.

Ceplair, Larry, ed. *Charlotte Perkins Gilman: A Nonfiction Reader.* New York: Columbia University Press, 1991.

Chase, Vanessa. "Edith Wharton, The Decoration of Houses, and Gender in Turn-of-the-Century America." In *Architecture and Feminism,* edited by Debra Coleman, Elizabeth Danze, and Carol Henderson, 130–60. New York: Princeton Architectural Press, 1996.

Cheadle, Dave, and W. H. "Bill" Lee. *Soapine Did It! An Illustrated History of Kendall's 19th Century Soap Advertising Campaign.* Englewood, CO: n.p., 2000.

Chodorow, Nancy. *The Reproduction of Mothering: Psychoanalysis and the Sociology of Gender.* Berkeley: University of California Press, 1978.

Clark, Clifford Edward. *The American Family Home, 1800–1960.* Chapel Hill: University of North Carolina Press, 1986.

Clarke, Norma. "Feminism and the Popular Novel of the 1890s: A Brief Consideration of a Forgotten Feminist Novelist." *Feminist Review* 20 (1985): 91–104.

Colquhoun, Ethel. "Modern Feminism and Sex Antagonism." *Quarterly Review* 219 (1913): 143–66.

Cook, Clarence. *The House Beautiful: Essays on Beds and Tables, Stools and Candlesticks.* New York: Scribner's, 1881.

Counihan, Carole, and Penny Van Esterik. *Food and Culture: A Reader.* New York: Routledge, 1997.

Cowan, Ruth Schwartz. "Coal Stoves and Clean Sinks: Housework between 1890 and 1930." In *American Home Life, 1880–1930: A Social History of Spaces and Services,* edited by Jessica H. Foy and Thomas J. Schlereth, 211–24. Knoxville: University of Tennessee Press, 1992.

———. *More Work for Mother: The Ironies of Household Technology from the Open Hearth to the Microwave.* New York: Basic, 1983.

Bibliography

Cunningham, Gail. *The New Woman and the Victorian Novel.* London: Macmillan, 1978.

Darwin, Charles. *The Descent of Man and Selection in Relation to Sex.* 2 vols. London: John Murray, 1871.

Davidson, Caroline. *A Woman's Work Is Never Done: A History of Housework in the British Isles, 1650–1950.* London: Chatto and Windus, 1982.

Davidson, Cathy N., ed. *No More Separate Spheres! American Literature* 7.3 (September 1998).

Davis, Lennard J. *Resisting Novels: Ideology and Fiction.* New York: Methuen, 1987.

D'Cruze, Shani. "Women and the Family." In *Women's History: Britain, 1850–1945; An Introduction,* edited by June Purvis, 51–83. New York: St. Martin's, 1995.

Dock, Julie Bates, ed. *Charlotte Perkins Gilman's "The Yellow Wall-paper" and the History of Its Publication and Reception: A Critical Edition and Documentary Casebook.* University Park: Pennsylvania State University Press, 1998.

Donovan, Josephine. *After the Fall: The Demeter-Persephone Myth in Wharton, Cather, and Glasgow.* University Park: Pennsylvania State University Press, 1989.

Doughty, Terri. "Sarah Grand's *The Beth Book:* The New Woman and the Ideology of the Romance Ending." In *Anxious Power: Reading, Writing, and Ambivalence in Narrative by Women,* edited by Carol J. Singley and Susan Elizabeth Sweeney, 185–96. Albany: SUNY Press, 1993.

Douglas, Mary. "Deciphering a Meal." In Counihan and Van Esterik, *Food and Culture,* 36–54. First published in *Implicit Meanings.* London: Routledge, 1975.

————. *Purity and Danger: An Analysis of the Concepts of Pollution and Taboo.* 1966. Reprint, London: Routledge, 1978.

Dowling, Linda. "The Decadent and the New Woman in the 1890s." *Nineteenth-Century Fiction* 33 (1979): 434–53.

Dyhouse, Carol. *Girls Growing Up in Late Victorian and Edwardian England.* London: Routledge, 1981.

————. "Social Darwinist Ideas and the Development of Women's Education in England, 1880–1920." *History of Education* 5 (1976): 41–58.

Eastlake, Charles L. *Hints on Household Taste.* 1878. Reprint, New York: Dover, 1969.

Edis, Robert W. "Internal Decoration." In S. Murphy, *Our Homes,* 309–64.

Elliott, S. Maria. *Household Hygiene.* Chicago: American School of Home Economics, 1907.

Elshtain, Jean Bethke. *Public Man, Private Woman.* Princeton, NJ: Princeton University Press, 1981.

Evans, Heather. "'Nor Shall I Shirk My Food': The New Woman's Balanced Diet and Sarah Grand's *Babs the Impossible.*" *Nineteenth-Century Feminisms* 4 (2001): 136–49.

Fernando, Lloyd. *"New Women" in the Late Victorian Novel*. University Park: Pennsylvania State University Press, 1977.

"Fiction New and Old." *Atlantic Monthly* 87 (January 1901): 127–32.

Flanders, Judith. *The Victorian House: Domestic Life from Childbirth to Deathbed*. London: HarperCollins, 2003.

Flint, Kate. *The Woman Reader, 1837–1914*. Oxford: Clarendon Press, 1993.

Forty, Adrian. "The Mary Ward Settlement." *The Architects' Journal* 2 (August 1989): 28–61.

———. *Objects of Desire*. New York: Pantheon, 1986.

Gallagher, Catherine. *The Industrial Reformation of English Fiction: Social Discourse and Narrative Form, 1832–1867*. Chicago: University of Chicago Press, 1985.

Gardiner, E. C. *The House That Jill Built, after Jack's Had Proved a Failure: A Book on Home Architecture*. Rev. ed. Springfield, MA: Adams, 1896.

Garrett, Rhoda, and Agnes Garrett. *Suggestions for House Decoration*. London: Macmillan, 1876.

Gavison, Ruth. "Feminism and the Public/Private Distinction." *Stanford Law Review* 45, no. 1 (November 1992): 1–45.

Gere, Charlotte, and Lesley Hoskins. *The House Beautiful: Oscar Wilde and the Aesthetic Interior*. London: Lund Humphries, 2000.

Gilbert, Sandra M., and Susan Gubar. *The Madwoman in the Attic: The Woman Writer and the Nineteenth-Century Literary Imagination*. New Haven: Yale University Press, 1979.

———. *Sexchanges*. Vol. 2 of *No Man's Land: The Place of the Woman Writer in the Twentieth Century*. New Haven: Yale University Press, 1989.

Gilligan, Carol. *In a Different Voice: Psychological Theory and Women's Development*. Cambridge: Harvard University Press, 1982.

Gilman, Charlotte Perkins. "According to Solomon." In *The Yellow Wall-Paper and Other Stories*, 122–29. First published in *Forerunner* 1 (December 1909): 1–5.

———. "The American Social Hygiene Association." *Forerunner* 7 (1916): 257–59.

———. "Apropos of Literature." In Knight, *Charlotte Perkins Gilman*, 104–5. First published in *Pacific Monthly* 2 (1890): 123.

———. "The Artist." *Forerunner* 2 (1911): 126.

———. "The Author's Strike." *Forerunner* 4 (1913): 244–45.

———. "Bee Wise." In *The Yellow Wall-Paper and Other Stories*, 226–34. First published in *Forerunner* 4 (1913): 169–73.

———. "Being Reasonable." In *"The Yellow Wall-Paper" and Selected Stories of Charlotte Perkins Gilman*, 185–92. First published in *Forerunner* 6 (1915): 197–201.

———. *Benigna Machiavelli*. Santa Barbara, CA: Bandanna Books, 1993. Originally serialized in *Forerunner* 5 (1914).

————. "Class Consciousness, World Consciousness and Socialism." *Forerunner* 3 (1912): 260–62.

————. "Coming Changes in Literature." *Forerunner* 6 (1915): 230–36.

————. "Comment and Review." *Forerunner* 1, no. 5 (March 1910): 23–24.

————. "Confidential Remarks about Our Advertising." *Forerunner* 1, no. 3 (January 1910): 32.

————. "The Cottagette." In *The Yellow Wall-Paper and Other Stories,* 130–38. First published in *Forerunner* 1, no. 10 (August 1910): 1–5.

————. "A Council of War." In *The Yellow Wall-Paper and Other Stories,* 235–43. First published in *Forerunner* 4 (1913): 197–201.

————. *The Crux.* New York: Charlton, 1911. Originally serialized in *Forerunner* 2 (1911).

————. "Cycles." *Forerunner* 3 (1912): 39.

————. *The Diaries of Charlotte Perkins Gilman.* Edited by Denise D. Knight. 2 vols. Charlottesville: University Press of Virginia, 1994.

————. "The Drama We Might Have." *Forerunner* 4 (1913): 242–43.

————. *The Dress of Women.* Serialized in *Forerunner* 6 (1915).

————. "The Ethics of Woman's Work." Lecture, 1 Feb 1894. In Ceplair, *Charlotte Perkins Gilman,* 77–79.

————. "An Extinct Angel." In *The Yellow Wall-Paper and Other Stories,* 48–50. First published in *Kate Field's Washington* (23 September 1891): 199–200.

————. "Feminism." In Ceplair, *Charlotte Perkins Gilman,* 183–87.

————. "Fighting, Growing and Making." *Forerunner* 4 (1913): 16–18.

————. "Five Girls." In *The Yellow Wall-Paper and Other Stories,* 83–86. First published in *Impress,* 1 December 1894, 4–5.

————. "Fulfillment." In *The Yellow Wall-Paper and Other Stories,* 244–52. First published in *Forerunner* 5 (1914): 57–61.

————. "Genius, Domestic and Maternal II." *Forerunner* 1, no. 8 (July 1910): 5–7.

————. "Girls and Land." In *The Yellow Wall-Paper and Other Stories,* 286–94. First published in *Forerunner* 6 (1915): 113–17.

————. "The Great Adventure." *Forerunner* 4 (1913): 251.

————. "The Great Change." *Forerunner* 5 (1914): 322–24.

————. *Growth and Combat.* Serialized in *Forerunner* 7 (1916).

————. "Hair Cloth and Public Morals." *Impress,* 9 February 1895, 3.

————. "Her Beauty." In *The Yellow Wall-Paper and Other Stories,* 210–17. First published in *Forerunner* 4 (February 1913): 29–33.

————. "Her Housekeeper." In *Herland and Selected Stories,* 195–207. First published in *Forerunner* 1, no. 3 (January 1910): 2–8.

———. *Herland.* New York: Pantheon, 1979. Originally serialized in *Forerunner* 6 (1915).

———. *Herland and Selected Stories by Charlotte Perkins Gilman.* Edited by Barbara H. Solomon. New York: Signet, 1992.

———. *The Home: Its Work and Influence.* 1903. Reprint, New York: Charlton, 1910.

———. "The Housewife." *Forerunner* 1, no. 11 (September 1910): 18.

———. *Human Work.* New York: McClure, Phillips & Co., 1904.

———. "In Modern Verse." *Forerunner* 3 (1912): 287.

———. "Instead of a Story." *Forerunner* 5 (1914): 309.

———. *In This Our World.* Boston: Small, 1898.

———. "Is Health Worth Having?" *Forerunner* 3 (1912): 204–6.

———. "The Jumping-Off Place." In *The Yellow Wall-Paper and Other Stories,* 148–58. First published in *Forerunner* 2 (1911): 87–93.

———. "Kitchen-Mindedness." *Forerunner* 1, no. 4 (February 1910): 7–11.

———. "The Labor Movement: A Prize Essay Read before the Trades and Labor Unions of Alameda County, Sept. 5, 1892." Oakland, CA: Alameda County Federation of Trades, [1893]. In Ceplair, *Charlotte Perkins Gilman,* 62–74.

———. *The Living of Charlotte Perkins Gilman: An Autobiography.* New York: Appleton, 1935. Reprint, New York: Harper, 1975.

———. *Mag—Marjorie.* In *Mag—Marjorie; and Won Over: Two Novels,* edited by Denise D. Knight, 13–148. New York: Ironweed, 1999. Originally serialized in *Forerunner* 3 (1912).

———. "Maidstone Comfort." *Forerunner* 3 (1912): 225–36.

———. *The Man-Made World; or, Our Androcentric Culture.* New York: Charlton, 1911. Originally serialized in *Forerunner* 1 (1910–11).

———. "Matriatism." *Forerunner* 5 (1914): 299.

———. "Mind Cleaning." *Forerunner* 3 (1912): 5–6.

———. "A Mischievous Rudiment." In *Herland and Selected Stories,* 276–84. First published in *Forerunner* 3 (1912): 1–5.

———. *Moving the Mountain.* In *Charlotte Perkins Gilman's Utopian Novels: Moving the Mountain, Herland, and With Her in Ourland,* edited by Minna Doskow, 37–149. Madison, NJ: Fairleigh Dickinson University Press, 1999.

———. "Mrs. Elder's Idea." In *The Yellow Wall-Paper and Other Stories,* 191–99. First published in *Forerunner* 3 (1912): 29–33.

———. "Mrs. Merrill's Duties." In *The Yellow Wall-Paper and Other Stories,* 277–85. First published in *Forerunner* 6 (1915): 57–61.

———. "The New Mothers of a New World." *Forerunner* 4 (1913): 145–49.

———. "On Some Recent 'Art.'" *Forerunner* 4 (1913): 111–12.

————. *Our Brains and What Ails Them*. Serialized in *Forerunner* 3 (1913).

————. "Our Ugliness." *Forerunner* 4 (1913): 187.

————. "A Partnership." In *The Yellow Wall-Paper and Other Stories*, 253–61. First published in *Forerunner* 5 (1914): 141–45.

————. "The Passing of the Home in Great American Cities." *Cosmopolitan*, December 1904: 137–47.

————. "Past, Present and Future." *Forerunner* 2 (1911): 16–18.

————. "A Personal Motive." *Forerunner* 4 (1913): 113–18.

————. "A Portion of Freedom." *Forerunner* 5 (1914): 224.

————. "A Question of Conscience." *Forerunner* 5 (1914): 229–31.

————. Review of *The Heavenly Twins*, by Sarah Grand. *Impress*, December 1893, 3.

————. "Six Hours a Day." In *In This Our World*, 136–37.

————. "Soapine." Advertisement. *Forerunner* 1, no. 2 (December 1909): 31.

————. "Something to Vote For." *Forerunner* 2 (1911): 143–53.

————. "Story Studies" [George Eliot]. *Impress*. 1 December 1894, 5.

————. "Summary of Purpose." *Forerunner* 7 (1916): 286–90.

————. "Superfluous Women." In Ceplair, *Charlotte Perkins Gilman*, 121–24. First published in *Woman's Journal*, 7 April 1900, 105.

————. "Their House." In *The Yellow Wall-Paper and Other Stories*, 20–09. First published in *Forerunner* 3 (1912): 309–14.

————. "Three Women." *Forerunner* 2 (1911): 115–23, 34.

————. "Thurston Gower." *Impress*, 24 November 1894, 4–5.

————. "To the Young Wife." In *In This Our World*, 129–31.

————. "Turned." In *The Yellow Wall-Paper and Other Stories*, 172–81. First published in *Forerunner* 2 (1911): 227–32.

————. "An Unnatural Mother." In *The Yellow Wall-Paper and Other Stories*, 98–106. First published in *Impress*, 16 February 1895, 4–5; *Forerunner* 7 (1916): 281–85.

————. *Unpunished: A Mystery*. New York: Feminist Press, 1997.

————. "The Vintage." *Forerunner* 7 (1916): 253–57.

————. *What Diantha Did*. New York: Charlton, 1910. Originally serialized in *Forerunner* 1 (1909–10).

————. "What Do Men Think of Women?" *Forerunner* 3 (1912): 15–16.

————. "Why I Wrote 'The Yellow Wallpaper'?" In *The Yellow Wall-Paper and Other Stories*, 331–32. First published in *Forerunner* 4 (1913): 271.

————. "Why Make Dust?" *Forerunner* 3 (1912): 61.

————. *With Her in Ourland*. Westport, CT: Praeger, 1997. Originally serialized in *Forerunner* 7 (1916).

————. *Won Over*. In *Mag—Marjorie and Won Over*, edited by Denise D. Knight,

149–270. New York: Ironweed, 1999. Originally serialized in *Forerunner* 4 (1913).

———. "The Work before Us." *Forerunner* 3 (1912): 6–9.

———. "The World and the Three Artists." *Forerunner* 1, no. 12 (October 1910): 8–9.

———. *The Yellow Wall-Paper and Other Stories.* Edited by Robert Shulman. Oxford: Oxford University Press, 1995.

———. *"The Yellow Wall-Paper" and Selected Stories of Charlotte Perkins Gilman.* Edited by Denise D. Knight. Newark: University of Delaware Press, 1994.

Girouard, Mark. *Sweetness and Light: The Queen Anne Movement, 1860–1900.* Oxford: Clarendon Press, 1977.

Glazener, Nancy. *Reading for Realism: The History of a U.S. Literary Institution, 1850–1910.* Durham, NC: Duke University Press, 1997.

Golden, Catherine J., and Denise D. Knight. Afterword to *Unpunished: A Mystery,* by Charlotte Perkins Gilman. New York: Feminist Press, 1997.

Goody, Jack. *Cooking, Cuisine, and Class: A Study in Comparative Sociology.* Cambridge: Cambridge University Press, 1982.

Gordon, Linda. "What's New in Women's History." In *Feminist Studies / Critical Studies,* edited by Teresa de Lauretis, 20–30. Madison: University of Wisconsin Press, 1986.

Gough, Val, and Jill Rudd, ed. *A Very Different Story: Studies on the Fiction of Charlotte Perkins Gilman.* Liverpool: Liverpool University Press, 1998.

Graff, Gerald. *Professing Literature: An Institutional History.* Chicago: University of Chicago Press, 1987.

Graham, Amanda. "Herland: Definitive Ecofeminist Fiction?" In Gough and Rudd, *A Very Different Story,* 115–28.

Grand, Sarah. *Adnam's Orchard.* New York: Appleton, 1913.

———. "At What Age Should Girls Marry?" In Heilmann and Forward, *Sex,* 1:113–18. First published in *Young Woman* 7 (1899): 161 64.

———. *Babs the Impossible.* New York: Harper, 1900.

———. *The Beth Book: Being a Study of the Life of Elizabeth Caldwell Maclure, a Woman of Genius.* New York: Appleton, 1897. Reprint, New York: Dial, 1980.

———. "The Boycott of 'Esther Waters.'" In Heilmann and Forward, *Sex,* 1:64. First published as letter to *London Daily Chronicle,* 3 May 1894, 3.

———. "A Case for Apology." In Heilmann and Forward, *Sex,* 1:67. First published in *London Daily Chronicle,* 17 August 1897.

———. "The Case of the Modern Married Woman." In Heilmann and Forward, *Sex,* 1:128–37. First published in *Pall Mall Magazine* (1913): 203–9.

————. "The Case of the Modern Spinster." In Heilmann and Forward, *Sex,* 1:138–45. First published in *Pall Mall Magazine* 51 (1913): 52–55.

————. "Court Her with Respect." Contribution to "How to Court the 'Advanced Woman.'" In Heilmann and Forward, *Sex,* 1:103. First published in *Idler* 3 (1894): 203–4.

————. "Does Marriage Hinder A Woman's Self-development?" In Heilmann and Forward, *Sex,* 1:121–25. First published in *Lady's Realm* 5 (1898–99): 576–77.

————. "Eugenia." In *Our Manifold Nature: Stories from Life,* 103–75.

————. "Foreword, 1893–1923." In *The Heavenly Twins.* London: Heinemann, 1923. v–xvi.

————. *The Future of the Novel: Famous Authors on Their Methods; A Series of Interviews with Renowned Authors.* By Meredith Starr, 202–8. London: Heath Cranton, 1921.

————. *The Heavenly Twins.* 1893. Reprint, Ann Arbor: University of Michigan Press, 1992.

————. "The Human Quest: Being Some Thoughts in Contribution to the Subject of the Art of Happiness." In Heilmann and Forward, *Sex,* 1:155–79. First published London: Heinemann, 1900.

————. "Illustrated Interview: Sarah Grand." By Jane T. Stoddart. In Heilmann and Forward, *Sex,* 1:211–19. First published in *Woman at Home* 3 (1895): 247–52.

————. "In the Days of My Youth: My First Success." In Heilmann and Forward, *Sex,* 1:200–204. First published in *M[ainly] A[bout] P[eople],* 22 May 1909, 493.

————. Letter to Professor Viëtor, Nizza, 15 December 1896. In Heilmann and Forward, *Sex,* 1:190–91. First published in Ernst Foerster, *Die Frauenfrage in den Romanen Englischer Schriftstellerinnen der Gegenwart,* 56–58. Marburg: N.G. Elwaer'sche Verlagsbuchhandlung, 1907.

————. "The Modern Girl." *North American Review* 158 (1894): 706–14.

————. "The Modern Young Man." In *The Modern Man and Maid.* New York: Crowell, 1898, 17–25.

————. "The Morals of Manner and Appearance." In Heilmann and Forward, *Sex,* 1:21–28. First published in *Humanitarian* 3 (1893): 87–93.

————. "The New Aspect of the Woman Question." *North American Review* 158 (1894): 270–76.

————. "On Clubs and the Question of Intelligence." In Heilmann and Forward, *Sex,* 1:94–99. First published in *Woman at Home* 9 (1900): 839–42.

————. "On the Choice of a Husband." In Heilmann and Forward, *Sex,* 1:106–11. First published in *Young Woman* 7 (1898): 1–3.

————. *Our Manifold Nature: Stories from Life.* London: Heinemann, 1894.

————. "A Page of Confessions." In Heilmann and Forward, *Sex,* 1:189. First published in *Woman at Home* 3 (1894): 65.

————. "Personal Sketch of Matilda Barbara Betham-Edwards, 1837–1919." In *Mid-Victorian Memories,* by Matilda Betham-Edwards, vii–lxvi. New York: Macmillan, 1919.

————. "The Salisbury-Stuart Treatment: A Chat with Mrs. Elma Stuart of Toutley Hall, Wokingham, Berks." *The Humanitarian* 9, no. 2 (1896): 108–11.

————. "Should Married Women Follow Professions?" In Heilmann and Forward, *Sex,* 1:121–25. First published in *Young Woman* (1899): 257–59.

————. "The Tree of Knowledge VI—Madame Sarah Grand." In Heilmann and Forward, *Sex,* 1:65–66. First published in *New Review* 10 (1894): 679–80.

————. *Two Dear Little Feet.* London: Jarrods, 1873.

————. "The Undefinable: A Fantasia." In *Emotional Moments.* London: Hurst, 1908, 303–58.

————. *The Winged Victory.* New York: Appleton, 1916.

————. "The Woman's Question: An Interview with Madame Sarah Grand." By Sarah A. Tooley. *Humanitarian* 8 (1896): 161–69.

————. "The Yellow Leaf." In *Our Manifold Nature: Stories from Life,* 1–101.

Guillory, John. *Cultural Capital: The Problem of Literary Canon Formation.* Chicago: University of Chicago Press, 1993.

Habermas, Jürgen. *Structural Transformation of the Public Sphere.* Translated by Thomas Burger. Cambridge: MIT Press, 1989.

Handlin, David P. *The American Home: Architecture and Society, 1815–1915.* Boston: Little, Brown, 1979.

Hansen, Karen V. "Rediscovering the Social: Visiting Practices in Antebellum New England and the Limits of the Public/Private Dichotomy." In Weintraub and Kumar, *Public and Private,* 268–302.

Hardy, Anne. *The Epidemic Streets: Infectious Disease and the Rise of Preventive Medicine, 1856–1900.* Oxford: Clarendon, 1993.

Harrison, Brian. *Separate Spheres: The Opposition to Women's Suffrage in Britain.* London: Croom Helm, 1978.

Haweis, Mrs. [Mary Eliza Joy]. *Beautiful Houses: Being a Description of Certain Well-Known Artistic Houses.* London: Low, Marston, Searle, and Rivington, 1882.

Hayden, Dolores. *The Grand Domestic Revolution: A History of Feminist Designs for American Homes, Neighborhoods, and Cities.* Cambridge: MIT Press, 1981.

Hedges, Elaine R. "The Needle or the Pen: The Literary Rediscovery of Women's Textile Work." In *Tradition and the Talents of Women,* edited by Florence Howe, 338–64. Urbana: University of Illinois Press, 1991.

————. "'Out at Last'? 'The Yellow Wallpaper' after Two Decades of Feminist Criticism." In *The Captive Imagination: A Casebook on The Yellow Wallpaper,* edited by Catherine Golden, 319–33. New York: Feminist Press, 1992.

Hedrick, Joan D. *Harriet Beecher Stowe: A Life.* New York: Oxford University Press, 1994.

Heilmann, Ann. *New Woman Fiction: Women Writing First-Wave Feminism.* New York: St. Martin's, 2000.

Heilmann, Ann, and Stephanie Forward. *Sex, Social Purity, and Sarah Grand.* 4 vols. London: Routledge, 2000.

Higonnet, Margaret R. "New Cartographies: An Introduction." In *Reconfigured Spheres: Feminist Explorations of Literary Space,* edited by Margaret R Higonnet and Joan Templeton, 1–19. Amherst: University of Massachusetts Press, 1994.

Hill, Mary A. "Charlotte Perkins Gilman: A Feminist's Struggle with Womanhood." *Massachusetts Review* 21 (1980): 503–23.

————. *Charlotte Perkins Gilman: The Making of a Radical Feminist, 1860–1896.* Philadelphia: Temple University Press, 1980.

Horn, Pamela. *The Rise and Fall of the Victorian Servant.* New York: St. Martin's, 1975.

Hoy, Suellen. *Chasing Dirt: The American Pursuit of Cleanliness.* New York: Oxford, 1996.

Huyssen, Andreas. *After the Great Divide: Modernism, Mass Culture, Postmodernism.* Bloomington: Indiana University Press, 1986.

Inness, Sherrie A. Introduction to *Kitchen Culture in America: Popular Representations of Food, Gender, and Race,* edited by Sherrie A. Inness, 1–12. Philadelphia: University of Pennsylvania Press, 2001.

James, Henry. "The Lesson of Balzac." In *The House of Fiction: Essays on the Novel by Henry James,* edited by Leon Edel, 60–85. Westport, CT: Greenwood, 1957.

Jameson, Fredric. "Reification and Utopia in Mass Culture." *Social Text* 1 (Winter 1979): 130–48.

Jennings, H. J. *Our Homes and How to Beautify Them.* London: Harrison, 1902.

Jordan, Ellen. "The Christening of the New Woman: May 1894." *Victorian Newsletter* 63 (Spring 1983): 19–21.

Kamm, Josephine. *Hope Deferred: Girls' Education in English History.* London: Methuen, 1965.

Kaplan, Amy. "Manifest Domesticity." In "No More Separate Spheres!" edited by Cathy N. Davidson, 581–606. Special issue, *American Literature* 7 (September 1998).

Katzman, David M. *Seven Days a Week: Women and Domestic Service in Industrializing America.* Urbana: University of Illinois Press, 1981.

Kelley, Mary. *Private Woman, Public Stage: Literary Domesticity in Nineteenth-Century America.* New York: Oxford University Press, 1984.

Kent, Susan Kingsley. *Sex and Suffrage in Britain, 1860–1914.* Princeton, NJ: Princeton University Press, 1987.

Kerber, Linda K. "Separate Spheres, Female Worlds, Woman's Place: The Rhetoric of Women's History." In *Toward an Intellectual History of Women: Essays by Linda K. Kerber,* 159–99. Chapel Hill: University of North Carolina Press, 1997. First published in *Journal of American History* 75 (June 1988): 9–39.

Kersley, Gillian. *Darling Madame: Sarah Grand and Devoted Friend.* London: Virago, 1983.

Kessler, Carol Farley. "Consider Her Ways: The Cultural Work of Charlotte Perkins Gilman's Pragmatopian Stories, 1908–1913." In *Utopian and Science Fiction for Women, Worlds of Difference,* edited by Jane L. Donawerth and Carol A. Kolmerten, 126–36. Syracuse, NY: Syracuse University Press, 1994.

King, Kathryn R. "Of Needles and Pens and Women's Work." *Tulsa Studies in Women's Literature* 14 (1995): 77–93.

Kinne, Helen, and Anna M. Cooley. *The Home and the Family: An Elementary Textbook of Home Making.* New York: Macmillan, 1919.

Knight, Denise D. "An 'Amusing Source of Income': Charlotte Perkins Gilman and the Soapine Connection." *The Advertising Trade Card Quarterly* 8, no. 2 (Summer 2001): 8–12.

———. *Charlotte Perkins Gilman: A Study of the Short Fiction.* New York: Twayne, 1997.

———. *"The Yellow Wall-Paper" and Selected Stories of Charlotte Perkins Gilman.* Cranbury, NJ: Associated University Press, 1994.

Kolodny, Annette. *The Lay of the Land: Metaphor as Experience and History in American Life and Letters.* Chapel Hill: University of North Carolina Press, 1975.

———. "A Map for Rereading: Gender and the Interpretation of Literary Texts." In *The New Feminist Criticism: Essays on Women, Literature, and Theory,* edited by Elaine Showalter, 46–62. New York: Pantheon, 1985.

Koven, Seth. "Borderlands: Women, Voluntary Action, and Child Welfare in Britain, 1840–1914." In *Mothers of a New World: Maternalist Politics and the Origins of Welfare States,* edited by Seth Koven and Sonya Michel, 94–135. New York: Routledge, 1993.

Kraditor, Aileen S. *The Ideas of the Woman Suffrage Movement, 1890–1920.* New York: Columbia University Press, 1965.

Kranidas, Rita S. *Subversive Discourse: The Cultural Production of Late Victorian Feminist Novels.* New York: St. Martin's, 1995.

Kucich, John. *The Power of Lies: Transgression in Victorian Fiction.* Ithaca, NY: Cornell University Press, 1994.

Lamb, Mary. "On Needle-Work." In *British Literature, 1780–1830,* edited by Anne K. Mellor and Richard E. Matlak, 50–52. New York: Harcourt, 1996.

Bibliography

Landes, Joan, ed. *Feminism, the Public and the Private*. Oxford Readings in Feminism. Oxford: Oxford University Press, 1998.

Lane, Ann J. *To "Herland" and Beyond: The Life and Work of Charlotte Perkins Gilman*. Charlottesville: University Press of Virginia, 1990.

Langland, Elizabeth. *Nobody's Angels: Middle-Class Women and Domestic Ideology in Victorian Culture*. Ithaca, NY: Cornell University Press, 1995.

Lebergott, Stanley. *The American Economy: Income, Wealth, and Want*. Princeton: Princeton University Press, 1976.

Ledger, Sally. *The New Woman: Fiction and Feminism at the Fin de Siècle*. Manchester, UK: Manchester University Press, 1997.

Leonardi, Susan J. "Recipes for Reading: Summer Pasta, Lobster à la Risehome, and Key Lime Pie." *PMLA* 104 (1989): 340–47.

Levine, George. *The Realistic Imagination: English Fiction from Frankenstein to Lady Chatterley*. Chicago: University of Chicago Press, 1981.

Lévi-Strauss, Claude. "The Culinary Triangle." Translated by Peter Brooks. In Counihan and Van Esterik, *Food and Culture*, 28–35.

Lewis, Jane. *Women and Social Action in Victorian and Edwardian England*. Aldershot, UK: Edward Elgar, 1991.

Lovell, Terry. *Consuming Fiction*. London: Verso, 1987.

Lubbock, Sybil. *The Child in the Crystal*. London: Jonathan Cape, 1939.

Lubove, Roy. *The Urban Community: Housing and Planning in the Progressive Era*. Englewood Cliffs, NJ: Prentice-Hall, 1967.

MacDonnell, Kevin. "Trade Cards by Charlotte Perkins Gilman: The Young Artist's Soapine and Non-Soapine Designs." *Advertising Trade Card Quarterly* 8, no. 3 (Fall 2001): 18–25.

Manger, Lois N. "Darwinism and the Woman Question: The Evolving Views of Charlotte Perkins Gilman." In *Critical Essays on Charlotte Perkins Gilman*, edited by Joanne B. Karpinski. New York: Macmillan, 1992.

Mangum, Teresa. *Married, Middlebrow, and Militant: Sarah Grand and the New Woman Novel*. Ann Arbor: University of Michigan Press, 1998.

Marin, Louis. *Food for Thought*. Translated by Mette Hjort. Baltimore: Johns Hopkins University Press, 1989.

McClintock, Anne. *Imperial Leather: Race, Gender, and Sexuality in the Colonial Conquest*. New York: Routledge, 1995.

McDermid, Jane. "Women and Education." In *Women's History: Britain, 1850–1945: An Introduction*, edited by June Purvis, 107–30. New York: St. Martin's, 1995.

McGee, Diane. *Writing the Meal: Dinner in the Fiction of Early Twentieth-Century Women Writers*. Toronto: University of Toronto Press, 2001.

McGurty, Eileen Maura. "Trashy Women: Gender and the Politics of Garbage in Chicago, 1890–1917." *Historical Geography* 26 (1998): 27–43.

Mill, John Stuart. *The Subjection of Women.* 1869. Reprint, London: Virago, 1983.

Miller, D. A. *The Novel and the Police.* Berkeley: University of California Press, 1987.

Mitchell, Sally. *The New Girl: Girls' Culture in England, 1880–1915.* New York: Columbia University Press, 1995.

Moore, George. *Literature at Nurse; or, Circulating Morals: A Polemic on Victorian Censorship.* 1885. Reprint, Brighton, UK: Harvester, 1985.

Morris, G. LL., and Esther Wood. "The Architecture of the Passmore Edwards Settlement." *The Studio* 16 (1899): 11–18.

Morris, Malcolm. "Arsenic in Wall-Papers and Paints." In S. Murphy, *Our Homes,* 365–72.

Morris, William. "The Beauty of Life." In *Collected Works of William Morris.* London: Longmans, 1910–15. 22:51–80.

Morse, Deborah Dehenholz. "Stitching Repentance, Sewing Rebellion: Seamstresses and Fallen Women in Elizabeth Gaskell's Fiction." In *Keeping the Victorian House: A Collection of Essays,* edited by Vanessa D. Dickerson, 27–73. New York: Garland, 1995.

Mouton, Michelle J. "Taking on Tennyson: Sarah Grand's *The Heavenly Twins* and the Ethics of Androgynous Reading." *Victorian Review* 23 (Winter 1997): 184–211.

Murphy, Patricia. "Reevaluating Female 'Inferiority': Sarah Grand versus Charles Darwin." *Victorian Literature and Culture* 26 (1998): 221–36.

Murphy, Shirley Forster, ed. *Our Homes, and How to Make Them Healthy.* London: Cassell, 1883.

Navarre, Joan. "Oscar Wilde, the Aesthetic Movement, and Victorian Trade Cards." *Advertising Trade Card Quarterly* 6, no. 3 (Fall 1999): 20–25.

"The Needs of Local Government." *Times* (London), 2 November 1910, 12, col. 4.

Nightingale, Florence. *Notes on Nursing: What It Is and What It Is Not.* New York: Appleton, 1860.

Noble, James Ashcroft. "The Fiction of Sexuality." *Contemporary Review* 67 (1895): 490–98.

Oakley, Ann. *Woman's Work: The Housewife Past and Present.* New York: Pantheon, 1974.

Ogle, Maureen. *All the Modern Conveniences: American Household Plumbing, 1840–1890.* Baltimore: Johns Hopkins University Press, 1996.

O[liphant], M. O. W. "The Anti-Marriage League." *Blackwood's Edinburgh Magazine* 159 (1896): 135–49.

Oliver, Lawrence J., and Gary Scharnhorst. "Charlotte Perkins Gilman v. Ambrose

Bierce: the Literary Politics of Gender in Fin-de-Siècle California." *Journal of the West* 32 (1993): 52–60.

Palliser, Mrs. Bury. *A History of Lace*. 3rd ed. 1875. Reprint, Detroit: Tower, 1971.

Panton, J. E. *From Kitchen to Garret: Hints for Young Householders*. 4th ed. London: Ward and Downey, 1888.

Parker, Rozsika. *The Subversive Stitch: Embroidery and the Making of the Feminine*. New York: Routledge, 1989.

Parkes, Louis C. *Hygiene and Public Health*. 3rd ed. Philadelphia: Blakiston, 1892.

Pateman, Carole. "Feminist Critiques of the Public/Private Distinction." In *The Disorder of Women: Democracy, Feminism and Political Theory*. Stanford, CA: Stanford University Press, 1989. 118–40.

Pearse, F. Mabelle. "To an 'Advanced Woman.'" *Idler* 161 (September 1896): 140–41.

Peterson, William S. "Henry James on 'Jane Eyre.'" *Times Literary Supplement* (London), 30 July 1971, 919–20.

————. *Victorian Heretic: Mrs. Humphry Ward's "Robert Elsmere."* Leicester, UK: Leicester University Press, 1976.

Plunkett, Mrs. H[arriette] M[errick]. *Women, Plumbers, and Doctors; or, Household Sanitation: Showing that, if women and plumbers do their whole sanitary duty, there will be comparatively little occasion for the services of the doctors*. 1884; New York: Appleton, 1885.

Pykett, Lyn. *The "Improper" Feminine: The Women's Sensation Novel and the New Woman Writing*. New York: Routledge, 1992.

Reverby, Susan M., and Dorothy O. Helly. "Introduction: Converging on History." In *Gendered Domains: Rethinking Public and Private in Women's History; Essays from the Seventh Berkshire Conference on the History of Women*, edited by Dorothy O. Helly and Susan M. Reverby, 1–26. Ithaca, NY: Cornell University Press, 1992.

Review of *The Beth Book*, by Sarah Grand. In Heilmann and Forward, *Sex*, 1:487–89. First published in *Bookman* (New York) 6 (December 1897): 363–64.

Review of *The History of David Grieve*, by Mrs. Humphry Ward. *Athenaeum* 1 (January 1892): 141–42.

Rich, Adrienne. "Vesuvius at Home: The Power of Emily Dickinson." In *On Lies, Secrets, and Silence: Selected Prose, 1966–1978*, 157–83. New York: Norton, 1971.

Richards, Ellen H. *The Cost of Cleanness*. New York: Wiley, 1908.

————. *The Cost of Living as Modified by Sanitary Science*. 3rd ed. New York: Wiley, 1910.

Richards, Ellen H., and S. Maria Elliott. *The Chemistry of Cooking and Cleaning: A Manual for Housekeepers*. 2nd ed. Boston: Home Science, 1897.

Richardson, Angelique. "Allopathic Pills? Health, Fitness and New Woman Fictions." *Women: A Cultural Review* 10 (1999): 1–21.

———. "The Eugenization of Love: Sarah Grand and the Morality of Geneology." *Victorian Studies* 42 (1999–2000): 227–55.

———. "'People Talk a Lot of Nonsense about Heredity': Mona Caird and Anti-Eugenic Feminism." In *The New Woman in Fiction and in Fact: Fin-de-Siècle Feminisms,* edited by Angelique Richardson and Chris Willis, 183–211. Basingstoke, UK: Macmillan, 2001.

Richardson, Benjamin Ward. *Diseases of Modern Life.* New York: Bermingham, 1882.

———. *The Field of Disease: A Book of Preventative Medicine.* Philadelphia: Henry C. Lea's Sonand, 1884.

Rombauer, Irma S., and Marion Rombauer Becker. *The Joy of Cooking.* Indianapolis: Bobbs-Merrill, 1975.

Romero, Lora. *Home Fronts: Domesticity and Its Critics in the Antebellum United States.* Durham, NC: Duke University Press, 1997.

Romines, Ann. "Growing Up with the Methodist Cookbooks." In *Recipes for Reading: Community Cookbooks, Stories, Histories,* edited by Anne L. Bower, 75–88. Amherst: University of Massachusetts Press, 1997.

———. *The Home Plot: Women, Writing and Domestic Ritual.* Amherst: University of Massachusetts Press, 1992.

Ruddick, Sara. *Maternal Thinking: Toward a Politics of Peace.* New York: Ballantine, 1989.

Ruskin, John. "Of Queens' Gardens." In *Sesame and Lilies. The Complete Works of John Ruskin,* edited by E. T. Cook and Alexander Wedderburn, 18:109–44. London: Allen, 1905.

Scanlon, Leone. "The New Woman in the Literature of 1883–1909." *University of Michigan Papers in Women's Studies* 2 (1976): 133–58.

Schaffer, Talia. *The Forgotten Female Aesthetes: Literary Culture in Late-Victorian England.* Charlottesville: University Press of Virginia, 2000.

Schaffer, Talia, and Kathy Alexis Psomiades, ed. *Women and British Aestheticism.* Charlottesville: University Press of Virginia, 1999.

Scharnhorst, Gary. *Charlotte Perkins Gilman.* Boston: Twayne, 1985.

———. *Charlotte Perkins Gilman: A Bibliography.* Metuchen, NJ: Scarecrow, 1985.

Schweickart, Patrocinio P. "Reading Ourselves: Toward a Feminist Theory of Reading." In *Gender and Reading: Essays on Readers, Texts, and Contexts,* edited by Elizabeth A. Flynn and Patrocinio P. Schweickart, 31–62. Baltimore: Johns Hopkins University Press, 1986.

Senf, Carol. Introduction to *The Heavenly Twins,* by Sarah Grand. Ann Arbor: University of Michigan Press, 1992.

Shapiro, Laura. *Perfection Salad: Women and Cooking at the Turn of the Century.* 1986. Reprint, New York: Random House, 2001.

Bibliography

Showalter, Elaine. *A Literature of Their Own: British Women Novelists from Brontë to Lessing.* Princeton: Princeton University Press, 1977.

————. "Syphilis, Sexuality, and the Fiction of the Fin de Siècle." In *Sex, Politics, and Science in the Nineteenth-Century Novel,* edited by Ruth Bernard Yeazell, 88–115. Baltimore: Johns Hopkins University Press, 1986.

Shulman, Robert. Introduction to *The Yellow Wall-Paper and Other Stories,* by Charlotte Perkins Gilman. Oxford: Oxford University Press, 1995.

Shuman, Amy. "The Rhetoric of Portions." *Western Folklore.* 40 (1980): 72–80.

Small, Helen. "Mrs. Humphry Ward and the First Casualty of War." In *Women's Fiction and the Great War,* edited by Suzanne Raitt and Trudi Tate, 18–46. Oxford: Clarendon, 1997.

Smith-Rosenberg, Carroll. *Disorderly Conduct: Visions of Gender in Victorian America.* New York: Knopf, 1985.

Spencely, Geoff. "The Lace Associations: Philanthropic Movements to Preserve the Production of Hand-Made Lace in Late Victorian and Edwardian England." *Victorian Studies* 16 (1973): 433–52.

Stage, Sarah. "Ellen Richards and the Social Significance of the Home Economics Movement." In *Rethinking Home Economics: Women and the History of a Profession,* edited by Sarah Stage and Virginia B. Vincenti, 17–33. Ithaca, NY: Cornell University Press, 1997.

Stamp, Gavin, and André Goulancourt. *The English House 1860–1914: The Flowering of English Domestic Architecture.* London: Faber, 1986.

Stephen, Barbara. *Emily Davies and Girton College.* London: Constable, 1927.

Stephen, Leslie. "Charlotte Brontë." In *Hours in a Library,* rev. ed., 3 vols. London: Smith, 1892. First published in *Cornhill Magazine,* December 1877.

Stowe, Harriet Beecher. *Uncle Tom's Cabin; or, Life among the Lowly.* 1852. Reprint, Harmondsworth, UK: Penguin, 1981.

Strasser, Susan. *Never Done: A History of American Housework.* New York: Pantheon, 1982.

Stuart, Elma. *What Must I Do to Get Well? And How Am I to Keep So? By One Who Has Done It.* London: David Stott, 1889.

Stutfield, Hugh E. M. "The Psychology of Feminism." *Blackwood's* 161 (1897): 104–17.

Suleiman, Susan Rubin. *Authoritarian Fictions: The Ideological Novel as a Literary Genre.* New York: Columbia University Press, 1983.

Sutherland, John. *Mrs. Humphry Ward: Eminent Victorian, Pre-eminent Edwardian.* New York: Oxford University Press, 1990.

Sutton-Ramspeck, Beth. "The Slayer and the Slain: Women and Sacrifice in Mary Ward's *Eleanor.*" *South Atlantic Review* 52, no. 4 (1987): 39–60.

Teale, T. Pridgin. *Dangers to Health: A Pictorial Guide to Sanitary Defects.* London: Churchill, 1878.

Thomas, Heather Kirk. "[A] Kind of 'Debased Romanesque' with 'Delirium Tremens': Late-Victorian Wall Coverings and Charlotte Perkins Gilman's 'The Yellow Wall-Paper.'" In *The Mixed Legacy of Charlotte Perkins Gilman,* edited by Catherine J Golden and Joanna Schneider Zangrando, 189–206. Newark: University of Delaware Press, 2000.

Tomes, Nancy. *The Gospel of Germs: Men, Women, and the Microbe in American Life.* Cambridge: Harvard University Press, 1998.

Tompkins, Jane. *Sensational Designs: The Cultural Work of American Fiction, 1790–1860.* New York: Oxford University Press, 1985.

Trevelyan, Janet Penrose. *The Life of Mrs. Humphry Ward.* New York: Dodd, 1923.

Trotter, David. *Cooking with Mud: The Idea of Mess in Nineteenth-Century Art and Fiction.* Oxford: Oxford University Press, 2000.

Tuttle, Jennifer S. Introduction to *The Crux* by Charlotte Perkins Gilman, 11–75. Newark: University of Delaware Press, 2002.

Visser, Margaret. *The Rituals of Dinner: The Origins, Evolution, Eccentricities, and Meaning of Table Manners.* New York: Grove Weidenfeld, 1991.

Walker, Alice. "In Search of Our Mothers' Gardens." In *In Search of Our Mothers' Gardens: Womanist Prose,* 231–43. San Diego: Harcourt, 1983.

Walker, Lynne. "Women Architects." In *A View from the Interior: Feminism, Women, and Design,* edited by Judy Attfield and Pat Kirkham. London: Women's Press, 1989.

Ward, Mary Augusta. "An Appeal against Female Suffrage." *The Nineteenth Century* 25 (1889): 781–88.

———. "Charlotte and Emily Bronte." In Trevelyan, *Life,* 166. First published in *Cornhill Magazine* 8 (1900) 289.

———. *Daphne* (in the United States, *Marriage à la Mode*). London: Cassell, 1909.

———. *Delia Blanchflower.* New York: Hearst, 1914; London: Ward, Lock, 1915.

———. *Diana Mallory* (in the United States, *The Testing of Diana Mallory*). London: Smith, Elder; New York: Harper, 1908.

———. "Discussions: Some Suffragist Arguments." *Educational Review* 36 (1908): 398–404.

———. *Eleanor.* London: Smith, Elder; New York: Harper, 1900.

———. *Elizabeth's Campaign* (in the United Kingdom, *The War and Elizabeth*). London: Collin's, 1917; New York: Dodd, 1918.

———. *A Great Success.* London: Smith, Elder; New York: Hearst, 1916.

———. *Harvest.* London: Collins, 1920; New York: Dodd, Mead, 1920 (dated 1919).

————. *Helbeck of Bannisdale*. London: Smith, Elder; New York: Macmillan, 1898. Reprint, Harmondsworth, UK: Penguin, 1983.

————. *The History of David Grieve*. London: Smith, Elder; New York: Macmillan, 1892.

————. Introductions to *The Life and Work of the Sisters Brontë*. 7 vols. New York: Harper, 1899–1900.

————. *Lady Connie*. London: Smith, Elder; New York: Hearst, 1916.

————. *Lady Rose's Daughter*. London: Smith, Elder; New York: Harper, 1903.

————. "Let Women Say! An Appeal to the House of Lords." *The Nineteenth Century and After* 83 (1918): 47–59.

————. *Marcella*. London: Smith, Elder; New York: Macmillan, 1894. Reprint, Peterborough, ON: Broadview, 2002.

————. *The Mating of Lydia*. London: Smith, Elder; New York: Doubleday, Page, 1913.

————. "Memoir of W. T. Arnold: Early Years." In *Studies of Roman Imperialism,* by W. T. Arnold, edited by Edward Fiddes. Manchester: Manchester University Press, 1906.

————. *Miss Bretherton*. London: Macmillan, 1884; New York: J. W. Lovell, 1888.

————. "Mrs. Humphry Ward and the Suffrage." Letter. *Times* (London), 19 December 1911, 8, cols. 3–4.

————. "A New Edition of Keats." Review of *The Poetical Works and Other Writings of John Keats,* edited by Harry Buxton Forman. *Macmillan's* 49 (March 1884): 330–40.

————. "On the Eve of the Bill." Letter. *Times* (London), 11 July 1910, 11, cols. 1–2.

————. Review of *Charlotte Brontë and Her Circle,* by Clement Shorter. *Times* (London), 23 October 1896, 8.

————. "Rhetoric and Revolution: Mrs. Ward's Reply to Mr. Lloyd George." Letter. *Times* (London), 27 November 1911, 9, col. 6.

————. *Robert Elsmere*. London: Smith, Elder; New York: Macmillan, 1888. Reprint, Lincoln: University of Nebraska Press, 1967.

————. *Sir George Tressady*. London: Smith, Elder; New York: Macmillan, 1896.

————. "Social Ideals: Address by Mrs. Humphry Ward." *Manchester Guardian,* 11 October 1897, 5.

————. "Some Thoughts on Charlotte Brontë." In *Charlotte Brontë, 1816–1916: A Centenary Memorial,* edited by Butler Wood, 11–38. London: T. Fisher Unwin, 1917.

————. "Speech to the Irish Central Bureau for the Employment of Women." 1905. In Bindslev, *Mrs. Humphry Ward,* 150–54.

————. "Style and Miss Austen." *Macmillan's* 51 (February 1885): 287–94.

———. "A Way Out." Letter. *Times* (London), 31 January 1913, 8, col. 5.

———. "Why I Do Not Believe in Woman Suffrage." *Ladies' Home Journal,* November 1908, 15ff.

———. "The Women's Anti-Suffrage Movement." *The Nineteenth Century and After* 64 (1908): 343–52.

———. *A Writer's Recollections.* 2 vols. London: Collins, 1919; New York: Harper, 1918.

———. *The Writings of Mrs. Humphry Ward.* The Westmoreland Edition. 16 vols. London: Smith, Elder, 1911–12.

Weintraub, Jeff. "The Theory and Politics of the Public/Private Distinction." In Weintraub and Kumar, *Public and Private,* 1–42.

Weintraub, Jeff, and Krishan Kumar, eds. *Public and Private in Thought and Practice: Perspectives on a Grand Dichotomy.* Chicago: University of Chicago Press, 1997.

Wilde, Oscar. "The English Renaissance of Art." In *De Profundis: Lectures and Essays,* vol. 11 of *The Complete Works of Oscar Wilde,* edited by Robert Ross. 1–47. 1907. Reprint, Garden City, NY: Doubleday, Page, 1923.

Williams, Susan S. "Writing with an Ethical Purpose: The Case of Elizabeth Stuart Phelps." In *Reciprocal Influences: Literary Production, Distribution, and Consumption in America,* edited by Steven Fink and Susan S. Williams, 151–72. Columbus: Ohio State University Press, 1999.

Wollstonecraft, Mary. *A Vindication of the Rights of Woman.* London: Penguin, 1992.

"Women on Borough Councils." *Times* (London), 21 October 1909, 4, col. 5.

Woods, Katharine Pearson. "Mrs. Ward and 'The New Woman.'" *Bookman* (New York) 4 (November 1896): 245–47.

INDEX

Index

Index

Index